Fresh Eyes to READ the BIBLE

Book 2

Fresh Eyes to READ the BIBLE

Book 2

The Real Jesus

Chung Duck Young

Copyright © 2010 by Chung DuckYoung. All rights reserved.

No part of this publication may be reproduced in any form, stored in a retrieval system or transmitted in any form by any means: electronic, mechanical, photocopy, recording, or otherwise without the prior written permission of the author, except as provided by United States of America copyright law.

Unless otherwise indicated, Scripture is taken from the King James Version of the Bible.

Scripture marked NIV is taken from the Holy Bible, New International Version, Copyright © 1973, 1978, 1984 by International Bible Society. Used by permission of Zondervan Publishing House.

Haggai Books

Printed in the United States of America

ISBN: 978-89-953885-5-6

Dedicated to the believers
who are eagerly waiting for the real Jesus
to have their sinful life changed to His life,
and to those who are exploited,
oppressed and deceived under the law
in the gospel's name.

The Spirit of the Lord is on me, because he has anointed me to preach good news to the poor. He has sent me to proclaim freedom for the prisoners and recovery of sight for the blind, to release the oppressed, to proclaim the year of the Lord's favor.

— Luke 4:18-19 NIV

CONTENTS

PREFACE —9

PART ONE Morals vs. Word of God

Morals vs. Word of God, Their Differences —13
A Garment Mingled of Linen and Woollen —19
Keep the Sabbath Day Holy —28
The Priests Profane the Sabbath and Are Blameless —33
Expo Science Park* —41
You Shall Not Commit Adultery —45
Sell that You Have, and Give to the Poor —55
You Shall Not Eat of the Flesh of Swine —69
Be Not Drunk with Wine —74
A Certain Taxi Driver* —80

* *Mark shows testimonies.*

PART TWO   The Hidden Manna

A Long Time Under the Law   —*87*
Cain and Abel   —*91*
Re-Illumination of Samson   —*100*
Adultery of David   —*112*
Traffic Violation in San Francisco*   —*129*
Blessed is the Man   —*136*
From Marketplace to Vineyard   —*143*
Dream of Reaping Grapes*   —*154*
Martha and Mary   —*155*
Faith Without Works is Dead   —*164*
The Unjust Steward   —*174*
Cannot Serve God and Mammon   —*192*
Law and Kingdom of God   —*200*
Trip to Charleston*   —*209*

PART THREE   The Real Jesus

The Real Jesus   —*219*
Faith of the Centurion   —*226*
Unjust Judge and Widow   —*240*
Daybreak Prayer and A Traffic Accident*   —*250*
A Certain Nobleman and Ten Minas   —*255*
One Sows and Another Reaps   —*272*
My Time is Not Yet Come: but Your Time is Always Ready —*280*
Boy that I Met in Orlando*   —*287*
Go, and Sin No More   —*291*

Finishing This Book... —*303*

PREFACE

I explained most of the important doctrines required for understanding the Scriptures in the first book of 'Fresh Eyes to Read the Bible.' Anyone who has well understood it would have had the eyes to read the word right.

I will describe the true meanings of the Scriptures in this second book based on these eyes. If the first book is the 'key' to open the Scriptures, then the second book opens the Scripture with the 'key.' Or, if I say the first book is the principle, then the second book is the actual application.

We, Christians, claim that we know and believe in Jesus. Generally, the Jesus that we know is the historical Jesus who came in the past, and the Jesus who will come to judge the world in the future. However, we do not know Jesus of the here and now. Unfortunately, only Jesus of the here and now can save us; neither Jesus in the past nor Jesus in the future.

Peter met Jesus and was saved and born again, and so did Paul. Now, any person desiring to be saved should meet Jesus individually as they did. Without meeting Him, there can be no salvation for us. It is incorrect to say that they met Him because they were special. They are not special, because all men are created equal especially in the sight of God.

The Jesus we are to meet here comes in both the word and in our walk with God. In particular, the word I mean here is not the word every church mentions, but the hidden true significance of the Scriptures. We will see through this book that what we traditionally understand about the Scriptures is far from its true meanings.

The Scriptures testify about Jesus Christ. Therefore, if we do not understand the true meaning of the Scriptures, we cannot but believe in another Jesus. He is Jesus in our imagination, who is created by ourselves based on man-made morals and traditions. No wonder our faith is misguided and feeble. This is because the Jesus that we have created has failed to save and heal us to be born again.

Nevertheless, we have one consolation: if we believe in the real Jesus, the power of love will project out of us as Christians as it was with the apostles Peter, Paul, John and so on.

Please check seriously whether the Jesus in whom you now believe is really testified to by the true meanings of the Scriptures, and also check whether you are really walking with God. This book will provide you with the opportunity to meet the real Jesus and be born again.

May the grace of the Lord be with you.

Chung Duck Young
2010

PART ONE
Morals vs. Word of God

The word of God is totally different from the commandments of men spoken of in various moral codes. However, we understand the word of God as moral instructions, the commandments of men. As a result, when we read the Word of God, we receive it as the commandments of men by receiving it as one of the moral codes.

In this case, our souls are dying irrespective of our decades-long Christian life, theological knowledge, or enthusiasm toward God in the church; simply because the commandments of men cannot save us.

In Part One of this title, I have explained the serious necessity for us to read the Word of God, the Scripture, correctly without being contaminated by human moral codes. I have also selected some passages that can be easily confused with the morals of men, and explained their true significance.

Morals vs. Word of God, Their Differences

The Way to Be Righteous

Every human being has the desire to live a good and righteous life in the world, even without the commandments of God. We wish to have a humble and meek heart and tolerate and love others in a broad-minded manner. For this reason, words such as love, kindness, humbleness, peace, justice and righteousness have power to make our hearts flutter.

Of course, if we go into further detail, the meanings of 'righteous,' 'good,' and 'just' will differ. Especially the word 'righteous' is used in relation with God, but over all, these represents the good that all human beings are striving for during their lives.

Now, our problem is that even though we hope for such good, we cannot live such a life for a single moment in our everyday life. Righteous life is pie in the sky. We can only live our lives on earth viewing this unattainable objective from afar.

How can we be changed into righteous persons and live such a life?

Method of Man: by Morals

When examining man's efforts to achieve righteousness in the world we see moral codes set up by men and enacted into law, and call those who have behaved to that standard righteous. Whether such men who conform to that standard are really righteous is another matter.

We, given over to this worldly way of thinking, try to read and understand the Scripture according to these traditional thoughts. That is, if we keep the just commandments made by God, He will call us just. So if we find the words such as "Love your neighbor as yourself," "Go and sell that you have, and give to the poor," and "You shall not commit adultery" while reading the Scripture, we understand that these words convey the same meaning as in human moral codes. So we try to keep these, thinking that if we manage to do this, God will call us the 'justified.' It would not be an exaggeration if I say that the purpose of the entire life of a Christian is to live by the Scripture in this way.

However, as we all know, it is not as easy as we imagine it to be. We have struggled to live according to the Scriptures for a long time in our Christian life. However, whenever we come to church on Sunday, our main prayers are to confess to having failed to live based on the words of God in the previous week.

What does this say? It says that the way we believe in Jesus fails to make us righteous. The Christian life we have led up to now serves to prove this. However, we do not realize this and we will therefore continue to make such efforts in our own way. And we will also continue to repent for our failure to live by the Scripture.

What on earth is the problem? Knowing that Jesus once forgave our sins, why should we repent repeatedly about not keeping the words of God throughout our life?

It is because we read and understood the Scriptures as human morals and ethics. If we understand the word of God as morals, superficially we have received the word of God, but actually, we have received the commandments of men. No wonder there was no change in us. The commandments of men cannot change unrighteous man into righteous man. Centuries of human history proves this.

▷ Method of God: by Faith of Jesus

How does God justify us? This is a very important question. Read Romans.

> Therefore, we conclude that a man is justified by faith without the deeds of the law. [Romans 3:28]

Paul says that a man is justified by faith. In this instance, the faith Paul describes does not mean the deed that "We have believed in Jesus." We generally think we can have faith by strengthening our resolution. So we repeatedly make up our mind in order to have strong and unshakeable faith. This is another type of deed of the law.

Faith means the 'faith of Jesus.' We are justified when the faith of Jesus comes to us. This is what justification by faith signifies.

In other words, faith is the life of Jesus. We cannot get His life through our deeds. We should give birth to it. When we meet Jesus in our personal life, we become pregnant with His life. After a certain period of healing by Him, we will then deliver the life of Jesus in us. At this moment, we receive the 'faith of Jesus' and will be concurrently born again and justified. This is the way in which God justifies us.

As described, the Scripture is the Word of God making us pregnant with the life of Jesus. However, if we change this word of life into moral commandments and try to apply them, shall we be changed? No, we will not be changed at all.

If we are not changed even though we have believed in Jesus for a long time, there is no other explanation. We have changed the Scriptures into the morals of the world.

Read Matthew below.

> [7] Ye hypocrites, well did Esaias prophesy of you, saying, [8] This people draweth nigh unto me with their mouth, and honoureth me with their lips; but their heart is far from me. [9] But in vain they do worship me, teaching for doctrines the commandments of men. [Matthew 15:7-9]

The Pharisees taught the Scriptures to their people, but unwittingly, converted it into the doctrines of men. If you think that Jesus only spoke these words to the Pharisees, and not to you, then you have not read the Scriptures properly. The Pharisees represent self righteous, sinful human beings. So you will be blessed if you can see the Pharisees in yourself, since then you shall be in a position to start receiving healing.

Anyway, if we believe in Him in this way, it means that we believe in 'another Jesus' (2Co 11:4). Surely, no one can save us from the sinful life into the righteous life, except the real Jesus.

To talk about salvation a little bit, salvation by Jesus referred to in the Scripture does not mean that one will be saved into heaven from hell in the afterlife. This kind of salvation is decided at the 'law stage' of our faith. So those who are eager to please God and fear God in their hearts under the law will go to heaven.

Of course, those readers who are reading this book must be pious believers. They will definitely go to heaven in the afterlife. However, even if I say this, intrinsically you cannot believe it one hundred percent, as this will only happen in the future.

Then how can you be one hundred percent sure that you are going to heaven? By going into heaven now! If you go in now, you will be in heaven from here to eternity. You do not have to worry whether you would be going to heaven or to hell. Jesus is the man who will bring heaven to you personally while you are alive here.

This is the kingdom of God and it will be given to you, if you believe in Jesus correctly. It would be sensible for you to hope to enter the kingdom now, and live righteously for the rest of life and for eternity.

Different Worlds, Different Laws

📂 Two Different Worlds Overlapping

In the world where we are living in, two kingdoms overlap. One is the world that is visible and that we can feel and catch hold of, and another is the invisible and everlasting kingdom. The Scripture says that the visible kingdom is the 'world' and the invisible kingdom is the 'kingdom of God.' The visible world is finite but the invisible kingdom of God is eternal. When I say the visible world is finite, this implies that our body has a time limit and the time will come when we leave this world and stand before God.

In addition, the kingdom of God is not the place where we go when we die physically. It exists here overlapping with this world. Read the following Scriptures verses.

While we look not at the things which are seen, but at the things which are not seen: for the things which are seen are temporal; but the things which are not seen are eternal. [2 Corinthians 4:18]

And the world passeth away, and the lust thereof: but he that doeth the will of God abideth for ever. [1 John 2:17]

Therefore, the visible kingdom and the invisible kingdom coexist in this world: the two are the 'world' and the 'kingdom of God' respectively.

📂 Two Different Laws

Different kingdoms have different laws to sustain them. People control and manage the visible world, and they make the laws of men so as to maintain and support the world. The laws are extended to include the principals of morals and ethics. The rulers of the world try by every available means to encourage life that fits with the moral and ethical codes that suit their particular agendas. This will enable their world to be maintained.

Differing from this, the invisible kingdom of God is controlled by the principle of life. Paul describes the different laws that control the two different worlds as follows:

> [1] There is therefore now no condemnation to them which are in Christ Jesus, who walk not after the flesh, but after the Spirit. [2] For the law of the Spirit of life in Christ Jesus hath made me free from the law of sin and death. [Romans 8:1-2]

This world is sustained by the law of sin and death made by men, and the kingdom of God is sustained by the law of the Spirit of life.

The Scripture is the word of God, the commandments relating to the kingdom of God. It is not the law of the world for sustaining the world of men. Therefore, if we read and apply the Scripture as the moral codes and legal systems of the world, we are substantially mistaken. It will be like applying one country's law to another.

Furthermore, the Scripture is written about Jesus. He did not come so as to reign over this world and reinforce it. This is the focus of the prince of this world. Jesus has come to give us the kingdom of God, which is not seen.

Read John.

> Jesus answered, My kingdom is not of this world: if my kingdom were of this world, then would my servants fight, that I should not be delivered to the Jews: but now is my kingdom not from hence. [John 18:36]

As described above, the Scripture and Jesus have little concern with the visible world and its associated legal systems. He came to build the everlasting kingdom in us. Therefore, we should not be so foolish as to apply the Scripture for the invisible kingdom of God in the same way as the law of this world.

Epilogue

The morals and ethics of the world is the law of death controlling the world, and the Scripture is the law of life of the kingdom of God. If we mix up the two, we shall face definite contradiction. With such contradiction around, we cannot expect salvation.

Now is the time to discard the approach of reading the word of God based on human morals and ethics. The passages of the Scripture that I will explain hereafter will look like the morals of this world at first sight, but I will show you whether they really are.

Let's go.

A Garment Mingled of Linen and Woollen

[Leviticus 19:19]
Ye shall keep my statutes. Thou shalt not let thy cattle gender with a diverse kind: thou shalt not sow thy field with mingled seed: neither shall a garment mingled of linen and woollen come upon thee.

God gives us three statutes to keep from this word: first, you shall not let your cattle gender with another kind, second, you shall not sow your field with seed of two kinds of mingled seed, and third, a garment mingled of two materials shall not come upon you.

We will have no difficulty in interpreting this verse if it is given for the purpose of controlling our deeds in the world of the flesh. If so, we will understand it in such a manner that we should not let different animals such as the dog and the cat gender with each other, we are not to sow fields with mingled seeds of cabbage and radish, and we must not wear clothes woven of linen and wool.

Is this really what God wished to say to us? Did God really write the Scripture so as to transfer such meaning to us? No man of common sense will have a dog and a cat gender with each other, and people will not plant their field with two different kinds of seed.

Furthermore, believers wear clothes woven of two kinds of material irrespective of this verse already. This type of commandment has no meaning at all, and God has no reason to command us to do such things.

We can guess that this word has another hidden meaning, and when we correctly understand it, we can have the 'spirit' of what the Word of God seeks to convey.

You Shall Not Let Thy Cattle Gender With a Diverse Kind

God has no intention of talking to us about gendering between dogs and cats. This word relates to the spiritual world, and in detail, it tells us not to mingle two kinds of life during our salvation, which is a 'born again' process. In fact, to be 'born again' has the same meaning as to 'be saved,' to 'have faith,' or to 'enter the kingdom of God.'

📂 What Are the Two Kinds

We have two different kinds of life while believing in Jesus.

The first one is the 'flesh,' which is the life that was given to us by natural birth. The second one is the 'spirit,' which is the life that we get by being born again of the spirit.

Consider John 3:6: "That which is born of the flesh is flesh; and that which is born of the Spirit is spirit."

We start with the life of 'flesh,' which is the life before being born again, and when we are born again by Jesus, we live the life of 'spirit.'

No 'spirit' life can come to us while we have the 'flesh' life, and the 'flesh' life is already dead if we have the 'spirit' life. These two kinds of life cannot co-exist in me and thus they cannot be mingled by nature.

📂 What is Mingling

God has given us the statute not to mingle the two kinds of life in Leviticus above. Paul says the same thing in this passage from 2 Corinthians.

> [14] Be ye not unequally yoked together with unbelievers: for what fellowship hath righteousness with unrighteousness? and what communion hath light with darkness? [15] And what concord hath Christ with Belial? or what part hath he that believeth with an infidel? [2 Corinthians 6:14-15]

These verses do not give us statutes for the things of the world such that believers should not run businesses together with unbelievers. And also they do not mean that the believers should not marry unbelievers or that they should not get along with gangsters.

What I am trying to say is that the Scripture is not a book of instructions for Christians to do or not to do regarding the matters of the world. Nevertheless, if you wish to know such things from time to time, you should ask the living Lord for help.

What Paul refers to is the principle of nature that if a man has new life, he cannot be mingled with old life. The word "Be ye (=believers) not unequally yoked together with unbelievers" can be considered to be Paul's version for the word "Thou shalt not let thy cattle gender with a diverse kind." They, though differently expressed, have the same meanings.

When the Christ (new life) comes on us, we cannot make friends with the Belial (worthlessness: old life), and when light comes on us, we cannot be mingled with darkness. This is what this principle means.

I will state my case. I used to post articles on an Internet forum when I started to realize the profound meanings of the Scripture. Not many people understood what I wrote, despite the fact that it was written in their native language. As you will see as you go on, the profound meanings of the Bible are not revealed to everyone. Only those who have ears to hear can hear.

However, some people, having read the postings and being deeply moved, wanted to have fellowship with me. I felt so happy because there were at least some who could understand what I had written. In fact, they had a good understanding of what I had explained. In some parts, their understanding of the depth, width, and breadth of the Scripture was excellent.

However, as I have already said, if a man has received and properly understood new life in God, he naturally has two elements: 'Profound words of the Scripture that shows the way to heaven' and 'walking with the living Lord.' Accordingly, I had to talk about walking with the living Lord while keeping company with them. However, knowing that they were not yet prepared to accept what I said, I refused friendship with them.

My behavior at that time did not originate from some sense of duty or desire to curry favor with Him. It was just a natural phenomenon coming from a man having received new life from Him. The light will naturally be separated from darkness.

As another example of mingling: many Christian leaders try to find a way to reconcile with other religions. However, believers cannot be equally yoked together with unbelievers because of the essential differences between the two groups. They are free to be conciliatory towards other religions, but such behavior does not guarantee true reconciliation. If someone thinks that different religions can be reconciled with each other through his endeavors, he is mistaken because then he has no true idea of who Christ is.

If we understood Jesus Christ properly such an attempt would simply not be made, because it attempts to make Christ have concord with Belial. It amounts to an impossible attempt to make light have communion with darkness.

True religious reconciliation will only be achieved when the people of all the respective religions come to know Jesus Christ.

Therefore, we should not let one life gender with another kind. It is impossible to do so.

📂 True Meaning of Statutes

If the believer and unbeliever, light and darkness, and new life and old life are obviously distinguishable and separate by nature, why did He tell us not to gender with each other and not to be unequally yoked? To explain I will take an example of "Do not mingle light and darkness" for "Not to gender with each other."

Light cannot be mixed with darkness. Therefore, this sentence cannot be a commandment. It only tells those who mingle light with darkness to think of their contradiction.

Who mingles light and darkness? Only those who cannot see will do so out of ignorance. If they are darkness itself, they do not know what is light. Furthermore, they do not even know whether they are darkness. So they mingle light and darkness since they cannot tell light from darkness.

Likewise, they mix up the things that are of the 'flesh' with the things that are of the 'spirit.' For example, we cannot tell whether our faith is under the law or under grace, but only when we meet the gospel will we know that we are under the law; so far unknowingly.

In contemporary Christianity, many people try to distinguish the law from grace, but fail. This is because grace cannot be seized by people under the law. Yet, they believe that they know something about grace. Under this circumstance, they have no choice but to mingle two lives, i.e., the life of 'flesh,' which is under law and the life of 'spirit,' which is under grace.

God says do not do that. Jesus will come to you like this time now if you pray hard to have such grace after being exhausted under the law. Only then, you will be able to separate one from another by nature.

This is what the statute "Do not let one life gender with another kind" means. This statute introduces Jesus Christ as the Life.

You Shall Not Sow Your Field with Mingled Seed

God subsequently instructs us not to sow a field with mingled seed. The field in Scripture does not indicate a field used for growing crops. The field signifies our heart.

In the parable of the sower in Matthew, Jesus also interprets the field as the heart and the seed as the word (Mat 13:18-23). So in the same manner, the field is the symbol of the heart and the seed symbolizes the word in Leviticus 19:19. "Do not sow your field with mingled seed" has the same meaning as "Do not receive mingled seed in your heart."

This word means that we should not sow two different interpretations of the word to our hearts. Then what do the two kinds of word sown in the heart mean?

The two kinds of word represent the law and the gospel. They are not different kinds of seed like, for example, the seed of cabbage and the seed of radish. They denote the same kind of seed which is the seed of the law at first and which then becomes the seed of the gospel. It is a very special kind of seed indeed.

For example, let's think of the relation between the egg and the chick. They are one because the chick hatches out of the egg. Concurrently, they are different as one kind is an egg and another kind is a chick.

In the same way, the word of God is distinguishable as two kinds that are one but separate: law and gospel. To the believers individually, the seed of law comes first, and thereafter comes the seed of gospel. If the believer who is under the time of the law takes the gospel, or he who is under the gospel takes the law, he is sowing his heart with the mingled seed of law and gospel. If the two kinds will be mingled and sown, they will come to nothing.

Actually, we cannot mingle these two and they do not mingle with each other. However, people do try to mingle these two and sow mingled seed because they do not understand that the law and the gospel are fundamentally different.

This feature is clearly revealed amongst believers. For instance, if I tell them to keep the law, they will escape by saying, "What kind of law do I have to keep? I am already saved through faith. We become conscious of sin through the law and for us the law is only a relic of the past!" Okay. Then, do the deeds of the saved come out of them? No, they do not. They only raise their voice saying that they are saved through faith, not knowing what the faith of Jesus is. They neither keep the law nor belong to the gospel, adopting a dubious attitude. Read Revelation.

> [15] I know thy works, that thou art neither cold nor hot: I would thou wert cold or hot. [16] So then because thou art lukewarm, and neither cold nor hot, I will spue thee out of my mouth. [Revelation 3:15-16]

They are neither cold (under the law) nor hot (under the gospel).

We are either cold or hot before God. The lukewarm state represents the cold man that pretends to be hot, which is sheer hypocrisy. So the Lord says He will spew them out of His mouth. This lukewarm status is naturally acquired when the law is mingled with the gospel. It is generated because they sowed two kinds of seed in their heart. Those who are born again receive one kind of word, that is, the gospel.

Consequently, the word "Thou shalt not sow thy field with mingled seed" means you should be born again and come into the world of the gospel. Then, you will not sow your field with mingled seed.

This statute reveals Jesus Christ as the Word.

Neither Shall a Garment Be Mingled of Linen and Wool

This statute does not mean that we should not wear clothes of mingled textiles such as 50% of polyester and 50% of cotton. However, if you want to think so, then you will have to say that you are sanctified because you are wearing clothes made of 100% wool.

This may appear absurd, but there are many Christians around us who think this way. For instance, they think they are sanctified because they do not eat pork according to the statute of the Bible. They belong to the same world as those who will not wear the mixed fabrics for sanctification.

📂 Two Kinds of Material of Garment

In the Scripture, clothes are the symbol of righteousness. This righteousness covers our shame so that we may stand before God openly and squarely. There are two kinds of clothes we can wear during our whole life: first, clothes according to the law, and then clothes according to the gospel, which is only given to the elect.

The former represents the self-righteousness that occurs when we kept the law, and the latter indicates the righteousness of God that we acquire when Jesus Christ has been resurrected in us. Therefore, there are two kinds of material for making clothes: one is the law and the other the gospel.

The expression of wearing clothes made from two kinds of material refers to mingling the law and the gospel of Christ, thereby seeking righteousness. However, it is impossible from the beginning to weave the law and the gospel into clothes because the law is darkness whereas the gospel is light.

It is light if it is not darkness, and it is darkness if it is not light. Likewise, it is the gospel if it is not the law, and it is the law if it is not the gospel. It is absolutely impossible to mingle the two.

However, some people appear to have the mighty power to mingle the two. These are they who are in darkness, and they do this out of ignorance. They understand the gospel as a part or continuation of the law and try to act based on such understanding. I will exemplify this from the book of John.

> A new commandment I give unto you, That ye love one another; as I have loved you, that ye also love one another. [John 13:34]

Jesus said this word to the disciples after the Last Supper. Many people accept this word as His will and make up their minds to love their brothers with all their heart. This attitude reveals that they receive the gospel as the law. That is, he gets the gospel mixed up with the law.

To the disciples at this stage, who were being healed while following Jesus for three and half years, the word is no more a commandment, but a declaration by Jesus that they have become those who can love one another. So they love.

If a man has never met and followed Him, then to him "Love one another" is purely a commandment to keep. However, he will think that he is following the gospel, which Jesus commanded. In reality, he is only mimicking the gospel, being under the law. All who are under the law will think and act this way, and so they are wearing a garment mingled of linen (law) and wool (gospel).

This statute reveals Jesus Christ as the Righteousness.

I Will Distinguish …?

We have considered verses from the book of Leviticus. Now, what is your conclusion in your heart? Are you not making a resolution like:

"I will not mingle 'flesh' and 'spirit.'" Or,

"I will distinguish the 'law' and the 'gospel.'"

However, even if you repeat the resolution over and over, it is meaningless simply because you cannot distinguish the 'flesh' and the 'spirit,' and the 'law' and the 'gospel' through your efforts. Only he who has the new life and who is in the gospel already can distinguish between the two concepts. Therefore, if you cannot identify them now, it proves that you belong to the law. You should wait and pray for Jesus to come to your life as a man.

The Scripture is to be interpreted in the same way. That is, spiritually. The garment in the Scripture is not the garment we generally think of, the field is not the agricultural field we know, and the seed is not the seed we sow. Further, "Keep the statutes" does not refer to the commandments that we know in general.

If we read the Scripture in accordance with common sense, it will be the morals and codes of conduct established by men. As long as we are reading the Scripture with these eyes, as we have been doing traditionally up to now, we are far from the salvation of Jesus.

The salvation of Jesus is the coming of the kingdom of God to me here.

Let us meet the real Jesus and be saved here and now.

Keep the Sabbath Day Holy

[Exodus 20:8-11]
⁸ Remember the sabbath day, to keep it holy. ⁹ Six days shalt thou labour, and do all thy work: ¹⁰ But the seventh day is the sabbath of the LORD thy God: in it thou shalt not do any work, thou, nor thy son, nor thy daughter, thy manservant, nor thy maidservant, nor thy cattle, nor thy stranger that is within thy gates: ¹¹ For in six days the LORD made heaven and earth, the sea, and all that in them is, and rested the seventh day: wherefore the LORD blessed the sabbath day, and hallowed it.

The Sabbath day means Saturday of the present time. It is the day of the week observed from Friday evening to Saturday evening as a day of rest and worship by Jews. The Sabbath day has its origin from the word of Genesis 2:2 in which God ended six days' creation and He rested on the seventh day.

God said to keep the Sabbath day holy. So the Jews keep the Sabbath holy very strictly, doing no works and prohibiting entertainment. We, Christians, also keep Sunday holy. Today's churches have applied the rule for the Sabbath to Sunday, and thus try to keep the day holy. The current service on the Lord's day is kept in memory of the first day of the week after the Sabbath, the day of His resurrection. However, the Sabbath the Scripture refers to is not Sunday but Saturday.

Meaningless Argument About the Sabbath

Some people insist that the Scripture instructs us to keep the Sabbath holy but it does not tell us to keep the Lord's day holy, and so they made a new sect. They gather together and worship God every Saturday, and then they criticize those who go to church on Sundays, which is the day of the sun god of heathens. Naturally, the traditional churches also judge them in return. Both parties argue with each other over which is the right day.

Some churches changed the commandment to keep the Sabbath holy in the Ten Commandments to keep the Lord's day holy. That is only a desperate countermeasure to fix the Lord's day as a service day.

However, all these arguments and efforts have digressed from the point of the Scripture.

The Sabbath in the Scripture does not refer to a day of the week. It indicates the born again man himself, which I will describe later. Therefore, it is totally meaningless to dispute whether the Sabbath that we must keep holy is Saturday or Sunday. It would only be a waste of time, if we argue over something which we understand incorrectly.

In chapter 16 of Matthew, when Jesus departed together with His disciples, they forgot to take bread. Knowing it, He says as follows for the purpose of enlightening them: "Take heed and beware of the leaven of the Pharisees and the Sadducees."

Upon hearing Him, they think of the leaven in bread.

"Ah, we forgot to take bread. He is pointing it out!"

When they are talking to each other about not taking bread, He hears them and then says:

"I did not speak to you concerning bread, but you should beware of the doctrine of the Pharisees and of the Sadducees."

The leaven He said was not the leaven of bread but their teaching.

Assume that He told us to beware of leaven. If we understand it as the leaven of bread and have a quarrel with each other over it, how pathetic will we be? We are quarreling about the wrong thing and are far from His intention.

Those having a quarrel over the day of the Sabbath are doing such a meaningless thing. As the leaven is not the leaven of bread

Morals vs. Word of God

in its true interpretation, the Sabbath is not the Sabbath of the calendar.

True Meaning of the Sabbath

Then, what does the Sabbath signify? The Sabbath means a born again man. Specifically, the man whom God created in the image of Himself through the born again process, which is the six days' work of God in Genesis chapter 1, is called the 'Sabbath.'
Read Genesis.

> ² And on the seventh day God ended his work which he had made; and he rested on the seventh day from all his work which he had made. ³ And God blessed the seventh day, and sanctified it: because that in it he had rested from all his work which God created and made. [Genesis 2:2-3]

He is the man in whom God is well pleased and He rests from all His work. Also, he is the holy man whom God has made holy. "Ye shall therefore be holy, for I am holy" (Lev 11:45) has been fulfilled in the man of Sabbath.

Ceasing From Works

Now I will explain what it means to cease from work on the Sabbath. When we individually meet Jesus in our life, our sinful nature starts to be healed by Him. This is the start of *my* new creation corresponding to the first day of Genesis Chapter 1. This process will be complete when *I* reach the sixth day of the creation whereby *I* become a man in His own image as stated in Genesis 1:2. It reads "So God created man in his own image, in the image of God created he him; male and female created he them."

During the above period, i.e., from the first day to the sixth day of the creation, *I* need to follow Him forsaking all, to the cross where *my* 'old man' will die united with Jesus. Read Matthew 16:24: "Then said Jesus unto his disciples, If any man will come after me, let him deny himself, and take up his cross, and follow me." During this period of time, God in Jesus works and *I* also work. Regarding the aspect of God's working, He leads *my* 'old man' to the cross to be crucified.

And regarding the aspect of *my* working, 'old man' in *me* tries to do something good for God in his *my* own way. 'Old man' labors to produce good works, which are self-righteousness, the fake good. In fact, salvation eliminates the 'old man' and its works. Therefore, *I* am working for self-righteousness, pending 'old man' being destroyed at the cross. However, on the seventh day, *I* will rest, as God commanded.

Think about the case of Peter. Whilst he was being healed and led to the cross, he tried to work for the Lord. Read John 13:37: "Peter said unto him, Lord, why cannot I follow thee now? I will lay down my life for thy sake."

This is the work that he thinks he can do for the Lord in the process of salvation. But, such work of his is not necessary at all. Only when Peter grows to know that his works profit nothing in life, he will stop and will only follow Jesus. This is the rest of the Sabbath day. And it was achieved in Peter at the cross.

There is a point in time when the work of Jesus and *my* work end and rest together. That is the time when the crucifixion of Jesus has occurred to *me*. At this time, the Lord has ceased from His works as *I* have been made complete, and *I* have ceased from the works of self-righteousness as my 'old man' died on the cross. Consider Hebrews.

> For he that is entered into his rest, he also hath ceased from his own works, as God did from his. [Hebrews 4:10]

Here, this verse mentions two aspects: one for God's ceasing and the other for *my* ceasing. God ceases from His works after having completed creation, and *I* cease from self-righteous works of the 'old man.' The Creator has completed the creation of creature and both creator and creature so have entered their rest.

On the Sabbath day all sons, daughters, manservants, maidservants, cattle, and strangers that are within the gates should not work. All these refer to *my* various thoughts and theories that are against

God. On the Sabbath they are supposed to be calm and at rest.

Epilogue

It is God's wish in the Scriptures that we are to be re-created to have new life. Jesus will come to us individually and he will create us in six days, and will finally lay down Himself united with our 'old man' at the cross. This completes the creation of myself as a born again being from heaven. Thus, *I* enter the rest and become holy. *My* seventh day begins from here onward and continues forever. Now *I* am the Sabbath day itself, thus, *I* keep the Sabbath holy.

Keep the Sabbath day holy!

The Priests Profane the Sabbath and Are Blameless

[Matthew 12:1-8]
¹ At that time Jesus went on the sabbath day through the corn; and his disciples were an hungred, and began to pluck the ears of corn, and to eat. ² But when the Pharisees saw it, they said unto him, Behold, thy disciples do that which is not lawful to do upon the sabbath day. ³ But he said unto them, Have ye not read what David did, when he was an hungred, and they that were with him; ⁴ How he entered into the house of God, and did eat the shewbread, which was not lawful for him to eat, neither for them which were with him, but only for the priests? ⁵ Or have ye not read in the law, how that on the sabbath days the priests in the temple profane the sabbath, and are blameless? ⁶ But I say unto you, That in this place is one greater than the temple. ⁷ But if ye had known what this meaneth, I will have mercy, and not sacrifice, ye would not have condemned the guiltless. ⁸ For the Son of man is Lord even of the sabbath day.

Jesus worked on the Sabbath. Superficially, He broke the commandment of God to keep the Sabbath holy. Naturally, the Pharisees were indignant and blamed Him for breaking the law, and they even schemed to put Him to death. Even to our eyes, Jesus broke the law of God, which commands us to keep the Sabbath holy. However, we are quite relaxed about His breaking the law. It is because we are simply on His side.

Some zealous believers try to defend His violation of the Sabbath with the following reasoning, which looks poor though:

First, Jesus did so as the son of God, and this was an exceptional case. So we should not follow such exceptional cases. However, the Scripture says that those who believe in Jesus will do what He did (Jhn 14:12). So if we believe correctly we can do works on the Sabbath day also as He did. Therefore, it is wrong to say that He can profane the Sabbath because He is special.

Second, the works Jesus did are allowed on the Sabbath. That is, things such as healing the people, laying hold of a sheep that fell into a pit and lifting it out, and plucking the ears of corn and eating them, *et cetera* are permitted. However, the Scripture simple says to keep the Sabbath holy, and allows no exceptions. One can either violate it, or keep it. That's all.

Third, some people defend Him with no clear reason. They think that the son of God cannot be wrong, and they side with Him blindly without thinking too deeply about it.

Any of the theories described above fails to provide a true defense for His profaning the Sabbath. The fundamental reason for the problems is that the Pharisees misunderstood the Sabbath. The Sabbath indicates neither one day of the week nor one week of one month, as we learned from the previous section.

Outline

Here, Jesus is doing what was not allowed on the Sabbath, and the Pharisees are unhappy. Jesus was giving reasons to them why His working on the Sabbath is blameless. He quotes two cases in the Old Testament. First case is that David entered the house of God, and ate the showbread with those who were with him, and second, the priests in the temple profane the Sabbath and are blameless.

Those who wish to protect Jesus for His violation of the Sabbath, need to come up with this reason, not the dubious reasons mentioned above.

Then, what are the true meanings of the incidents that Jesus mentioned in Old Testament? Further, He continued to talk about mercy and sacrifice, and the Son of man being Lord even of the Sabbath day. It is hard to grasp the contextual connections of mercy, sacrifice, and Lord of the Sabbath day.

Jesus is mentioning a very precious truth through which we can be set free from the law. Now I will explain it in detail.

Characteristics of the Pharisees

> [Matthew 12:1-2] [1] At that time Jesus went on the sabbath day through the corn; and his disciples were an hungred, and began to pluck the ears of corn, and to eat. [2] But when the Pharisees saw it, they said unto him, Behold, thy disciples do that which is not lawful to do upon the sabbath day.

The Pharisees lived according to the Scriptures. They kept the Sabbath day holy by not working as commanded by the Scripture. They defined what they could do and what they could not do on the Sabbath in their own way, and lived a thorough life following the established law.

They made such a laborious endeavor and so they had to show off their efforts to other people and win their admiration. When they had accumulated such self-righteousness, they automatically gained 'judging power' over others. This is what they did. When they found fault with Jesus and His disciples and judged them, it was a perfect chance for them to display their observance of the Sabbath to others.

We quite often meet such self-righteous people. They will say that we should love our neighbors, and we should not commit adultery, and so forth. They are saying this because they have done this themselves, and wish to force others to do as they do. Pharisees are such people.

When the Pharisees scolded Jesus by insisting that He had profaned the Sabbath, He refuted them by quoting two examples from the Old Testament, the cases of David and the priests.

The Priests Profane the Sabbath and Are Blameless

> [Matthew 12:3-5] [3] But he said unto them, Have ye not read what David did, when he was an hungred, and they that were

Morals vs. Word of God 35

with him; ⁴ How he entered into the house of God, and did eat the shewbread, which was not lawful for him to eat, neither for them which were with him, but only for the priests? ⁵ Or have ye not read in the law, how that on the sabbath days the priests in the temple profane the sabbath, and are blameless?

It would have been easier for us to understand, if He had said that the hungry people should eat first and thereafter comes observance of the Sabbath. This would be more humane. However, He claims His justice citing the case of David and the priests.

Referring to 1Samuel 21:1, when being chased by king Saul and being hungry, David went into the house of God in Nob to meet Ahimelech the priest, and he ate the bread that the priest gave him. At that time, there was only the showbread, and Ahimelech gave it to David and his men so that they may eat it. According to the law, only the priests could eat the showbread, but David and his followers ate it and were blameless. This is the story, which Jesus cites.

As another example, He mentions the case in which the priests were blameless when they profaned the Sabbath in the temple. Even though the Israelites should keep the Sabbath holy and do no work at all, the priests in the temple were allowed exceptions from the law.

🗁 In the Temple

There is one thing in common between David who did what he was not allowed to do on the Sabbath and the priests who were blameless. It is that they were in the temple. David went into the temple and ate the showbread, and the priests profaned the Sabbath in the temple. Once in the temple, they are blameless even if they eat the showbread or profane the Sabbath day.

It is hardly possible that the Pharisees did not know of these two cases. However, it is not certain whether the Pharisees correctly understood what Jesus had explained, but they would argue as follows:

"Are you in the same category as David and his men at that

time? Are you the very priests in the temple? Even if we accept that the persons in the temple are blameless, you are not in the temple but in the cornfield."

Both cases in the Old Testament foreshadow the things that will be achieved when Jesus comes. Jesus says in response to their thoughts as follow:

One Greater Than the Temple

> [Matthew 12:6-8] ^{6} But I say unto you, That in this place is one greater than the temple. ^{7} But if ye had known what this meaneth, I will have mercy, and not sacrifice, ye would not have condemned the guiltless. ^{8} For the Son of man is Lord even of the sabbath day.

Here, Jesus is revealing that the temple is only a shadow of the reality, which is Jesus, to come. Reality is greater than its shadow. So in this sense, He said He is greater than the temple. The disciples violated the Sabbath, but they were blameless because they are with Jesus who is the reality of the temple itself.

Before Jesus comes, a man should enter the temple in order to be blameless even if he profaned the Sabbath. However, after He came, the temple as a tabernacle or a building is switched to the temple as a man. The temple as a man walks around. So if we walk with Him, we can be free from the law whatever we do anytime and anywhere.

This is not limited only to the law regarding keeping the Sabbath holy, but it covers the whole of the Law.

The disciples will be one with Jesus receiving Him in them as the Holy Spirit after His death on the cross and resurrection. Then, the body of disciples individually becomes the living and walking temple. Read 1Co 3:16: "Know ye not that ye are the temple of God, and that the Spirit of God dwelleth in you?" Thus, they are freed from the law. Jesus came to achieve this salvation for us also.

Jesus who came in the past could set them free who were his disciples and people in His day. Then, where and how can we meet Him, be one with Him, and be set free from the law? Jesus comes to us through men who have the Word in them, they are like Peter, Paul, John, *et cetera*. Men who have the Word will lead us to receive the Holy Spirit in us. Then our body will become a living and walking temple of God. We then will also become those who profane the Sabbath and are blameless.

🗁 Temple of Idol

If Jesus has not yet come on us as the Holy Spirit, our body is not a holy temple but a temple of the idol. Each one of us who call ourselves Christians believe that Jesus stays in us, the Holy Spirit abides in us, and that God is with us, and every other good thing.

However, if God is really in our heart, we do not judge others. Nevertheless, we do judge others, envy them, feel jealous of them, and finally do not love our neighbors as ourselves. This is because we have another Jesus in us. This God is an idol made by me based on Bible common sense, which is the commandment of men. God made in our image.

God will come on us when the temple of the idol in us has been destroyed and a new temple has been built through the real Jesus at the cross. After this process has been completed, the Spirit of God will come on us.

I Will Have Mercy and Not Sacrifice

Jesus continues to say in Matthew 12:7: "If you had known what this means, I will have mercy, and not sacrifice, you would not have condemned the guiltless." This does not mean to say that we should show our mercy to others around us. Its true meaning is as follows:

"Lay down all your own endeavors to serve God, which means sacrifice, and simply follow and obey Jesus seeking His mercy, then you will be healed and will receive the Holy Spirit. It is your priority. If you have known that believing in God is to seek His mercy, not to accumulate your self-righteousness (sacrifice), you would have understood us and said we are blameless."

Jesus points out our inevitable digression while we believe in

Him, quoting from Hosea 6:6. The following is the mind of Jesus towards us:

"If you present your self-righteousness acquired from the deeds of the law to God, you will have to condemn others with reference to the works you have done. For example, when you have kept the Sabbath, you will soon boast that you have kept it, and concurrently you will watch others and judge them when they break the Sabbath. This is the root of the struggles and this causes no peace in this world.

So you have to have the mercy of God. Be humble, do not behave as if you know anything in front of God, otherwise all you will do is develop the self-righteousness of the Pharisees. And you will go the way that they went. You should be like the prodigal son and ask Him to have mercy on you. If your prayer is sincere, then God will send you the Savior, and He will put the Holy Spirit in your heart after healing your soul.

This is the mercy of God, which the Scripture speaks of. Then, you will understand Me and will not judge and blame for the profanation of the Sabbath."

Indeed, the Pharisees took their self-righteousness as sacrifices and gave it to Him boastfully. They quite naturally pointed out what Jesus and His disciples did wrong and judged them because they had such self-righteousness. They did not believe in God in the right manner. And we are not much different from them.

The Son of Man is Lord even of the Sabbath Day

Jesus calls Himself the Lord of the Sabbath. The word 'Lord' is translated from the Greek word *kurios* meaning the 'master,' 'leader,' or 'ruler' according to the lexical definition. The disciples called Him Lord many times, which refers to the lexical meaning of the Lord spoken by the public in general in those days.

However, the phrase 'Lord of the Sabbath day' in this verse has a deeper meaning. It represents the Lord as the author and finisher of salvation who shows the way to salvation, leads us, and finally makes us reach the kingdom of God by laying down His life on the cross. He is the only one who can do this, and He is the Lord of this salvation. Salvation is to enter His rest.

So the disciples who can truly call Jesus the Lord are those in whom the entire process of salvation has been completed by Jesus. Read Acts 2:21: "And it shall come to pass, that whosoever shall call on the name of the Lord shall be saved."

This is what Peter said at the Pentecost. Finally Peter had accepted Jesus as his Lord. Whoever wishes to call Jesus his Lord, should reach the Pentecost stage of faith. Then Jesus will be his Lord truly.

So He is the Lord of those who are saved and enter His rest. He is the Lord even of the Sabbath day.

It is clear that the Sabbath does not mean the day or the date, but those who are saved and who entered His rest. The Son of man is the Lord of such Sabbaths.

Epilogue

Here you can see that Jesus and the Pharisees have a totally different view of the Scriptures. The Pharisees are absolutely blind to the real meaning of the Scriptures. Under these circumstances, how can they believe in God properly? Not a chance.

Likewise, if you do not know the true meanings of the Scripture, how can you expect to believe in Jesus properly? You will definitely go astray in your walk of faith. Be humble in front of the Word of God, and listen to what the Scriptures are really saying. If you think that you know something about the Scripture, the Scripture will keep silent to you.

In the passage discussed above (Mat 12:1-8), Jesus reveals to us the real meaning of the temple. You should be the temple itself having received the Holy Spirit through meeting the real Jesus. For this, you have to pray to God as one of the prodigal sons for mercy. Then you will be sinless. You will be the Sabbath itself, having Jesus as your Lord in the real sense.

Expo Science Park*

I will now tell you a story that happened not much after I met the Lord. I had three days off including Saturday, Sunday, and Monday that was a national holiday. Unexpectedly, I had to go to Busan on business during the same days. My wife suggested to me to make a trip with the family, and I accepted her idea because we had not traveled together for a long time.

However, I thought it would not be a full enough schedule if we visited Busan only, and so I made a schedule to drop by the city of Daejon located in-between. On Friday evening, I went down to Daejon alone ahead of our family.

Early next morning, I went to a church to attend the daybreak prayer service. I recall that the persimmon trees in the middle of the garden looked impressive. The sermon about Joel that the preacher gave moved me very much.

In the daytime, I finished my official work, and I went to the express bus station to receive my family. We met easily and happily. They told me what they heard from the woman sitting next to them in the bus. "The woman said, if we wanted to visit the Science Park, we should go there very early in the morning. Otherwise, we will have to spend most of the day waiting for the entrance standing in line."

My wife and kids were thinking of waking up early on the Sunday morning to go to the park. They were in great expectation of the Science Park.

Sunday came. I attended the early morning service at the church on that day too, and I asked one of the church members:

"I'd like to know the time when the first Sunday morning service begins."

"The first one starts at 9 am and the second one begins at 11 am."

On hearing it, I felt embarrassed. I thought if the first service was given 7 am, we would attend the first service and then visit the park. On the way back to hotel, I was troubled a lot. I was frequently told to keep the Lord's day by the Lord. I sincerely wanted to go to church, but in consideration of my family who came a long way with great expectation, I could not go to the park late after attending the 9 am service.

Reaching the hotel, in agony for a while, I just decided to sing a hymn instead in the hotel room without going to church, and then departed for the park. We hurried to reach there, but as we had heard, there was a long queue of those who came earlier than us before the gate of the park. Although we entered the park after a long wait, it was not as exciting and interesting as I had anticipated. My wife and kids felt the same way.

After visiting the science park, we went down to Busan on the same day. Upon arrival, my son had a great evening on the beach alone. However, he was laid up in bed with a severe headache and a high fever until the next morning. As he was so serious, our original plan to walk around Busan had to be cancelled. I had to take them back to Seoul early in the morning.

Our trip that was planned with such a great expectation was thus messed up. It resulted in a half tour and we were not happy at all.

Coming back to Seoul, I had no idea why the tour which all of our family had looked forward to so much, had got into this mess. After several days of thinking, I finally realized what the problem was.

In Daejon, I should have gone to the church service with my family, and thereafter to the park. Priority should have been given to the service at the church, not the amusement park. God was not pleased with my decision.

In fact, while singing a hymn in the hotel room, I felt uneasy, which was an indication from the Lord. It was natural that the park we visited ignoring God's will was not exciting to us at all. In consideration of my ignorance about the will of the Lord, the Lord was rather generous and merciful to allow us even half of our itinerary. So I repented.

Though too late, I regretted that I did not decide to go to church at that time. However, when I thought deeply, I could not decide otherwise. That was the best I could do with my faith that I had at that moment. I thought many things through this trip.

Usually, I gave priority to go to church every Lord's day. For instance, whenever I attended the service on Sunday, I compared my attendance at the service with my personal comfort, and I laid weight on attending church. I had the faith to overcome annoyance at that level.

However, the Lord prepared something to increase the level of my faith, which was this trip. I was offended by this case and I accordingly got hurt by it. Further, this hurt was impressed on my heart deeply and my faith grew in this process. Through this trial, my faith increased to think of God first even though my family had high hopes of doing something else.

Some people having heard my testimony may ask, "Does the commandment to keep the Sabbath day holy mean to keep the Lord's day holy?" Yes, the Lord wants us to keep the Lord's day holy even in the literal sense.

I read a testimony of one couple. They promised to the Lord to go to church regularly from the coming week. But that week was consecutive golden holidays, including Sunday, so they thought "All right. This time only, we will go on a trip, and from next week onward we would go to church for sure." They both agreed on this idea and went on a trip, but the trip was not interesting at all.

The next morning, the husband went jogging and met with an accident and he fell into a coma. She could not do anything but nurse him indefinitely with little hope of his recovery. She cried and prayed hard every day and night. Miraculously, one day, her husband rose up after six years in a coma and his first word was "Amen."

This testimony also shows us God's will for us to keep the Lord's day holy. Through making us keep the Lord's day, the Lord will make us the priests in the temple who profane the Sabbath, and are blameless.

You Shall Not Commit Adultery

[Hosea 2:2-7]

² Plead with your mother, plead: for she is not my wife, neither am I her husband: let her therefore put away her whoredoms out of her sight, and her adulteries from between her breasts; ³ Lest I strip her naked, and set her as in the day that she was born, and make her as a wilderness, and set her like a dry land, and slay her with thirst. ⁴ And I will not have mercy upon her children; for they be the children of whoredoms. ⁵ For their mother hath played the harlot: she that conceived them hath done shamefully: for she said, I will go after my lovers, that give me my bread and my water, my wool and my flax, mine oil and my drink. ⁶ Therefore, behold, I will hedge up thy way with thorns, and make a wall, that she shall not find her paths. ⁷ And she shall follow after her lovers, but she shall not overtake them; and she shall seek them, but shall not find them: then shall she say, I will go and return to my first husband; for then was it better with me than now.

"Thou shalt not commit adultery," says Exodus 20:14. When we read this in the Bible, we think of adultery between a man and a woman. This way of thinking reveals that we have read the word of God as a moral code of man.

While we are still infant believers, there are times when the word reads to us as such. However, that stage should be only for a short period of time. If we continue to be such infants for thirty or forty years, we cannot say we are saved.

The Bible is not written for preventing adultery. It is obvious if we think that atheists and believers of other religions also try not to commit adultery even without the Bible. Then what is the difference? What is the particular reason we believe in Jesus?

We should know that even though the Bible introduces the concept of physical adultery, it is only an expedient for conveying the spirit to the readers. We, therefore, when we read the Scriptures, should not get stuck at the literal meanings, but we always have to find the spiritual meanings of them.

I will now explain what God wants to talk to us about through the concept of the adultery.

Outline

In Hosea Chapter 1, God speaks to the prophet Hosea as follows: "Go, take unto thee a wife of whoredoms and children of whoredoms: for the land hath committed great whoredom, departing from the LORD" (Hos 1:2b).

So Hosea married Gomer and had the son Jezreel (which means 'God scatters'), the daughter Lo-Ruhamah (it means 'no mercy'), and the son Lo-Ammi (meaning 'not my people'). We can imagine from their names that they are not loved by Him.

In Chapter 2, He speaks to the people of Israel: "Plead with your mother. She is not my wife and I am not her husband because she has committed adultery. If you do not get her to put away her whoredom out of her sight and her adulteries, I will strip her naked and set her like a dry land and slay her with thirst. I will not have mercy on her children."

The mother of Israel says, "I will go after my lovers who give me my bread, my water, my wool, my flax, my oil, and my drink."

God then foresees that she will not find her way and will say, "I will go and return to my first husband for then was it better with me than now."

Now, I shall explain the following points:

First, what does it mean to play the harlot? It is not what we generally think.

Second, God said to plead with you mother regarding the matter of playing the harlot. And who is this mother? We will be able to plead with her only when we know who she is.

Third, the mother of Israel left God and followed her lovers, and who are these lovers?

What is It to Play the Harlot?

We already know well the act of playing the harlot or the act of adultery. Adultery is defined in the dictionary as sex between a married person and someone who is not their husband or wife. The person who does this kind of act is called an adulterer.

However, this Scripture does not refer to this adultery or fornication. As I said, the Scripture explains the spiritual world by borrowing the concept of physical adultery. It likens the relation between God and the Israelites to the relation between the husband and the wife. Read Isaiah below:

> For thy Maker is thine husband; the LORD of hosts is his name; and thy Redeemer the Holy One of Israel; The God of the whole earth shall he be called. [Isaiah 54:5]

The people of Israel are the wife of God. He says they are adulterous and played the harlot, which means that they left God and had sex with other persons. And, of course, the Israelites are us, the believers, the chosen people of God in the spiritual sense.

God says the mother of Israel has committed adultery and He says, "Plead with your mother, plead." If the mother has committed adultery, why does God not tell her directly not to? Is it reasonable to tell the children to put away the whoredom from your mother? You may defend yourselves by saying that you are not the mother who committed adultery.

However, God is right. He cannot be wrong. We should thank God for revealing the secret of being born again by allowing the mother to come on stage here.

▷ Who is the Mother?

Who is our mother? The mother is us. We are the mother, and

the child of the mother is us, too. I will now explain the reason why we are our mother.

We all recall the dialogue about being born again between Jesus and Nicodemus in John.

> ³ Jesus answered and said unto him, Verily, verily, I say unto thee, Except a man be born again, he cannot see the kingdom of God. ⁴ Nicodemus saith unto him, How can a man be born when he is old? can he enter the second time into his mother's womb, and be born? [John 3:3-4]

In this instance, before thinking that Nicodemus was a man of ignorance, we should realize we too, are as ignorant. If we had known the truth about being born again, we would have correctly identified who God was referring to as the mother. If we have no idea about who she is, we are asking the same question as Nicodemus, "Can I enter the second time my mother's womb and be born?"

Jesus speaks about being born again spiritually. That is, a man can go into the kingdom of God when he is born again. The born again man has to have two beings, one is the 'self before being born again' and the other is 'self after being born again.'

How can the 'self before being born again' be born again? Will he have to enter his mother womb again and come out of it? No. Self that is not born again will be born again when he receives the seed of God and gives birth to a child.

Therefore, the mother of the 'me after being born again' is, in fact 'me before being born again.' Both of them represent me. Thus, my mother is me.

📂 Whose Seed Does My Mother Receive?

Here is the most crucial part of the passage. We are the wife of God who is supposed to receive the seed of God to be pregnant and deliver the life of Jesus in us. When we deliver the life, we will be saved and born again by the very life we delivered (Mat 1:21, 1Ti 2:15).

The life we deliver is dependant upon the seed we receive. I mean if we receive God's seed, we will deliver the son of God. If we receive 'non-God' seed, which is called adultery, we will deliver a 'non-God' child. They are not sons of God, and they will be called Jezreel (God scatters), Lo-Ruhamah (No Mercy), Lo-Ammi (Not My People) as mentioned in Hosea Chapter 1.

God says we are adulterous because we receive seed other than the seed of God.

Then, how are we receiving different seed other than of God? We all receive the word of God from the Scripture and without doubt, we keep it as instructed.

Some of us may think like this:

"I, as a Christian, read the Scripture, study it, pray, and experience spiritual gifts and so I am deadly sure that I receive the word of God this way. What else can I do to receive the word? God must be talking to somebody else but me…"

Yes, I agree. All who believe in Jesus will receive the seed from the Scripture, not from the books of other religions. If this is true, then we should have known the meaning of adultery; and would not have repeatedly committed sins and repented of the same; we would not have thought that the completion of sanctification would come only after death, while leading a laborious and heavy-laden life. Because the Scripture makes us holy as God is and it gives us once-and-for-all forgiveness. Unfortunately, we are not so.

The reason for this paradox is this. Even though we read the Scripture, if we fail to understand its spiritual meanings, we receive the superficial and literal meanings of it, which are actually the commandments of men.

For example, regarding the word, 'thou shalt not commit adultery,' if we understand this commandment as physical adultery; we have substantially received the word of men, even though we think we received the word of God. Thus, the Scripture is transformed into the word of men in us unwittingly. Can this word make us pregnant and deliver the new life? No. If so, all those non-believers who did not commit adultery out there would have been born again with the new life.

Therefore, as long as we read the Scripture in such a fashion, it can never bring us to being born again, and we will remain as sinners regardless of what we do in church. We can see those who sow the commandments of men wrapped up as the word of God, and those who receive the same, are committing the fornication that the Scripture warns of.

This is adultery that we are committing everyday. No wonder our faith in Christ is so powerless. This is the very reason why we are not changed even though we have believed in Jesus for several decades. And many people have left and are leaving the church being fed up with the shallow teachings of the church. So sad, they try to seek truth in other religions. Nevertheless, there is no truth, except Jesus.

Now, most of you will think that you are born again. Okay. Then, what kind of seed have you been receiving? Doctrines of men, right? What do you expect your faith, your spiritual child, would be? Don't tell me you are expecting he would be the son of God. He should be one of the following three: Jezreel, Lo-Ruhamah, Lo-Ammi.

If you think your being born again should be re-looked at, then now is the time for you to plead with your mother not to take the seed of men, but God. Then, you will be able to deliver the son of God, which is the born again you!

Let us look at the father, the seed-giver.

Whose Father is God?

In John Chapter 8, Jesus disputes with the Jews. Both of them insist that God is their father. Here father refers to God. The father is the one who gives seed to the mother of the Israelites. The Jews thought that they had received the seed of God, but Jesus said they had not. Read John below:

> [41] Ye do the deeds of your father. Then said they to him, We be not born of fornication; we have one Father, even God. [42] Jesus said unto them, If God were your Father, ye would love me: for I proceeded forth and came from God; neither came I of myself, but he sent me. [John 8:41-42]

Whose father is God? Needless to say, God is the father of Jesus. Jesus and the Jews are mentioning the same God who appears in the Scripture. Then, what is the difference between Jesus and the Jews?

The Jews read the Scripture as morals and ethics, the commandments of men. This is how the mother of the Jews received the words of men from the Scripture. For this reason, Jesus tells the Jews, who say that God is their father, that their father is the devil, not God (Jhn 8:44). The children who are born through the commandments of men are the children of devil. They are children of whoredoms in Hosea's expression.

In general, we use the term devil when we speak ill of others. So we may mistakenly conclude that Jesus has cursed the Jews by saying something like "Go to hell!"

No, not so. Jesus, being love itself, cannot do so by nature. The definition of devil in the Scripture is the man who has left God. They left God, being deceived by thinking that the Scriptures are the morals and ethics of men. They are deceived by themselves and are therefore seized by the devil.

Jesus has come to take back the captives of the devil and to give them life. He wishes to enlighten them to repent and have them back to God. This book also serves that purpose.

The Jews are insisting that God is their father, but they do so out of ignorance. The Jews represent us, who believe in Jesus in the same way.

The Lover of the Mother of Israel

Who is the lover of the mother of Israel? The lover who is their father, is the God created by themselves (in their own image). They created God to their taste based on their morals and ethics taken from the Scripture. Naturally, they will love the God that they made, and worship Him. But, that is not God but Baal (Baalim), the idol.

Read Hosea below:

[Hosea 2:13] And I will visit upon her the days of Baalim, wherein she burned incense to them, and she decked herself with her earrings and her jewels, and she went after her lovers, and forgat me, saith the LORD.

This is how they served the idol. They prayed (burned incense), and accumulated self-righteousness of good deeds to show off to others proudly (decked herself with earrings and jewels), and believed in the idol, forgetting God (went after her lovers). All these days of idol worship will be visited upon them and judged by the Lord.

At first glance, the moral and ethical interpretation of the Scripture looks good, pleasing to the eye, and desirable, so we follow. This is how our mother is 'after the lover,' and thus we are adulterous now. If we carry on this faith, we will face the following day of visitation from the Lord:

[22] Many will say to me in that day, Lord, Lord, have we not prophesied in thy name? and in thy name have cast out devils? and in thy name done many wonderful works? [23] And then will I profess unto them, I never knew you: depart from me, ye that work iniquity. [Matthew 7:22-23]

Let him hear who has ears to hear.

I Slay Her with Thirst

[Hosea 2:3] Lest I strip her naked, and set her as in the day that she was born, and make her as a wilderness, and set her like a dry land, and slay her with thirst.

God says if the mother does not put away her whoredom out of her sight, she will be like a wilderness and die of thirst. This means that if she will not receive the right word of God, He will make her a wilderness and slay her.

It sounds like terrible punishment. However, it is not punishment, but natural law. For instance, if you drink no water, you will become like a dry land and then finally die of thirst. When He said that He would strip her naked and 'set her as in the day that she was born,' He meant that if the person remained in the state of having left God, serving a self-created God, then he will be dead. If a man leaves life, he faces death naturally. It is not a punishment, but a natural law.

We can find many persons in the Scripture who have been stripped naked in their lives. The typical character is the younger son having left his home in the parable of the prodigal son. He left his father, he was plundered of all he had, and he almost starved to death. It is the natural result of his leaving the father who is life itself.

The case in which the prodigal son leaves his father means fornication the Scripture says to us. When he was starving to death, he then tried to find his father because he realized he was much better off in the house of his father.

The prodigal son finally said, "And when he came to himself, he said, How many hired servants of my father's have bread enough and to spare, and I perish with hunger" (Luk 15:17).

I Will Go and Return

[Hosea 2:7] And she shall follow after her lovers, but she shall not overtake them; and she shall seek them, but shall not find them: then shall she say, I will go and return to my first husband; for then was it better with me than now.

If we have whoredom on our face now, we are living in the wilderness. Such life will go on until we are exhausted and fall down. After that, we will show interest in the spiritual meanings of the Scripture and seek God truly. This is the return of us to our first husband. From then, we can believe in Jesus in the right manner.

The prodigal son finally said, "I will arise and go to my father, and will say unto him, Father, I have sinned against heaven, and before thee" (Luk 15:18).

Epilogue

In the parable of the lost son in Luke Chapter 15, when the

younger son came back the father celebrated his return. However, the older son complained saying, "But as soon as this thy son was come, which hath devoured thy living with harlots, thou hast killed for him the fatted calf" (Luk 15:30).

In living with the father, the older son was only concerned about doing moral deeds, such as, working hard according to his father's orders, increasing his father's wealth, not going around with harlots, *et cetera*. However, it turned out that he could not stay with his father and his brother (Luk 15:28).

On the other hand, the father was well pleased that the younger son had returned. He did not care whether or not the younger son was adulterous, or whether he had gathered a fortune. He only hoped for the return of his son day and night.

If we interpret adultery in the Scripture as physical adultery and live to show God how good we are, then we are like the older son. If we understand adultery in a spiritual sense, however, then we will be returning to God, our Father, as the younger son.

Let us stop the adultery now. God awaits our return day and night.

Sell that You Have, and Give to the Poor

[Matthew 19:16-22]

[16] And, behold, one came and said unto him, Good Master, what good thing shall I do, that I may have eternal life? [17] And he said unto him, Why callest thou me good? there is none good but one, that is, God: but if thou wilt enter into life, keep the commandments. [18] He saith unto him, Which? Jesus said, Thou shalt do no murder, Thou shalt not commit adultery, Thou shalt not steal, Thou shalt not bear false witness, [19] Honour thy father and thy mother: and, Thou shalt love thy neighbour as thyself. [20] The young man saith unto him, All these things have I kept from my youth up: what lack I yet? [21] Jesus said unto him, If thou wilt be perfect, go and sell that thou hast, and give to the poor, and thou shalt have treasure in heaven: and come and follow me. [22] But when the young man heard that saying, he went away sorrowful: for he had great possessions.

Jesus said, in order to be perfect we need to sell what we have and give to the poor. Maybe this is one of the strongest commandments for believers to help the poor.

However, no one can keep this commandment strictly, because we also need possessions to make our living. So we only try to keep this commandment at large. Then in this case, did we keep His commandment? I do not think so. Because He commanded us to simply sell what we have and give to the poor. No excuse for not doing so. We just have to do it.

However, if you, as a believer, are keen to hear what Jesus is saying, I say to you that that is not what Jesus is saying. It has a different meaning. All the sayings of Jesus are not commandments, but the spirit that leads you to eternal life. Read John 6:63, "It is the spirit that quickeneth; the flesh profiteth nothing: the words that I speak unto you, they are spirit, and they are life."

Here, Jesus reveals the truth that we all have to believe in a self-created God, and when the time is ripe, Jesus comes and reveals the true God. When we live under a self-created God, we read the Scriptures as commandments, which are the superficial meanings of it, and that is the only reading that we have at that stage. So we would not know even our readings are commandments or not, as there is nothing to compare, until Jesus comes and shows us the true spiritual meanings

The young man here had the superficial meanings of the Scriptures. That proves he believed in a self-created God. And we will know that we are the young man who left Jesus as we read this message. This revelation by the word is a judgment to save us from sin and death.

If we are misguided and continue to worship this self-created God, we face final judgment. And it will be too late to repent. Blessed are those who are judged by the word now, for they will have sound faith before final judgment.

Let us see how this word gives us life, the spirit.

What Is the Good Thing?

> [Matthew 19:16-17] [16] And, behold, one came and said unto him, Good Master, what good thing shall I do, that I may have eternal life? [17] And he said unto him, Why callest thou me good? there is none good but one, that is, God: but if thou wilt enter into life, keep the commandments.

A rich young man asked Jesus that what good thing he should do to have eternal life. Whatever his understanding of eternal life was, eternal life as set out in the Scripture does not mean life that lasts eternally in time. But, it means the new life of Jesus, which is the spirit, compared to the depraved life we already have, which is of the flesh.

Jesus wanted to enlighten him about one thing first before He answered this question, so He said, "Why do you call me good? There is none good but one, that is, God."

This means that there is no one or no deed in the world that is good by itself. Therefore, in order to do good things, they should be connected to God, the only good. Without this, all endeavors will be in vain.

The young man thought that if he would do good things as he was, God would allow him eternal life, the kingdom of heaven, and all kinds of blessings. So he asked Him "What shall I do?" He is already in the wrong position and is thus asking the wrong question.

Our thinking is not much different from his. We think that we will be qualified for eternal life if we do good things, such as almsgiving, prayer, fasting, donation, loving our neighbor, and so forth. Based on this, we will ask Jesus, "What else shall I do?"

However, these good things are not only done by good men. Anybody can do such good things. Even evil men, who cannot have eternal life, can also do such deeds. For instance, the Pharisees in the Scripture did many good things. They donated, fasted, stole nothing, and committed no adultery. They honored their father and mother. However, Jesus rebuked them as hypocrites (Mat 6:1-8).

By this, we know that even if a man has done good things, he may not be a good man who is eligible for eternal life. Also, even if a man does a good thing, that deed, of itself, cannot make good either. As explained, good things and good deeds are not good by themselves. It depends on who carries out the deed. If a good man does it, it would be good. If an evil man does it, it would be evil.

So, in order for us to do good things, we need to become a good man first, and then we can do good things. This is the truthful approach to performing good deeds. And to be a good man, we should be connected to God, the only good, by being born again.

This is the meaning of what Jesus said, "There is none good but one, that is, God."

Remember this: Having eternal life is not a matter of a reward from Jesus for works done according to the Scriptures, but a matter of being transformed into a new man by Jesus according to the Scriptures.

📂 Self-Created God

I will explain further with the case of the rich young man, to show that you should be changed by Jesus. The young man did all the necessary deeds mentioned in the Scriptures. Nothing lacks in that sense. So when Jesus says something, he will automatically say "I have done that from my youth up."

But the point is not that whether he did something or not. The point is whether he is connected to God properly or not. Of course, to this word he will say also, "Yes! Properly." He is deadly sure on all occasions. So when Jesus said, "There is none good but one, that is, God." He thought, "I know that, I only do all these things being connected to God."

Unfortunately not. This is his blind spot. He is connected to his self-made God, that is, he is not connected properly to God. He unknowingly believes in the God that he made through the moral and ethical meanings of the Scriptures.

So in this case, even though he thought he did good things of God, in reality he did not. He did good things for himself to show people, being deceived by his self-created God. That good deed is called self-righteousness. No wonder a self-created God produces self-righteousness. In faith, you should not perform self-service. Have Jesus, the servant attend you.

Simply speaking, it is apparent that the young man was serving a self-created God when we see the way he interprets the Scriptures. He read it as commandments, not as the spirit.

He did not understand what Jesus said, but he thought he understood, and the dialogue goes on. Jesus is now answering his question, "What good thing shall I do, that I may have eternal life?"

📂 If You Will Enter Life, Keep the Commandments

"If you will enter life, keep the commandments," Jesus answered to young man. The young man, understanding this word based on a self-created God, talked to himself as follows:

"Yes, the commandments that I take from the Scripture are good, because they are God's words. I decided in the right way and I did the good things up to now. Now the eternal life is mine. I will have to ask Him which commandment He indicates. Undoubtedly, He will mention the commandments recorded in the Scripture, the words of God. I had done all these things for the sake of God."

Therefore, naturally he asks Him in the next verse, which commandment he should keep. The young man was talking about his self-created God, thinking Jesus also was talking about the same God that he has.

Then, what is the spiritual meaning that Jesus wanted to convey to the young man by: "Keep the commandments?"

📂 The Significance of Keep the Commandments

The young man understood the word to keep the commandments as observing the commandments. Jesus did not mean to imply this. The word 'keep,' *tereo* in Greek, here can be construed in two ways; first, to 'observe,' and second, to 'guard,' or to 'retain.' When it comes to the meaning of 'keep' in the word 'keep the commandments,' it is to be construed as second meaning. Therefore, to keep the commandments in the Scripture represents to have them in him and to retain them.

How does he do this? He has to meet Jesus and have his sinful nature destroyed on the cross, and after that Jesus will come into him again as Christ, the Holy Spirit. This way he can have the law and the commandments, which are of God Himself, written in his heart, and can keep them. This is the true connection with God as one, the only good. This is how he can keep the word or the commandments. This is what Jesus was saying to the young man. This will become evident as we go on.

As for the young man, doubtlessly, he was connected to God, but to the wrong God. The wrong God asks him to do something good, but true God asks him to be healed first by Jesus to do something good, as Jesus reveals here.

Having not yet realized what Jesus was really asking him, the

Morals vs. Word of God 59

young man showed his readiness to do good things for eternal life, and so asked Jesus, "Which commandments?"

Which Commandments?

> [Matthew 19:18-20] [18] He saith unto him, Which? Jesus said, Thou shalt do no murder, Thou shalt not commit adultery, Thou shalt not steal, Thou shalt not bear false witness, [19] Honour thy father and thy mother: and, Thou shalt love thy neighbour as thyself. [20] The young man saith unto him, All these things have I kept from my youth up: what lack I yet?

In response to his question "Which?" Jesus mentioned the well-known commandments from the Scripture. Then, he asked Him again, by saying, "I have kept all these things from my youth up. What do I lack yet?"

In fact, the commandments are not something that men can keep. However, to say the least of it, he did no murder, he did not commit adultery, he did not steal, he did not bear false witness, he honored his father and mother, and he loved his neighbor as himself to his standard. Therefore, he wished to show them before Him and people with pride.

When he asked Him by saying, "What do I lack yet?" he was so sure that he had been doing all right. He might have expected that He would tell him "Yes, you really did a good job. You have received eternal life."

▷ The Young Man is *Me*

As we can see, what the young man was aiming to do is not different from what we are aiming for in believing Jesus.

We did no murder, we did not commit adultery, we did not steal, we did not bear false witness, we honored our father and mother: and, we loved our neighbor as ourselves. On top of that, we attended church service, prayed, participated in the missionary team, sang at church choir, studied Bible, helped the needy and donated, all from our youth up. We are proud of these works.

This is how we believed in Jesus in order to have eternal life, and so will say to Jesus, "What do I lack yet?" This is exactly what the young man said. As a matter of fact, he said what we want to say to Him in place of us. Maybe we would be reluctant to accept such a fact, because the young man left Jesus sorrowful. We want to be different from him. Obviously, we did not leave Jesus, as we are following Him in the church. Nevertheless, we are not much different from him. No, we are him.

Some believers may say:

"This guy wanted to be righteous by the works of the law, but I am totally different from him, because I believed in Him and consequently, I am saved and have received eternal life by faith. Out of thanks for this amazing grace of God, I love my neighbors now."

Regarding the faith that the Scripture refers to, it is not that 'we believe' or 'try to believe' in Jesus. This is another type of works to believe in order to have eternal life. True faith is the 'faith of Jesus' that comes when we meet the real Jesus here. Jesus will heal our soul and will come into us as Holy Spirit, which is the faith of Jesus, Only then, can we believe in Him in the real sense.

Therefore, even if we may say we are saved by faith, it is not the real faith that brings us to salvation, but works and endeavors from us. So we are not in the least different from the young man who tried to be righteous by works. On the contrary, we can never catch up with him in doing the commandments of God. He kept all the commandments, but most Christians would not keep them all on the pretext that they are saved by faith.

Then, are we really saved by faith? No, we are not. We are lukewarm, and neither cold nor hot (Rev 3:16). In fact, we are cold (under the law), thinking hot (under grace) by ourselves.

If you cannot understand and agree with what I have said above, just think about your eyes to read the Scripture. Is it the eye of flesh, or eye of spirit? If you have any thing or many things to show to God, you are in the flesh.

What Is It 'That the Young Man Has'?

[Matthew 19:21-22] [21] Jesus said unto him, If thou wilt be perfect, go and sell that thou hast, and give to the poor, and thou shalt have treasure in heaven: and come and follow me. ²² But when the young man heard that saying, he went away sorrowful: for he had great possessions.

Many people insist based on this word, saying, "Look, Christianity also upholds no possession. Pastors should not own expensive cars, but they better ride small cars or bicycles." If Christians agree to this kind of interpretation, they have to sell all they have and give to the poor. Then, they will be called true believers.

The key point of the matter we are dealing with is; what are 'that he has' that he was told to sell? In consideration of verse 22 saying 'for he had great possessions,' we naturally think 'that he has' means material possessions. Yes, it could be so; however, that is not what Jesus meant to say.

What He told him to sell was not the material possessions, but his mental possession, that is, self-righteousness. His thoughts of "I have done this," "I have done that also," *et cetera* were the 'that he has' that Jesus mentioned. The young man was full of such self-righteousness that was accumulated by keeping the commandments of the Bible.

He had to sell 'that he has' to have the eternal life. How?

🗁 Sell That Which You Have

When Jesus told him to sell that he had, he went away sorrowful: for he understood 'that he has' as his material possessions.

Strangely enough, this young man could not sell his possessions, even though he claimed that he kept all the commandments of God. If he had really kept the commandments, why could he not sell his possessions? This proves that his statement that he had kept all the commandments was based on his own standard.

Anyway, how can a man sell his self-righteousness? The fundamental problem is this: The reason why we have such self-righteousness is that the 'old man' is alive. The 'old man' is the 'flesh,' which is one's life before he is born again. This 'old man' makes efforts to do good things without God and tries to negotiate an entrance ticket to kingdom of heaven with God. Jesus intends to destroy our 'old man' on the cross. When this is completed, our self-righteousness will be gone simultaneously. Thus, we sell 'that we have,' our possessions.

In the case where we believe in a self-created God, we tend to accumulate increasingly 'possessions' that is, self righteousness as time goes by. Ironically enough, the more we serve God, the more we go against God. We should not be expecting blessings from God under these circumstances.

If you want blessings, sell 'that you have.' Destroy your self-created God on the cross by following Jesus, and then all good things will be yours at once.

📂 Give to the Poor

"Sell that thou hast, and give to the poor." This is a really difficult word to understand. I will now try to explain this and it is up to you to understand. Those who have experienced the spiritual world will know that this makes sense.

Regarding what the 'poor' means, I will first explain what the 'rich' is, which is the antonym of the poor. The rich means the one who is full of self-righteousness, like the young man in this case. The poor is opposite to the rich. That is, the poor represents the one whose 'old man' has been destroyed, being united with Jesus at the cross, and thus, whose self-righteousness has ceased to exist. He is poor because he has nothing to display and boast of.

Read Matthew 5:3: "Blessed are the poor in spirit: for theirs is the kingdom of heaven." The poor are already in the kingdom of heaven because their 'old man' was destroyed on the cross, and as a result, the spirit of Christ has come upon them.

The relationship between the self-righteousness and the Holy Spirit is darkness versus light. If a person has self-righteousness, the Holy Spirit has not yet come on him, and if he has the Holy Spirit, his self-righteousness has been destroyed.

When a man sells 'that he has,' he becomes a poor man, who is in the kingdom of heaven. By giving up self-righteousness, he gains a poor state for himself. This is what it means to sell what you have and give to the poor. Jesus will lead us there, if only we do not refuse Him by wandering around trying to keep the commandments of a self-created God.

📂 Illustration

"Jesus said unto him, If thou wilt be perfect, go and sell that thou hast, and give to the poor, and thou shalt have treasure in heaven: and come and follow me," Matthew 19:21 says.

Here, to help understanding I will give a simple illustration. If we are in the flesh, no matter what good things we do by the Scriptures or in the church, we will only be producing self-righteousness. Even if the things of the 'spirit' look superb and we imitate them, all will be in vain.

If we wish to do good things, then we go through the death barrier that is the boundary between the two different worlds. No one can go through the death barrier and live. That is why we must meet and follow Jesus and be united with Him to go through the death barrier and live (Rom 6:5-7).

The Scripture testifies to this Jesus. But, we who are seized by the devil inside us, being deceived by him, want to work hard for eternal life, instead of going through death with Jesus. This is what the young man here did from his youth up, and all other believers also.

In fact, believers do not like Jesus who brings them to the death barrier. So they want to interpret the Scripture, which testifies to Jesus, in their own way, and consequently to their eyes the Scripture is so difficult to understand. We, the believers who have ears to hear, should wake up and go through the death of the cross being united with Jesus. Thereafter we in Christ will have to save our nations.

In the illustration, if we go through the death barrier, we will become spirit and will be perfect, poor in spirit, having treasure in heaven, able to follow Jesus with eternal life simultaneously. If we think of this verse (Mat 19:21) as a conditional sentence, it becomes a difficult passage to interpret. This is not a conditional verse. All these good things will be achieved at once when we go through death barrier.

	'ME'
Comes First	Comes Last
Law/Self-Created God	Grace/true God
Natural Life	Eternal Life
Self-Righteousness/Possessions	Possessions Sold
Rich	Poor
Imperfect	Perfect
Have Dung	Have Treasure
Earth/World	Heaven
Follower of self-created Jesus	Follower of Jesus

▲
DEATH Barrier
CROSS/JESUS

Let me continue to explain the remaining parts of the verse.

📂 Perfect Man

When your self-righteousness is gone, you become perfect. The perfect man is the one to whom the Christ, which is another name of the Holy Spirit, has come. You might feel awkward called perfect. However, it is the point where all true believers reach whilst they are alive in this world. Read Matthew below.

> Be ye therefore perfect, even as your Father which is in heaven is perfect. [Matthew 5:48]

In order for you to be perfect as God is perfect, the attribute of God should come to you, which is the Holy Spirit. Perfect is he on whom the Holy Spirit has come. He is poor in spirit and eternal life is his.

Considering that the original question was how to have eternal life, you will agree that this context explained in here is quite natural and reasonable.

📂 Treasure in Heaven

"And thou shalt have treasure in heaven."

This word does not intend that if the young man sells what he has, God will give him treasure in return when he ascends into heaven in the afterlife.

Here, heaven is neither the sky nor the kingdom of heaven where you go afterlife. Heaven is the place where God is. Therefore, when God, as Holy Spirit, has come on you, then you yourself will be heaven itself. And, the treasure, which is Christ, abides in you.

📁 Then Come, Follow Me

Here, 'follow' does not mean to imitate His deeds as a role model, but it means to have His life and live.

Think about Peter's case. When he met Jesus, he 'followed' Him as role model for three and half years, but during this time Peter could not 'follow' His life. At his Pentecost and thereafter, he could really 'follow' Him in his life because he had His life, the eternal life.

So we can see that in believing in Jesus, we have two stages of following Him; first to follow to be healed, and second to follow His life after healing and the forgiveness of sin.

In this verse, 'follow Me' means the second stage of following, because He is saying to the man who is made perfect and in heaven, that he has eternal life. We also should go through the process that the disciples experienced. Then we can live the life of Jesus, doing what He did. This is the meaning of following Him.

Why Did the Young Man Go Away?

> [Matthew 19:22] But when the young man heard that saying, he went away sorrowful: for he had great possessions.

In fact, He did not tell him to sell his earthly property, but he misunderstood Him and went away sorrowful. Some of us may wonder why He allowed the young man to misunderstand and go away. We may suppose that if He had told him that the possessions to sell were not his material ones, then he would not have gone away. No, it is not like that.

He could not follow Him from the very outset. It is because he could neither obey Him nor understand Him due to his self-righteousness and pride. So he could not follow Him anyway. He had to spend more time living his self-righteous life under the law. When he became exhausted and fell down, he would then be ready to follow Him. The time for him was not ripe. So he departed from Jesus quite naturally.

Here we can notice that this story has a double meaning. That is, the young man was rich and he departed from Jesus, This mirrors the spiritual truth. That he who is rich with self-righteousness cannot stay with Jesus, who is eternal life itself. The young man was rich and left Jesus, both in a natural and spiritual sense.

If we have self-righteousness, we cannot follow Him even though our body is in church every Sunday.

Epilogue

I want to make sure that I am not conveying the impression that our endeavors to keep the commandments are wasted, so please continue to do so. This is a faith-growing course; no one can skip the legalistic faith stage. Nevertheless, we have to think about what comes next. Now is the time to put an end to legalistic faith and receive true faith.

This book is a cry for those believers who are really exhausted and want to get out from under the law.

> Verily, verily, I say unto you, The hour is coming, and now is, when the dead shall hear the voice of the Son of God: and they that hear shall live. [John 5:25]

They that hear this cry shall live. It is time to live. In the past we have carried out the will of the self-created God, and we should not be deceived by him any more.

The Scriptures are not commandments or doctrines of men. It only testifies of the living Jesus who will make you one with the true God, the only good. Once we become one with Him, then we will have eternal life, become perfect, enter heaven, and be real followers of Jesus.

Follow this Jesus!

You Shall Not Eat of the Flesh of Swine

[Deuteronomy 14:8]
And the swine, because it divideth the hoof, yet cheweth not the cud, it is unclean unto you: ye shall not eat of their flesh, nor touch their dead carcasses.

The swine is described to be unclean in the Bible. Influenced by such teachings, some believers do not eat of swine flesh, and judge others who eat it as unclean. However, the Bible does not refer to swine in the natural world. It uses the swine to disclose the spiritual world of truth. That is, the characteristics of swine are borrowed in order to explain the spiritual world. So these believers who follow this literal meaning are in error, if they want to understand and believe correctly.

I will now tell you the true meaning of "You shall not eat of swine's flesh."

We Live By Eating

The Scripture testifies of Jesus, the giver of eternal life to believers. As such, all of Scripture is about the life of Jesus, not about the affairs of the world.

In order for us to have eternal life, we have to eat something, as we eat food in order to sustain our natural life. So we should eat if we desire to have eternal life. What should we eat? The flesh and blood of Jesus. Read John below.

> [53] Then Jesus said unto them, Verily, verily, I say unto you, Except ye eat the flesh of the Son of man, and drink his blood, ye have no life in you. [54] Whoso eateth my flesh, and drinketh my blood, hath eternal life; and I will raise him up at the last day. [55] For my flesh is meat indeed, and my blood is drink indeed. [John 6:53-55]

We shall have eternal life when we eat the flesh of the Son of man and drink His blood. In this passage of Scripture, the flesh and blood of the Son of man represents the Word. However, if we eat something other than His flesh, what will we be? We will remain dead because we have failed to receive eternal life. So we should be alert to what we eat. Is it the flesh of Jesus or something else? Verses in the Scriptures that command not to eat various unclean animals are meant to be read in this manner.

What Does the Flesh of Swine Mean?

Swine are classified as one of the unclean animals. The Scripture gives reason why swine are unclean. The reason is that they do not chew the cud. Chewing the cud is the process for a herbivore to bring the food back from the stomach into the mouth and chew it again. Through this characteristic of the herbivore, the Scripture reveals to us what we should do in eating the word, the flesh of Jesus. That is, we should chew the cud when eating the word of Jesus.

How can we chew the cud? When we reading the Scriptures we need to pray, meditate on it, study it, and think on it deeply again and again. This is the way we chew the cud. The Bereans are an example. Read Acts 17:11: "These were nobler than those in Thessalonica, in that they received the word with all readiness of mind, and searched the scriptures daily, whether those things were so."

By chewing the cud, we can find the true meaning of the word. Without it, we will only know the superficial meaning, which is, in reality the morals and ethics of men. This way we will be eating something else, not the word.

The swine represent those who receive the word of God without serious meditation and prayer, and so they only grasp the literal and superficial meaning of it. Superficial meanings of the Scripture are referred to as a gnat and hidden true meanings to a camel in Matthew 23:24: "Ye blind guides, which strain at a gnat, and swallow a camel."

They are swine. And their teachings (words) are the flesh of swine, as Jesus' teachings are His flesh. Therefore, learning and receiving their teachings is eating the flesh of swine.

Then why are swine and their flesh unclean? That which makes us clean is clean. Consider John 15:3: "Now ye are clean through the word which I have spoken unto you." The swine and their flesh are unclean because it cannot give us cleanness of spirit, that is, forgiveness of sin, even if we eat it. However, the one who chewed the cud has the spiritual meanings of the word. They will provide us the flesh of Jesus, the real clean food.

Therefore, even though the same word of God in the Scriptures is preached, some preachers give it as the flesh of swine, and some give it as the flesh of Jesus. Watch from whom you are hearing and learning! Below is the description of men who are giving and taking the teachings of swine from the Scriptures. Read Isaiah.

> Which remain among the graves, and lodge in the monuments, which eat swine's flesh, and broth of abominable things is in their vessels. [Isaiah 65:4]

Men are born sinners. Unless they are saved by the word of God, they remain in the grave, the symbol of death. The monuments mean their self-righteousness accumulated by doing many good things in the eyes of man, not God. They teach and receive doctrines of men (the flesh of swine) as that of God. Here in Isaiah 65:4 men are likened to 'vessels,' and the 'abominable things' are such as evil thoughts, adulteries, fornications, murders, thefts, covetousness, wickedness, deceit *et cetera* (Mar 7:21-22).

The true meaning of the word of God will be revealed to you when you chew the cud deeply by thinking and praying. If you will have eternal life, you should not eat the flesh of swine. If so, you are dead.

📁 Swine and Pearls

> Give not that which is holy unto the dogs, neither cast ye your pearls before swine, lest they trample them under their feet, and turn again and rend you. [Matthew 7:6]

Jesus says, "Neither cast ye your pearls before swine." In this case, the swine signifies those who do not think on the word deeply and know it as if it were the commandments of men. If we preach to them the gospel, likened to pearls, they blaspheme in opposition to us, saying, "It is an arbitrary interpretation," or "It's heresy." If they go further, they will harm us. This is their trampling of pearls under their feet.

You can remember the Pharisees who fought against Jesus, and the Jews who tried to kill the apostles. As to be expected, they were swine who had been receiving the word of God without chewing the cud.

Divide the Hoof

In the mean time, if the hoof is divided, we can eat of it. The one who can divide the law and gospel; he is the man who can divide the hoof. We can have teachings from him.

Many believers do not know even whether there are hidden meanings in the Scriptures. They only know the superficial and natural meanings. They are they who do not and cannot divide the hoof. If we receive their teaching, we will not be saved, and remain as dead. So the Scripture instructs not to eat of the flesh of such animal.

In the swine's case, its hoof is divided, but it does not chew the cud. Dividing the hoof and chewing the cud is saying one and the same thing. Therefore, if either of the two is not met, none is met.

Epilogue

Some people in the church prohibit eating of the flesh of swine. Such behavior is caused by their sincere desire to live by the Scripture. However, such conduct is already the result of 'eating the flesh of swine.' That is, they do not eat pork because they have already eaten the flesh of swine from the Scriptures.

Our eyes to read the Bible are blind. We should be humble in front of God in reading the Bible, and then God will lead us to the right truth. We have believed in Jesus blindly. That is clear if we think about that in so far that we have been reading the Scriptures, which testifies to Jesus, in a very different way. Quite naturally, a self-created Jesus would be very different from who Jesus is in reality.

So much for the flesh of swine. Now is the time to eat of the flesh of Jesus.

Be Not Drunk With Wine

[Ephesians 5:17-21]

17 Wherefore be ye not unwise, but understanding what the will of the Lord is. 18 And be not drunk with wine, wherein is excess; but be filled with the Spirit; 19 Speaking to yourselves in psalms and hymns and spiritual songs, singing and making melody in your heart to the Lord; 20 Giving thanks always for all things unto God and the Father in the name of our Lord Jesus Christ; 21 Submitting yourselves one to another in the fear of God.

In most churches, we are encouraged to stop drinking and smoking. The wine drinker, however, insists that the Bible only instructs us not to get drunk. It does not tell us not to drink at all. Furthermore, Jesus also made wine and drank it too.

Maybe he is referring to the case of marriage in Cana in John Chapter 2. Some people try to defend Jesus by saying, what He made was not wine but grape juice.

Although we can understand their loyalty towards Him, it is a tough controversy. Because the guests said in John 2:10: "Every man at the beginning doth set forth good wine; and when men have well drunk, then that which is worse: but thou hast kept the good wine until now."

What Jesus made at the banquet, was real good wine, not grape juice. Obviously, Jesus drank wine (Luk 7:34).

Anyway, it is sad that the Scripture, which is given to us to show the way to salvation, is used as a guidebook for eating and drinking in this sinful world. All the words in the Scripture including not to be drunk or not to eat the flesh of swine relate to the salvation of people. Wine does not refer to whiskey or beer, as the flesh of swine does not indicate edible pork.

The Structure of This Word

Let us look at the text. If we understand wine as alcohol, we will make a resolution as follows:

"I will not drink, but I will be filled with the Holy Spirit! I will try to give thanks in everything, and I will submit myself one to others. Also, I will speak in psalms and hymns and spiritual songs, singing and making melody in my heart to the Lord!"

Good resolution! May it all be yours! However, if you think that way, you are already drunk with wine. Since you are drunk, you understand this word as a legalistic commandment to do something. If you have read this word on sober reflection, you would not have understood it in that way.

This word has two parts: first, be not drunk with wine, and second, be filled with the Spirit. In detail, the first part is; be not unwise, do not be a man who cannot understand what the will of the Lord is, and so do not be drunk with wine.

All these are referring to one and the same thing. A man who has not been born again.

The second part is; be filled with the Spirit, speak to yourselves in psalms and hymns and spiritual songs singing and making melody in your heart to the Lord. Give thanks for all things to God, and submit yourselves one to another. Also, all these are referring to one and the same thing: the state of man who is born again.

See the illustration below.

ME

Before Born Again ⇨	⇦ After Born Again
Drunk with Wine	Filled with Holy Spirit
Unwise, No understanding of the Lord, In excess	Speak in psalms singing to Lord, Give thanks, Submit myself.
Unsaved state	Saved state

▲
CROSS/PENTECOST

Morals vs. Word of God 75

I emphasize once again that the above descriptions are not commandments. They show the way to heaven, in other words, the way to become a born again man. Therefore, in order for us to know and understand the will of the Lord, we should be men who are not drunk with wine first, and in order to speak to ourselves in psalms and hymns, we should be men who are filled with the Spirit first.

Now I will explain who the drunken man is and who the one filled with the Holy Spirit is.

He Who Got Drunk

📂 What is Wine?

The words in the Bible can be interpreted in two ways: one is a commandment, which is the law, and the other is the spirit that quickens within us. The commandments, the legalistic meaning of the Bible, look like the words of God, but they are the teachings of men. Read Matthew 15:9: "But in vain they do worship me, teaching for doctrines the commandments of men."

The teachings of men derived from the Scripture are likened to wine here. We can find the word of wine many times in the Scripture, and it is used to indicate the teachings of men as follows:

> Woe unto him that giveth his neighbour drink, that puttest thy bottle to him, and makest him drunken also, that thou mayest look on their nakedness! [Habakkuk 2:15]

> Awake, ye drunkards, and weep; and howl, all ye drinkers of wine, because of the new wine; [Joel 1:5]

> Nor thieves, nor covetous, nor drunkards, nor revilers, nor extortioners, shall inherit the kingdom of God. [1 Corinthians 6:10]

He who teaches the commandments of men is the man who gives his neighbor drink, and they who learn such teaching are drunkards. Knowing how most believers read the Bible, you will realize that most of them are drunk. Naturally, they cannot inherit the kingdom of God (1Co 6:10).

🗁 How About Alcoholic Wine?

Now it is clear that the wine in the Scripture is not the alcoholic drink we generally know. So now we know that the Scripture does not prescribe to us whether to drink wine or not. Nevertheless, the Lord is not pleased with our drinking wine. The consistent testimonies of those who have experienced God prove it. Ignore someone who says that a little wine will do you good. Only hear what the living Lord says to you.

We will not drink alcohol and smoke, not because it is written so in the Scripture, but because of the leadership of the living Lord who is walking with us. Walking with Him is one of the two major pillars in our steps to growing in faith, together with the word of God. We should not neglect one of them.

🗁 Drunken Man

In this world, if a person gets drunk, he will be easily excited, he will be bold to say anything, which he normally would not do, and he will talk utter nonsense. It is the state of being drunk.

Peter before the day of Pentecost tended to speak recklessly: "I will die with you," "Though all men will be offended because of You, I will never be offended," "Why cannot I not love?" and "You are the Christ, the Son of the living God," and many more. In fact, all of his sayings tended towards the reckless. All that he said proved empty promises. He spoke that way, being 'drunk' and knowing nothing clearly. He received the Holy Spirit on the day of Pentecost after Jesus had risen, and then he came out of the state of the drunken man.

In Ephesians 5:18, "And be not drunk with wine, wherein is excess," the Greek word translated into 'excess' is *asotia*, which is a compound of a, a negative particle and *sotia* a derivative of *sozo* (to save). This word has the same structure and meaning as *a+sotos* that is translated into 'riotous (living)' in the parable of the prodigal son (Luk 15:13). Both words mean 'state of unsaved.'

So if translated literally, in accord with the original Greek meaning, the verse 18 will be "And be not drunk with wine, wherein is the state of unsaved." Paul refers to the unsaved as drunkards. They are unwise, do not understand what the will of the Lord is, are unsaved, and are out of the kingdom of God.

Therefore, if we think of this as a commandment and pledge ourselves to speak in psalms and give thanks always to God, it reveals that we are drunken men. It is because we haughtily try to do something that is completely impossible. We ought to meet and follow Jesus first to become such a man.

Man Filled With the Holy Spirit

Paul links the unsaved state to 'being drunk,' and the saved state to 'being filled with the Holy Spirit.' In fact, when Peter and his friends were filled with the Holy Spirit at the Pentecost, the crowd said that these men were drunk. Read Acts.

> [13] Others mocking said, These men are full of new wine. [14] But Peter, standing up with the eleven, lifted up his voice, and said unto them, Ye men of Judaea, and all ye that dwell at Jerusalem, be this known unto you, and hearken to my words: [15] For these are not drunken, as ye suppose, seeing it is but the third hour of the day. [Acts 2:13-15]

Being filled with the Holy Spirit indicates baptism by the Holy Spirit. If you want to be filled with the Holy Spirit, you should meet the real Jesus and be healed by Him. After that, you will be baptized with the Holy Spirit at your own personal Pentecost. Thus, you are freed from the state of being a drunkard, and you become a man filled with the Holy Spirit.

This way, the text of Eph 5:19-21 quoted at the beginning is achieved in (or by) you. That is, you will speak to yourself in psalms and hymns and spiritual songs, singing and making melody in your heart to the Lord. You will give thanks always for all things to God and the father in the name of our Lord Jesus Christ. Also, you will submit yourself one to another in the fear of God.

This is what you have been dreaming about for several decades as a believer.

Epilogue

When we believe in Jesus under the law, we are drunk, and when under grace, we are filled with the Spirit. How do we know we are drunk? Very simple. If the word 'drunk' in the Scripture reads to us as drunk by alcoholic wine, we are drunk.

How do we get out of a drunken state? Also very simple. Follow the real Jesus according to the true meanings of the Scripture, and be saved. Thus, we will get out of the drunken state, and will be filled with the Spirit.

No more drunken believing, please!

A Certain Taxi Driver*

In the past, I used to preach Jesus to taxi drivers whenever I took a taxi. I will now tell you a testimony of one driver I met in those days.

One day, I took a taxi to my office from south of the river. Having easier communication with the driver in mind, I took the front seat. He was skinny, stubborn-looking, and about sixty years of age. The taxi started. I tried to find an opportunity to talk about Jesus with him.

A few moments later, I got into conversation with him. I first talked about how things were going in general, and then I started on what I wanted to share with him.

"Do you go to church by any chance?"

Most of the taxi drivers I had met replied negatively to this question. Some said, they were disappointed and no longer went to church, some said, they were too busy to go to church. I imagined one of these answers from him.

However, his answer was very unexpected.

"Yes, I attend it every Sunday," he said.

"Oh, really?"

For a short time, I was at a loss as to what to say, because I did not expect him to be a believer. While I was trying to figure out what to say, he began to talk to me about how he first went to church. At first, I wanted talk to him, but now he started to talk to me. His whole story is as follows:

He said that he was obstinate. His acquaintances told him to believe in Jesus on many occasions. He refused. He was holding fast to his own views by saying, "As the eldest son in the family, I have to do the duty of sacrificial rites for my ancestors. If I go to church, they will not allow me to do that, saying that that is idol worship. So please go to your church as you wish, and leave me alone."

In the meantime, one day his 25-year-old second son was riding on the rear seat of his friend's motorcycle and fell off and, injuring his backbone, became paralyzed in both legs. What made matters worse was that he was beyond medical treatment, and so the doctors gave up. Therefore, he had to leave the hospital and stayed home in care. His legs swelled up badly, and started to go septic when the swelling subsided. This happened repeatedly. We can easily guess how painful it was for the father who had to watch helplessly his son's misery.

Many days passed, and one of his neighbors advised him: "If it is incurable, why don't you go to the prayer house to pray to God?" And he gave him some information about a prayer house located in the north of the city of Seoul. He had never ever been near a church, but he took his son to the prayer house with the hope of enabling his son to get well. When they arrived at the prayer house, the man in charge asked him,

"Do you or your family go to church?"

"No."

"I'm sorry, but you are not allowed in if not."

He was embarrassed about this unkind reply and stubborn attitude. However, he had no choice but to return home.

After returning home, as he was so desperate, he visited a church nearby for the first time in his life, and requested to meet the senior pastor. He told the whole story to the pastor. Having heard, the pastor kindly agreed to register him as a church member. He then, acquired a registration certificate and ran to the prayer house again.

This time, they were allowed to enter and stayed there. In the prayer house, he prayed to God desperately so that his son would be healed. Painfully, however, his son did not show any improvement in health. They stayed there about six months, and then came back home.

He did not and could not give up, and attended the church, and cried out to the Lord from the bottom of his heart in prayer. In spite of his earnest desire and prayer, his son died two years after the accident happened. Facing death, the son said his last word to his father.

"Dad, you are attending church, aren't you? Yes, you must go on."

The son then passed away at last, wearing a happy expression on his face.

With this as a motivation, his whole family has changed to become pious Christians. He testified thus to me.

I was moved very much upon hearing what he said. God sent this stubborn man many prophets saying to him to believe in Jesus, but he refused. So He made another plan for him. That is, He let him know God through the accident that happened to his younger son. God knew he would soon stop going to church if He quickly took the life of his son after the accident. Therefore, He allowed the son to remain in a miserable state two years so that he may continue to pray desperately and to have his faith take root deeply.

We may think attending church is a small thing, but to God it is something that is more important than the life of his son. That is because it relates to eternal life.

I recall the testimony of a Korean doctor who was working for the hospital as a cancer specialist in the U.S. He had to watch cancer patients dying miserably. It made his heart bleed to see them who were worn to a shadow and suffered from great pains until death.

He could not understand why God did not quickly take those who were without hope of recovery, but left them in long-term suffering. When he asked the Lord, His answer was:

"I do so for the purpose of showing My mercy to you."

At first hearing, this is difficult to understand. However, God sometimes allows patients to live on in agony so that the people around them may think about God and pray to know Him.

This same mercy came to the taxi driver. Because of the drawn out pain of his son, he could pray to Him for a long time and he could be near to Him. The son was an angel God sent to him and his family to bring them to church.

Here, we can understand that it is not God's purpose to eliminate suffering, pain, agony, and the troubles of this world. What God wants is that through this process He can draw His people closer to Him, and finally become one with them.

That's it. That is God's mercy. God will not spare anything or everything in the world to show this mercy to us.

Are we ready to receive this mercy of God?

PART TWO
The Hidden Manna

The Lord said, "To him that overcomes will I give to eat of the hidden manna" (Rev 2:17). The hidden manna signifies the hidden but true meaning of the word of God.

The hidden true meaning judges the faith we have had for several decades and discloses that the faith is false. Because of this, many people turn a deaf ear to it and close their eyes. Accordingly, not all men can receive it. Only those who have undergone long trials and tribulations under the law and have no further regrets about such faith life can receive it. They are those who overcome.

Please pray with a humble heart to God so that you may receive and understand as many of these messages as possible. If you are ready to acknowledge the legalistic reality of your faith and thus want to be healed, you will be made well. Through this process, you whose souls are heavy laden will enter God's rest (Hbr 4:1-2).

A Long Time Under the Law

Moses Whom We Meet First

Let's think about the manner in which the Israelites left Egypt and went through the wilderness into Canaan. This is a representation of the process of salvation. They wandered for forty years in the wilderness under the leadership of Moses, and those who came out of Egypt all died there. The remaining new generations were led into Canaan by Joshua.

About seven years passed thereafter before they had conquered the land of Canaan.

This records our journey of faith. We believe in Jesus and read the Scripture in order to enter Canaan, the kingdom of God. However, we cannot immediately come into the kingdom of God when we come to church to believe in Jesus. Whether we want it or not, we spend forty years in the wilderness, guided by Moses.

What does this mean? When we come to church and read the Bible, we meet the literal meaning of the word of God, and interpret it as the morals and commandments of men. This surface meaning corresponds to Moses who leads us in the wilderness in the spiritual sense.

Do you wonder why you follow Moses? Moses is the sign of the law. When you come to church you are to keep the laws given by Jesus, for example, do not judge, love your neighbor as yourself, attend church, give tithe, *et cetera*. Yes, it is the laws that you are to keep. So in this way you are under Moses, even if you are superficially under Jesus.

So we attend church and join various activities such as; missionary work, serving table, donating to charity, praying and fasting, loving neighbors, and so on. All of these things are signified by what the Israelites did, wandering in the wilderness while following Moses.

However, unfortunately, the ending of such faith is predestined—we cannot make a single step into the kingdom of God, but will be exhausted and fall away in the wilderness. This is the spiritual reality of the Israelites in those days that could not reach Canaan but died in the wilderness. No one can come into Canaan through Moses, and no one can come into the kingdom of God through the law, the superficial meanings of the word of God.

In fact, so far we have believed in Moses in the name of Jesus. We can know right away if we simply check whether we have believed in Him in accord with the hidden spiritual meaning of the Scripture or not. Or do we even know that there are such meanings of the Scripture other than literal?

The period in which believers are led by Moses is common to all of us. So no one can simply judge whether it is good or bad to be guided by him. What matters is whether it is time for us to listen to the hidden meaning of the word of God and move on from our past faith.

Those whose time has not yet come will have to live under Moses further until they are fully desolate and driven to despair.

Moses' Role

God speaks to us through the literal meaning of the word when we are spiritually immature. And this is the only way. It is because we can only read it at that level. The literal meaning has a role of its own in accordance with His providence. Just as He created Moses, He permitted the superficial meaning of His word.

This surface, literal meaning of the word drives us to give up hope and fall. Following this literal meaning of the word, we did many good things and repented on occasion for not doing certain things, but nothing has changed within us. Spinning round in a vicious circle, we will be finally exhausted and fall down.

Moses' role is to make the Israelites fall down and die in the wilderness, in the spiritual sense. Some of you may feel upset at the expression of 'make them die,' but to die is to live. It is because Joshua, the pattern of Jesus, will lead them into Canaan. Joshua will only come to them who are desolate and hopeless under the law of Moses.

In this context, Paul says as follows:

> [3] Even so we, when we were children, were in bondage under the elements of the world: [4] But when the fulness of the time was come, God sent forth his Son, made of a woman, made under the law, [5] To redeem them that were under the law, that we might receive the adoption of sons. [Galatians 4:3-5]

In this instance, 'the elements of the world' represent the doctrines of men, i.e., the literal meaning of the Scripture, which is symbolized by Moses. When our time is up under the law, God will send us Jesus. And Jesus will open our eyes to see the true meaning of the Scripture and open our ears to hear it. The words that were hidden in the past are now revealed to us. Now we are to enter the kingdom of God, for the adoption as sons. The word "To him that overcometh will I give to eat of the hidden manna" (Rev 2:17) is fulfilled in us at this stage.

Long Time Under the Law

During the course of going into Canaan, the Israelites spent a long time in the wilderness after coming out of Egypt. The wilderness represents 'under the law,' and Canaan 'under grace.' So it means that we have to spend a long time under the law to go into the grace of God.

As we proceed in Part Two of this title, the true significance of the word of God will be illuminated. You may realize that so far you have unknowingly believed under the law. You might have been a very long time in the church, but do not be disappointed it is natural that the period is so long.

What is important is that you now receive the true spiritual meaning of the Scripture. If you cannot, you should further undergo life under the law. But, if you can hear, you can go into the kingdom of God in a short period of time if you walk with the living Jesus.

Blessed is he who can hear the true and spiritual meaning of the word of God.

Cain and Abel

[Genesis 4:1-8]
¹ And Adam knew Eve his wife; and she conceived, and bare Cain, and said, I have gotten a man from the LORD. ² And she again bare his brother Abel. And Abel was a keeper of sheep, but Cain was a tiller of the ground. ³ And in process of time it came to pass, that Cain brought of the fruit of the ground an offering unto the LORD. ⁴ And Abel, he also brought of the firstlings of his flock and of the fat thereof. And the LORD had respect unto Abel and to his offering: ⁵ But unto Cain and to his offering he had not respect. And Cain was very wroth, and his countenance fell. ⁶ And the LORD said unto Cain, Why art thou wroth? and why is thy countenance fallen? ⁷ If thou doest well, shalt thou not be accepted? and if thou doest not well, sin lieth at the door. And unto thee shall be his desire, and thou shalt rule over him. ⁸ And Cain talked with Abel his brother: and it came to pass, when they were in the field, that Cain rose up against Abel his brother, and slew him.

The story of Cain and Abel, positioned at the opening part of the Scripture, has been one of the most contentious passages for a long time. "Why didn't God have respect unto Cain and his offering?" Many theologians and pastors have tried to solve this question and failed.

Some of them insist that it is because Cain offered a sacrifice to God without faith by quoting the passage of Hebrews 11:4: "By faith Abel offered unto God a more excellent sacrifice than Cain, by which he obtained witness that he was righteous, God testifying of his gifts: and by it he being dead yet speaketh." However, this answer is not helpful if we have no idea of the meaning of 'a sacrifice by faith.'

Others point out that when God had respect for the offering of Abel, the younger brother, it is wrong that Cain, the older, could not tolerate his brother. However, the Scripture does not aim to correct one or two of our deeds. Bearing in mind that the Scripture reveals the fundamental nature of human beings, we know that this interpretation is not right either.

Does God receive no fruit of the ground that the farmer gathered in, but does He only prefer the firstlings of his flock and of the fat that the shepherd raised? Why did He have no respect for the offering of Cain and no respect for Cain himself? We will consider this now.

Cain and His Offering (Gen 4:2-5)

Cain brought an offering to God in the same way that Abel did. One thing we know from this is that Cain is not a villain who does not know God, does not offer a sacrifice to Him, and kills others. Considering that Cain offered a sacrifice to Him as Abel did, he was one of those who believed in God and expected to receive blessings in reward for their belief.

Therefore, it will be inappropriate if we conclude and ease our mind as follows:

"I am not Cain because I never killed any man and I am a sincere worshipper. I regularly go to church, pray to God, and do many good things. I am totally different from Cain, the murderer."

Each of the characters in the Scripture shows features of believers, good or evil, who go to church and believe in God. This is the basic point of view we should have in connection with the Scripture when we read it. The characters we find in the Scripture are not people who have nothing to do with me and are far away from me. They all indicate me. In the same context, if I have the same believer's pattern as Cain, I am Cain.

We will now think about the way in which Cain believed in God.

📂 The Fruit of the Ground

What is the fruit of the ground that Cain offered to God? It does not literally refer to crops such as rice, barley, cabbage, *et cetera*. By contrast, with the concept of heaven, the ground represents man himself who has left God in heaven. Read the following verses from 1 Corinthians.

> [47] The first man is of the earth, earthy: the second man is the Lord from heaven. [48] As is the earthy, such are they also that are earthy: and as is the heavenly, such are they also that are heavenly. [1 Corinthians 15:47-48]

Paul the Apostle contrasts Adam who is the prototype of earth (ground) with Jesus Christ who is that of heaven. So the earth signifies the sinner having left God, and heaven indicates those who have become one with God through Jesus Christ.

People who are 'earth' worship God and offer sacrifices to Him. It is a great mistake if you think that sinners include only those who never go to church, speak ill of Him, and insult Him. Consider how Adam and the woman disobeyed Him and left Him, and their descendants offered sacrifices to Him. Sinners also serve Him, worship Him, and praise Him, but they never realize that they have left Him.

On the contrary, in the church people encourage them with high commendation that they are the nearest to Him because of their sincere eagerness. Cain represents such believers.

Cain cultivated the land and offered God the fruit of the ground. This means that he offered Him what he did according to his own righteousness, which is self-righteousness. It was the best that Cain could do as a man who was cultivating the land. However, it was intrinsically the fruit of the ground, which were the thorns and thistles that He does not accept.

📂 The Fruit of the Ground We Offer to God

Upon experiencing the living God or having been moved by

some great event in our lives, we begin to make an enthusiastic Christian life. We do many things we never did before for Him. For example, we read the Bible, give tithes, aggressively participate in missionary work, pray in an unknown tongue, sing praises, and practice spiritual gifts.

When we are changed this much, our fellow-Christians applaud us for our good faith, and we also place confidence in the faith we have, because we did it fervently and with our utmost sincerity. But it corresponds to laying the foundation only; when we plan to build a tower. So if we stop and remain at this stage, all the eagerness and devotion we have had up until today, will prove futile. This is because it is not the final fruit of faith, the tower. Read Luke below:

> [28] For which of you, intending to build a tower, sitteth not down first, and counteth the cost, whether he have sufficient to finish it? [29] Lest haply, after he hath laid the foundation, and is not able to finish it, all that behold it begin to mock him. [Luke 14:28-29]

God will not have respect for such an offering because we have brought forth no fruit. This is the reason why He did not have respect for the offering of Cain.

Abel's Sacrifice

Now, let us think about the sacrifice that Abel offered to God. He brought of the firstlings of his flock and the fat. The lamb he offered is symbolic. The lamb in the Scripture symbolizes Jesus who is offered to God as a sacrifice, and the firstlings of the flock (Exd 13:2) symbolize the same. The fat, the choicest part, symbolizes the Holy Spirit who comes after Jesus.

It is very significant that Abel was a keeper of sheep and that he brought of the firstlings of his flock and of the fat thereof. It reflects the fact that he has met Jesus (the firstborn of sheep) and has received the Holy Spirit, which is the Christ (the fat) that Jesus sent.

There is only one sacrifice that God has respect for, that is, Christ who is formed in us through the word of God. Read Galatians 4:19: "My little children, of whom I travail in birth again until Christ be formed in you,"

Abel is the symbol of such men. If God has respect for the works of man, it means that He sees Christ who is formed in him, not his works. Consequently, the sacrifice we should offer to Him is not of our works (the fruit of the ground), but of Christ formed in us (firstling and fat).

Sacrifice Expresses the Man who Offered the Same

We can understand that God's rejection of Cain's offering is serious, but why did He, in addition, not have respect for Cain himself? We may not have the insight to grasp this but it does stimulate our curiosity.

The sacrifice we offer to Him relates not to the sacrifice itself but to the person who offers it. The sacrifice is an expression of the person making the offering, and so it is one with him. God recognizes Cain and his sacrifice as one. Therefore, even if Cain would offer his sacrifice to Him truthfully and whole-heartedly, He would not have had respect for it. Accordingly, all the problems occurred because he was Cain. Cain is symbolic of the sinner, and so He will not have respect for anything the sinner offers to Him.

The same principle will be applicable to Abel. Abel was made righteous by having Christ in him, and offers himself as a sacrifice to God. Since he has become righteous, God has respect for all he offers to Him. Abel and his sacrifice are one and so He has respect for both.

Now, I would like to give you something to think about. Frequently, we think Cain will be Cain forever. However, Cain and Abel in the Scripture are not proper nouns. They are common nouns. Cain symbolizes the sinner, the life born of the flesh and Abel is the symbol of the righteous man, the life born of the spirit (Jhn 3:6). Cain is not an eternal Cain, but he has an opportunity to be changed into an Abel through Jesus.

We may easily think that we shall remain as we are now throughout our lives. Based on that thinking, we will then mistakenly conclude that we will become righteous when we change some of our deeds. However, what we should change is not the deeds, but our beings. We should be born again to change ourselves from Cain to Abel. This is what God wants from us through the illustration of the offerings of Cain and Abel.

You do not need to be upset or disappointed even if this message has revealed by chance that you are Cain. On the contrary, it is a blessing because Cain will be changed into Abel only based on such disclosure and understanding. When Cain has been changed to be Abel, his offering will also be changed to be the offering of Abel for which God has respect.

Cain is me before I am born again, and also Abel is me after I am born again.

Cain Whose Countenance Fell (Gen 4:6-7)

We can think as follows about God's reason for rejecting Cain's sacrifice: "Cain offered a sacrifice to Him inattentively and without his whole heart. So his sacrifice was rejected. He should have offered it in all sincerity." However, he did his utmost to offer the sacrifice. On what ground am I saying this to you? You can know this from verse 5: "But unto Cain and to his offering he had not respect. And Cain was very wroth, and his countenance fell."

If he had offered Him a superficial and insincere sacrifice, he would not have been angry even when it was refused. Because he would have thought that it served him right. But he would have been angry when he had put all his effort into the offerings only to have them rejected. Thus, "Cain was very wroth" proves that he had devoted himself to the sacrifice with all his heart.

It is difficult to admit, but almost all believers are currently offering God a sacrifice similar to that made by Cain. They do their utmost with eagerness thinking that God will accept their works. However, all these things are self-righteousness, the fruit of the ground.

The Pharisees in the time of Jesus were Cain, and offered sacrifices to God with all their hearts. However, they were declined. Read Luke below.

> [11] The Pharisee stood and prayed thus with himself, God, I thank thee, that I am not as other men are, extortioners, unjust, adulterers, or even as this publican. [12] I fast twice in the week, I give tithes of all that I possess. [Luke 18:11-12]

And Jesus said that God did not have respect for their sacrifices (Luk 18:14). The Pharisees had to be angry, thinking to themselves, "I did it with all my heart…" As a natural consequence, they tried to stone Jesus, as Cain killed Abel.

Today, the true gospel requires the collapse of the self-centered faith of believers. At that moment, all will be angry at the gospel, whether severely or slightly according to the amount of eagerness that they put into believing in Jesus, as Cain was also.

📂 Desire of Sin and Ruling Over It

"If thou doest not well, sin lieth at the door." This signifies that if we do good things that are not of God, who is the author of good, this already conceives of the desire for sin. Cain offered the sacrifice, which did not please God, and he was angry eventually when he did not receive respect for it. His anger was connected to sin, and the Scripture describes this situation as 'sin lying at the door.' In this instance, Cain had to control his tendency to sin, but he failed and killed his brother.

The Pharisees and the scribes in the time of Jesus are descendents of Cain. Upon hearing that their sacrifice was unacceptable to God, they got angry and crucified Jesus. Any wise believer will now think that he should offer a sacrifice that pleases God.

By Faith… A More Excellent Sacrifice…

The writer of Hebrew says Abel offered unto God a more excellent sacrifice by faith. Consider Hebrews.

> By faith Abel offered unto God a more excellent sacrifice than Cain, by which he obtained witness that he was righteous, God testifying of his gifts: and by it he being dead yet

speaketh. [Hebrews 11:4]

The passage does not mean that Abel offered a sacrifice with superior trust in God, but it means that he offered a sacrifice of the Christ formed in him. We can know it from "Abel brought of the firstlings of his flock and of the fat thereof." Abel represents the man who had the Christ in him after being healed by Jesus. The Christ formed in him means that faith increased in him. So, "By faith Abel..." means "By the Christ who was formed in Abel, he..."

Limit of Biblical Knowledge

The issue of Cain and Abel has troubled Bible readers for a long time. Many believers have not yet found a clear answer as to why God did not have respect for the sacrifice of Cain. It will require several decades for them to study and realize the hidden meanings, or may be not ever, if they try alone.

So when we understand such hidden meanings of the Scripture we will be so happy to share and teach such understandings to others. Encouraged by the commendations of people with whom we share these revelations, we tend to try to study and interpret other difficult verses of Scripture.

I know a man who studied and understood some profound meanings of the Scriptures, and he was so happy. He was also proud because everybody commended him.

However, if we think a little bit deeper, what he actually got was the fact that he was a Cain, nothing more than that. He must aim to be changed to Abel by following Jesus, if he really understood what the story of Cain meant for him. So I admonished him in this respect. Nevertheless, he did not want to accept my words, and he insisted on his way. Consequently, he still remains as Cain even though he has hidden biblical knowledge in his memory.

Understanding of the hidden meanings itself will not change us into Abel. It only shows us the way to heaven, that is, to be Abel, and we must not forget that we should actually walk the way to get into heaven. Can there be any more serious matter than that we are the very Cain?

If a man has realized that he is a Cain, he will naturally repent, and will follow Jesus forsaking all others from that time on. And Jesus will make him to be born again as Abel in this lifetime. Consequently, he will cease to offer the sacrifice of Cain, but he will offer the sacrifice of Abel.

Epilogue

Cain was a tiller of the ground and Abel was a keeper of sheep. It is quite natural for Cain to offer the fruit of the ground, and Abel the firstling of his flock.

What type of occupation do you have? If you believe in Jesus under the law, you are a tiller of the ground, and if you believe in Jesus by meeting the real Jesus, you are the keeper of the sheep.

Cain signifies natural or carnal man and Abel spiritual man. We all start our faith with that of Cain, when we meet Jesus, we will be revealed as Cains, and those who repent at this point, they will be given the faith of Abel in due course.

Now is the time to offer the sacrifice of Abel.

Re-Illumination of Samson

[Judges 16:15-21]

¹⁵ And she said unto him, How canst thou say, I love thee, when thine heart is not with me? thou hast mocked me these three times, and hast not told me wherein thy great strength lieth. ¹⁶ And it came to pass, when she pressed him daily with her words, and urged him, so that his soul was vexed unto death; ¹⁷ That he told her all his heart, and said unto her, There hath not come a razor upon mine head; for I have been a Nazarite unto God from my mother's womb: if I be shaven, then my strength will go from me, and I shall become weak, and be like any other man. ¹⁸ And when Delilah saw that he had told her all his heart, she sent and called for the lords of the Philistines, saying, Come up this once, for he hath shewed me all his heart. Then the lords of the Philistines came up unto her, and brought money in their hand. ¹⁹ And she made him sleep upon her knees; and she called for a man, and she caused him to shave off the seven locks of his head; and she began to afflict him, and his strength went from him. ²⁰ And she said, The Philistines be upon thee, Samson. And he awoke out of his sleep, and said, I will go out as at other times before, and shake myself. And he wist not that the LORD was departed from him. ²¹ But the Philistines took him, and put out his eyes, and brought him down to Gaza, and bound him with fetters of brass; and he did grind in the prison house.

The name of Samson is very familiar to us. This may be because his story was filmed and we have heard stories about him in Sunday school. The highlight of them will be the sad story of his love for Delilah, a harlot. This story is seen as marring his reputation as a judge, chosen by God. So in general, we misunderstand him. We believe that he was elected by God, but then was enticed by a harlot and disobedient to Him. As a result, he died a miserable death.

Accordingly, he has become known as a person who should not be imitated. To tell the truth, however, he was one of the elders of faith who obeyed His will through and through.

Now, we will consider him in this light.

Records About Samson in the Scripture

Judges Chapters 13-16 give the story of Samson, a Nazarite. The name Samson means the 'sun,' and he was a judge of Israel for twenty years. Manoah, his mother, had no child but she heard from the angel of the LORD that she would bear him, and she also knew that he should be a Nazarite who would deliver Israel from the Philistines. The Nazarite is a consecrated man; he should drink no wine nor strong drink, no razor should touch his head, and he should not eat unclean things. God chose him from birth and led him to live a hallowed life.

Returning to the original passage, Samson loved a Philistine woman named Delilah who lived in the valley of Sorek. However, she was promised a reward of eleven hundred pieces of silver from each of the lords of the Philistines, if she could find out the secret of his great strength. Despite her repeated attempts to get the information from Samson, he lied and misled her.

When she realized that Samson did not want to let her know the secret of his strength, she pressed him by saying, "How can you say you love me when your heart is not with me?" His soul was sorely vexed. Finally, he told his secret to her; a razor had not come near his head since birth for he had been a Nazarite unto God. He would become weak if his head was shaved.

Accordingly, he got faced with a miserable situation. When he slept upon her knees, she called for a man, caused him to shave his head, and they took him. The Philistines put out his eyes, bound him with fetters of brass, and had him grind in the prison house.

However, the hair of his head began to grow again after he was shaved, and the Philistines gathered together in the temple of Dagon and wanted Samson to entertain them in commemoration of his capture. At this time, he prayed to God saying, "I may be avenged of them for my two eyes," and he took hold of the two middle pillars, braced himself against them and pushed them down with his great strength. He and all the Philistines in the temple were killed.

A Point to Think About

Samson, the hero, having led the Israelites triumphantly, died a miserable death as a consequence of loving Delilah. Upon reading his story, we conclude that this is a natural consequence for a man who violated God's commandment not to commit adultery. We then accept the lesson that we should obey the word of God.

In another way, we take Samson's story as a lesson that women entice men and men should therefore avoid them since they have the potential to bring ruin and the destruction of families.

I would like readers to consider three questions regarding such a superficial interpretation of the story of Samson.

First, the Scripture is the word of God and so will it not have a far deeper significance than a superficial interpretation? After all we can learn such lessons in our everyday life without the help of the Scripture. For example, we read in newspaper or magazine articles that a certain famous entertainer was taken to court for adultery and was ruined. All of us can learn from this. If so, what the Scripture teaches and what the newspapers report give us substantially the same lesson of not committing adultery. However, will not the word of God provide a far deeper meaning than the lesson of preventing adultery? This is the first question.

Second, the question is about the viewpoint of the writer of Hebrews. We think of Samson as the man who disobeyed God's commandments, lived with a harlot, and was finally ruined. However, the writer of Hebrews describes him as one of the elders of faith. Read the verse below from Hebrews.

And what shall I more say? for the time would fail me to tell of Gedeon, and of Barak, and of Samson, and of Jephthae; of David also, and Samuel, and of the prophets: [Hebrews 11:32]

Is the Samson we know different from the Samson the writer of Hebrews describes? Did the writer of Hebrews read the record that Samson lived with the harlot Delilah? Or, did he call him the 'elder' because he was a negative example we should not follow?

If the Scripture says that he is an elder, and we say otherwise, then it is we that are mistaken. We are mistaken somewhere in appraising him.

Third, he was a Nazarite: "For, lo, thou shalt conceive, and bear a son; and no razor shall come on his head: for the child shall be a Nazarite unto God from the womb: and he shall begin to deliver Israel out of the hand of the Philistines" (Jdg 13:5).

He was a man of faith walking with God as a Nazarite, and he was a great servant that He used. Could such a Samson fall? The actual mission given to him was to save the Israelites out of the hand of the Philistines, and it was achieved by his killing far more Philistines than ever when he pulled their temple down on their heads. Is it correct to say that he fell who was a Nazarite unto God from the womb and did all the things assigned to him? This is the third question.

Samson Who was Just

He was not a man chastened by God because he was enticed by a harlot. He walked with God from the beginning to the end including during his relationship with Delilah. Some may raise questions about what I describe.

"Does He let sin happen?"

"Did He allow him to lead a fast life with a harlot?"

Yes, He did. He allowed him to fall in love with her in order to save Israel.

📂 God Lets Samson Marry a Woman in Timnath

In order to understand God, we should first read Chapter 14 of Judges carefully. Here, Samson wanted to marry a woman of Timnath in the land of Philistines. His parents were entirely against him because the people of Israel were not allowed to take a wife from among uncircumcised heathen. What is worse, the Philistines were the enemies of the Israelites. In spite of all these environmental handicaps, he married her.

Had we been there, we too would have been against his marriage to the woman of Timnath since it was contrary to the law. However, the Scripture clearly says that he married her according to His will. Consider Judges.

> ³ Then his father and his mother said unto him, Is there never a woman among the daughters of thy brethren, or among all my people, that thou goest to take a wife of the uncircumcised Philistines? And Samson said unto his father, Get her for me; for she pleaseth me well. ⁴ But his father and his mother knew not that it was of the LORD, that he sought an occasion against the Philistines: for at that time the Philistines had dominion over Israel. [Judges 14:3-4]

His marriage ran counter to the law of Israel. Did he not know this? Obviously he did. As a Nazarite, he would naturally have asked God about his marriage to a Philistine and God gave his blessing. So he tried to marry her. However, his parents had no idea of this and so they were not with him according to the law. However, he could pursue his marriage even against the law because God had answered him.

Once having understood this, we can see that his marriage to her is no sin at all. Neither had He turned aside from the law, since God who has made the law allowed him to marry her. In addition, the true meaning of the law is different to what we understand literally. Anyway, as consequence of his marriage, he defeated the Philistines with great slaughter and thus fulfilled the mission that God had given him.

To explain further, God sought an occasion against the Philistines by allowing Samson to marry the woman of Timnath. Read Chapters 14 and 15 in Judges.

Samson gets married to her and makes a seven-day feast. He puts forth a riddle to the thirty Philistine companies that have joined the wedding feast, and this must be solved before the feast ends. But they could not unravel it. So they threatened the bride on the seventh day, and weeping, she pressed him for the solution to the riddle. When Samson told the answer to her out of pity, she told it to the wedding guests. And they told it to Samson within the period.

Knowing that they had intimidated his wife to get the answer, he killed thirty Philistines, took their clothes, and gave a change of garments to the guests who had answered the riddle.

His wife was then given to another man. When he later visited his wife again, her father refused to give her to him. Angry at the father, he caught 300 foxes, tied them tail to tail, attached burning torches to each pair and set them loose in the Philistines' grain fields. The resulting fire destroyed grain and corn fields as well as vineyards.

The Philistines got angry and burned the bride and her father to death. Samson revenged himself on the Philistines and killed them with a great slaughter (Jdg15:8). If you are interested in the next story about him, I want you to read the Bible by yourself.

As you can see, Samson's marriage to the woman of Timnath triggered a chain reaction that resulted in him killing a large number of Philistines, the enemies of Israel. For the salvation of Israel, the chosen ones, God allowed him to marry her to kill more of the enemy.

📂 Love with Delilah Also, God Allowed

As a Nazarite, as in the case of the woman of Timnath, Samson also definitely sought God's will in the matter of Delilah. It was natural for him to seek God's will before he had a date with Delilah, a gentile and a harlot. He could love her because God allowed him to love her.

We can conclude this if we consider that he obeyed God regarding his marriage with the woman of Timnath. These two cases progressed in the same way. Marriage with the woman in Timnath is a sign of loving Delilah. There are many reasons why I can adopt this viewpoint.

First, both the women he loved were Philistines, or gentiles. He could neither love them nor marry them according to the law.

Second, he loved them wholeheartedly. As he told the woman of Timnath the answer of the riddle when she pressed him, he told Delilah the secret of his strength knowing he would die. These two cases indicate that he loved these women wholeheartedly.

Third, just as in the marriage to the woman of Timnath caused a chain reaction to kill Philistines with great slaughter, his love for Delilah generated another chain reaction of destruction of Philistines.

When Samson got married to the woman of Timnath, it was precipitated by the plan of God to defeat the Philistines. This is also applicable to his love for Delilah. This too was caused by God's plan for the destruction of the Philistines.

When I use the expression "It is caused by the plan of God," I mean that he had no sin. If you guess that he was chastened for the sin of loving Delilah, and so his eyes were put out and he had to grind in the prison, then where can you find the verse that he was chastened by the sin of loving the woman in Timnath? You can find it nowhere in the Scripture. Samson loved Delilah according to God's will, and this cannot be chastened.

Otherwise, what do the sufferings of Samson mean? I will explain it later.

📂 Samson's True Love

What was his love like? Did he try to enjoy himself by carelessly saying, "She is just a harlot?" No. He loved her until he died. He already knew there would be no way out if he told her his secret. Although he cherished her and loved her, he could not tell it to her. He dodged her and delayed time and again.

He said, "If they bind me with seven green withs that were

never dried," "If they bind me fast with new ropes that never were occupied," and "If thou weavest the locks of my head with the web." When he said such childish things, he did not mean to play a game of questions to kill time. He tried to stall knowing that he would die if he gave away the secret and that she would leave if he would not. He told her such answers, full of distress, not wanting to let her leave.

However, she urged him by saying that he teased her because he did not love her. The Scripture says what he felt at that time as follows:

"And it came to pass, when she pressed him daily with her words, and urged him, so that his soul was vexed unto death" (Jdg 16:16).

He was troubled to death while she pressed him and he could not tell the secret. He loved her truly and he gave himself up to her. Finally, he revealed his heart to her and he consequently faced a miserable situation.

We usually say that we should stay away from harlots, and conclude that all the things that happened to Samson occurred because he was reckless in his love for Delilah. However, as some of you may know, we may happen to love a woman we should not love no matter how cautious we are. What can we do then? The only thing we can do is to love. Samson loved her in this way.

Plan of God

Then, what plan did God want to realize through Samson? God knew that if he loved Delilah, he would not be able to get away with it and that he would have a hard time. Nevertheless, He worked with purpose so that all these things that happened to Samson would result in the fulfillment of God's plan for the destruction of the Philistines, the enemies of Israel.

By allowing Samson to have a relationship with Delilah, God planned to destroy many more Philistines than had already perished as a result of Samson's tragic marriage to the woman of Timnath. As He willed, by collapsing the temple of Dagon, Samson killed more Philistines than during the rest of his life (Jdg 16:30).

God's plan for him was fulfilled at this time. God used him in this way. This is how God uses His people.

However, nowadays we believe that we are being used by God if we do not become involved with the Delilahs of this world.

This story is not merely about God choosing Samson to be a merciless killer of Philistines. It is a spiritual allegory. Israelites refer to the believers of today, the chosen people of God, and the Philistines symbolize the desires of our human, sinful nature, and are therefore, obstacles to faith. So to destroy the Philistines means to remove various elements of sin from the Israelites so that God may purify their faith. The more completely they are destroyed, the better it is for the people of Israel.

This refers to the spiritual process occurring in us while we are being healed by Jesus in our life.

Samson, the Elder

God prepared a plan to use Samson to save the Israelites. The plan required him to suffer and die a painful death. Superficially, his death resulted from the love of Delilah. So it appears as though Samson's death is part of God's chastening and wrath. However, this is not correct. All these things were planned and worked by Him. It is because God does not chasten him for loving Delilah since Samson was a Nazarite, walking with Him always and already dead to the law.

Today, many people enjoy the pleasures of harlots, but they do so being led by sexual desires irrespective of His will and this will inevitably invite God's judgment.

In contrast to them, Samson who represents the born again man, is essentially different from those who are under the law. He undergoes a series of processes under the control of God and delivers the Israelites out of the hand of the Philistines through his relationship with Delilah and his consequent death. Because of this, the writer of Hebrews calls him the elder who was worthy to be used to carry out God's will.

God will work today in the same way that He delivered Samson into the hands of the Philistines. He first sends born again men to save those who are taken by the wicked power.

In this instance, as the wicked power that ensnares the people of God is destroyed perfectly, they come nearer to salvation. During this salvation process, He does not spare the life of born again men, and this is exemplified in the case of Samson.

It is further clarified by the example of His allowing Jesus to be crucified for our salvation.

Samson's Eli, Eli, Lama Sabachthani (Jdg 16:20-21)

People generally think that Samson underwent sufferings because he was disobedient to God, and so they ascertain that they are right by citing the passage, "And he wist not that the LORD was departed from him" (Jdg 16:20b) and then conclude:

"Look! Samson sinned against God, and so He left him!"

This is not true. Samson is a type of Jesus Christ who is to come. That is, he functions as a shadow of the reality to come. As Jesus had no sin, Samson also had no sin. The Scripture speaks of his birth as follows:

> ² And there was a certain man of Zorah, of the family of the Danites, whose name was Manoah; and his wife was barren, and bare not. ³ And the angel of the LORD appeared unto the woman, and said unto her, Behold now, thou art barren, and bearest not: but thou shalt conceive, and bear a son. ⁴ Now therefore beware, I pray thee, and drink not wine nor strong drink, and eat not any unclean thing: ⁵ For, lo, thou shalt conceive, and bear a son; and no razor shall come on his head: for the child shall be a Nazarite unto God from the womb: and he shall begin to deliver Israel out of the hand of the Philistines. [Judges 13:2-5]

His birth is similar to that of Jesus Christ who was born of the Virgin Mary who was with child of the Holy Spirit. Further, the word, "He shall begin to deliver Israel out of the hand of the Philistines" says in advance that Jesus will finally come to save us from our sin. When Samson finally pulls down the temple of Dagon to annihilate the evil power, it foreshadows Jesus crucifixion that pulls down and destroys the works of the devil and its idol temple built inside us.

In the same way, we believe that Jesus experienced crucifixion because He sinned. If I say so, some believes may say, "The Jews may think so, but I don't." What they are saying is that they believe that Jesus suffered without sinning. Do they really think in this way? We all know that Jesus in his time on earth was a good person whom we should love and honor. We are on His side. However, this is because we simply think of Jesus as a figure in history.

When the time comes, Jesus will have to rebuke us in earnest to heal us in our present life on earth. And then we will refuse to listen and curse Him. We will furthermore probably do this because Jesus comes to us as an ordinary man, a carpenter maybe, with the Word in him. Think about the apostles Peter, Paul, John and so forth that come to us as ordinary men, but with the Word in them.

Do you think that you can tell a man with the Word in him from a man without? You dare not say yes!

If you do not know Jesus who comes to you as an ordinary man in the flesh, then your will treat Him carelessly. This will be especially so, when He seeks to correct you in your understanding of the Word, not to mention, when He rebukes severely to correct those who are possessed of sin (Rom 7:21-24, Mat 16:23).

For example, when the pastor with the Word in him rebukes you, you will not be able to see Jesus in him but only judge him in the 'fleshly' manner. So you will insist on your own opinions that are different from those of the pastor, and will probably hold a grudge against him. When some mishaps happen to him, you will think in yourself "He did me wrong, and so he deserves it. God punished and he paid for that." You would not have criticized him so if you had known that the word from the pastor had Jesus in it.

Therefore, what Isaiah said is correct. We consider Him stricken and afflicted of God. Consider Isaiah.

> Surely he hath borne our grief, and carried our sorrows: yet we did esteem him stricken, smitten of God, and afflicted. [Isaiah 53:4]

Just as the Jews failed to recognize Jesus who came to them as an ordinary man, we also cannot recognize Him coming to us as an ordinary man.

Since the LORD left Samson, he suffered the agony of having his eyes put out, but as a result, he could destroy many of God's enemies and thereby deliver the Israelites. So did Jesus. When He died on the cross, God turned away and He suffered the torment of crucifixion. However, He saved many people because of it.

Read Matthew.

And about the ninth hour Jesus cried with a loud voice, saying, Eli, Eli, lama sabachthani? that is to say, My God, my God, why hast thou forsaken me? [Matthew 27:46]

Epilogue

God did work through Samson and Jesus following the same principle. In detail, He delivered many people based on their sacrifices. We love and praise Jesus, but very few praise Samson. However, as a matter of fact, Samson is the same Savior as Jesus. If you say you can understand who Jesus is but you cannot understand who Samson is, it means that you know neither of them.

Samson is a righteous man and an elder of the faith. Now, let us bury our past when our eyes were blinded by human moral criteria that led us to conclude that Samson merely loved a harlot. As result of this, we misinterpreted the story of Samson and consequently failed to recognize him for whom he really was.

Let us restore his reputation and our understanding!

Adultery of David

[2 Samuel 11:1-5]

¹ And it came to pass, after the year was expired, at the time when kings go forth to battle, that David sent Joab, and his servants with him, and all Israel; and they destroyed the children of Ammon, and besieged Rabbah. But David tarried still at Jerusalem. ² And it came to pass in an eveningtide, that David arose from off his bed, and walked upon the roof of the king's house: and from the roof he saw a woman washing herself; and the woman was very beautiful to look upon. ³ And David sent and enquired after the woman. And one said, Is not this Bath-sheba, the daughter of Eliam, the wife of Uriah the Hittite? ⁴ And David sent messengers, and took her; and she came in unto him, and he lay with her; for she was purified from her uncleanness: and she returned unto her house. ⁵ And the woman conceived, and sent and told David, and said, I am with child.

When we are growing in faith, we go through the stage of law first. When the time is ripe, we will meet the real Jesus who will heal our souls, and this is the stage of healing. And when the healing is complete at the cross, the Holy Spirit will come to us, and thus we will live as a life-giving spirit for the rest of our lives. This is the stage of life-giving spirit.

At each stage, we have to face troubles and sufferings. But these troubles have different meanings at each stage. At the law stage, it is the result of transgressions, and at the healing stage, it is caused by the healing of a sinful soul. At the life-giving spirit stage, it comes from the opposition from other sinful men.

As an analogy, if you have cancer, you suffer from the cancer (sin) itself. This is the law stage. When you meet a doctor (Jesus) for an operation, you will feel pain due to the operation. This is the healing stage. And when the operation is complete you will become healthy (without sin) and will operate on others (sinners) with Christ inside us. However, you will face opposition from them, and be troubled. This is the life-giving spirit stage.

You can see here the same troubles and sufferings of man, but they have different meanings according to each stage. However, our eyes are blind, so we can only see that the troubles and sufferings of man have only one reason, that is, the punishment of God as a result of sins. This proves that we are under the law. That is why we only see and understand the affairs of the law.

In this passage, I will explain the troubles and sufferings that David underwent due to his adultery with Bath-sheba and murder of Uriah.

As expected, we tend to simply read and understand this case as the punishment of God. However, it has a far deeper meaning, which leads us to true salvation. David's troubles and sufferings refer to the stage of healing by Christ the life-giving spirit, not a simple punishment for his sin.

Now I will show you what this story really means.

Outline

To understand this message, we should read the whole book of 2 Samuel, but to save time, we must read at least Chapters 11:1 to 12:14 in 2 Samuel.

In summary, Saul the first king of Israel dies, David succeeds him to be king in Hebron and he later ascends the throne of Israel. God was with him to allow him to subjugate the neighboring hostile countries and win everywhere he went.

In this situation, King David committed adultery with Bath-sheba, the wife of Uriah, and he plotted to kill Uriah to hide his adultery. He then fetched her to his house as his wife.

For this sin of David, God allows him various troubles and sufferings. For example, His son, born to Bath-sheba died not much later, and his daughter Tamar was raped by her brother of a different mother. This caused conflict among his sons. He sought refuge escaping from the rebellion of Absalom, and Absalom slept with David's concubines. When all these hardships and sufferings ended, David was restored as king, and he was accepted as a great king by God and his people.

After knowing what happened to David, all of us will think in this way:

"If we commit adultery, we must pay for it. So we must not do it."

Yes, that's right. No adultery is permitted. However, we may inevitably face the situation of committing adultery and may be entangled in it. That is life. There may be a time when people are obliged to commit adultery, although knowing that they must not do it. The purpose of this story written in the Scripture is not merely to teach that we shall pay dearly if we transgress the law of God, but to show the hand of God who made David a man of God through suffering.

Now, I will describe where and how the hand of God worked in the sufferings of David, which is hidden.

Adultery of David (2Sa 11:2-4)

Regarding the background to this story, Israel destroyed the children of Ammon and besieged Rabbah. At that time, David staying in Jerusalem woke up one night and walked on the roof of the king's house. He saw a very beautiful woman washing herself and he sent to inquire about her and found out that she was Bath-sheba, the wife of Uriah. He sent messengers to get her and after she had purified herself from her uncleanness, slept with her, and let her go back home. After a time passed, she sent word to him that she was pregnant.

People usually focus on analyzing the possible reasons for his sin. Some of them say that he remained idle in Jerusalem instead of going to join the battle along with his soldiers, and this was his mistake. Others make an issue of the fact that he did not sleep but went up to the roof, questioning if he cherished a dark design. Others insist that he became as proud as a peacock and committed adultery unhesitatingly as God blessed him to conquer all the surrounding countries.

However, all these guesses have failed to reach the essence of the event.

Depending on the situation, the king may not go to the front or he may go up to the roof of his house. In addition, it was unlikely that he did this out of arrogance simply because he was the king. This is obvious if we consider that he tried to hide the fact of his adultery.

🗁 The Incompleteness of David's Walk with God

David was modest and so he took counsel with God about everything. When going to war, he used to ask Him "Shall I attack that army or not?" and he followed God's instructions (2Sa 5:19). However, having always tried to find the will of God in every case, he stumbled over his adultery with Bath-sheba.

David knew that adultery was evil and that God hated it. He knew well that adultery would provoke God to chastise him harshly. Accordingly, he was not a man who would easily commit adultery. Nevertheless, he did it, which shows that the temptation at that time was far beyond his self-control.

This was not a stand-alone simple mistake, but it showed the fundamental incompleteness of David's walk with God under the law. God tempted him beyond the limitations of his current walk with Him, so David could not but fail. By committing the sin, David realized that his current walk with God was not sufficient or complete, and so prayed to have a perfect relationship and walk with God; which is being one with God.

🗁 God's Plan

This was what God wanted David to pray. God wanted to lead David to a new level in his walk with Him. So He allowed him to experience a crisis in his relationship with God through David's adultery with Bath-sheba.

Consider Matthew 1:6: "And Jesse begat David the king; and David the king begat Solomon of her that had been the wife of Urias;"

The family tree of Jesus Christ includes David the king and Solomon, the successor to David. We can understand from this that his adultery was not an independent and simple transgression that ended as an act of adultery. His adultery with her was unavoidable and it was included in God's plan. God's plan was to refine David who was under the law, and as a result bring him under grace. In other words, He wanted to have Christ in him.

With this plan, He had all these sufferings happen to David. In fact, this is the salvation, which will be achieved by Jesus Christ in us, and it is foreshadowed here by the case of David. Remember this plan of God, as it will be the plan for every individual, including you.

Pregnancy by Bath-sheba

Having called her and slept with her, David received a message like a bolt from the blue: She was pregnant. Some people may say he did not consider it as a big problem to sleep with her since he was, after all, the king. This is not true. As a king who walked with God and was held in great respect by his people, he was very embarrassed and concerned that his adultery would become public knowledge. We can gather this from the plans he made to conceal his adultery.

🗁 Problem of David

In fact, the mistake he made as a man walking with God was not committing adultery, because man does err. His mistake was that, upon hearing she became pregnant; he developed a scheme to make it appear that Uriah was the father and when this failed, he sought to kill him.

If she had not become pregnant, this affair would not have been a problem. David should have sought God's will after he learned of her unexpected pregnancy. It was God who caused Bath-sheba to become pregnant. When Abraham went down to Egypt, who caused all the wombs of the house of Abimelech (Gen 20:18) to close up? Who made Rachel barren (Gen 30:2)? When Hannah prayed, who opened her womb and ensured that she became pregnant (1Sa 1:5)? God did! It was part of God's plan that Bath-sheba became pregnant.

However, David, who had been walking with God, missed His hand in these events. If he had realized this and repented, the case would not have escalated. However, he did not seek Him but used his natural brain to make things calm down. This reflects the limitations of those who walk with Him under the law.

🗁 David's First Plan

David was bewildered. If she bore a child, Uriah, her husband, would come down hard upon her, but she could not tell him a lie because he was on the battlefield during that period. If she gave birth to a child, it would prove that she had slept with another man.

David was in big trouble. If he were living in present times, he would tell her to go to hospital and have an abortion, but this was impossible at that time. David in an awkward position developed a scheme to recall Uriah from the battlefield and grant him leave for a day so that he would sleep with his wife. Then, when she gave birth to a child, nobody would doubt who the father was. Read 2 Samuel 11:6: "And David sent to Joab, saying, Send me Uriah the Hittite. And Joab sent Uriah to David."

When Uriah came to David, David superficially asked about the military situation and ordered him to go down to his house, sleep there, and then go back to the battlefield. However, instead of going home, Uriah slept at the door of the king's palace. When he reported in the next day, David asked Uriah

"Why didn't you go down unto your house?" and Uriah said

"While the army are encamped in the open field and fight the enemies in the field, how shall I go into my house, eat, drink, and lie with my wife at leisure?"

David called Uriah again the next day to eat and drink with him and made him drunk, expecting that he would go to his house and sleep with his wife this time. However, he did not go home. David's scheming came to nothing because of Uriah's loyalty.

Nevertheless, David still had a chance to redeem himself if he had repented. If he had realized that it was truly the hand of God that had caused his schemes to fail repeatedly, and if he had repented of his actions, he could have avoided making matters worse. Unfortunately, he could not think of Him, but continued with his own ideas. This was the reality of David's faith in those days. And he could not do any better. This shows the limitations of those who believed in God under the law.

Until David sinned in this way, he would not confess he was such a man. However, once he had committed these sins, he could not help but admit it. Obviously, he would not have committed these sins if he were not such a man. God controlled things to make progress with David so that David may confess that he is a man who sins in this way.

Of course, it does not mean that God forced David to do so, but it does mean that He let David's own scheme take its course.

📂 David's Second Plan

Having found that things did not turn out as he wished, he tried to take another step: that is, to do away with Uriah. So David wrote a letter to Joab who was at war, saying, "Set Uriah in the forefront of the hottest battle and order our forces to retire from him that he may be smitten and die." David asked Uriah to take the letter. Having no idea at all, he took the letter to return to the battlefield and deliver it to Joab by command of David. His machinations came off at last, and Uriah died (2Sa 11:14-15).

David made many attempts to hide his faults, but he failed, and he finally achieved his will by killing Uriah. However, the thing David had done displeased the LORD.

The Evil of David in the Sight of the LORD

Read 2 Samuel 11:27: "And when the mourning was past, David sent and fetched her to his house, and she became his wife, and bare him a son. But the thing that David had done displeased the LORD."

We get agitated about the things David did since he fornicated with the wife of his officer and then murdered him and took his wife. If God stands still, we will refuse to accept Him as our God. Thankfully, the Scripture says that the thing that David did displeased the LORD. This word comforts us very much!

Now we naturally think that He is a God of justice and judgment. However, if you think of Him in this way, you totally misunderstand Him.

Each of Us Can Commit Adultery

If you think long and hard, and if you were David, it is highly probable that you would have done as he did. In the sight of God, David having committed adultery is not much different from you having failed to do it because you had no opportunity.

You have avoided committing adultery because you have not yet seen a woman as beautiful as Bath-sheba, and even if you have met such a woman, you have probably not committed adultery since she is completely indifferent to you.

The murder of Uriah can be explained in the same way. David had no intention of killing him. However, when things went awry, David plotted to put him to death and then killed him. It does not mean that he did so because he was so much more wicked than other men. Any of us could behave like this if we are in such a situation.

The following story line is popular in TV dramas. Popular because it arouses our sympathy.

A married man is having intercourse with a girl. One day, she visits him at the office, saying, "I am pregnant. So I have to move into your house with all my belongings." With his heart in his mouth, he soothes her and persuades her to go to hospital and have an abortion. If she says no, he tries to pacify her with money, and if she persists to the last, he starts thinking of killing her. It is a very common story. In some cases, he actually murders her. The story ends. This reveals how we generally react and behave.

Now, considering all circumstances, we can conclude that committing adultery and homicide does not depend on who we are but the situation that we find ourselves in.

Following the same logic, the man who commits adultery is not more wicked than another man who does not. Naturally, God does not distinguish between the two types of man based on whether they have committed adultery or not. Sinners are sinners, regardless of what they do. As a result, He did not chasten David because he committed adultery and killed his officer. Punishment of such acts will be the job of men in the world.

God only will use this case to cause David to repent to God, just as He always does with all human beings.

📁 Evil of David

Then, what does the suffering of David that was caused by adultery and murder, mean and why did He say, "The thing that David had done displeased the LORD?"

The reason why He allowed David to undergo such suffering was to heal him spiritually and lead him to become one with God. It was to enable him to escape from a law-based relationship with God and give him the blessing of uniting with Him as one forever.

Further, when the Scripture said that the thing that David had done displeased the LORD, He did not mention his commitment of adultery and murder. He pointed out that David had not depended upon Him in the course of what he did. It displeased God that he did not follow Him at all. As already explained, if he had tried to find Him and rely on Him in each situation, he would have not slain Uriah.

Open Psalm 51. The introductory paragraph is: "To the chief Musician, A Psalm of David, when Nathan the prophet came unto him, after he had gone in to Bathsheba."

> Against thee, thee only, have I sinned, and done this evil in thy sight: that thou mightest be justified when thou speakest, and be clear when thou judgest. [Psalm 51:4]

David confesses that he has sinned only against Him, without mentioning his commitment of adultery and manslaughter. So it looks like he was denying his sin against people. However, when he confessed as above, it does not mean he is innocent of sinning against other people. He realized that all his sins had arisen from the one sin that "he did not pursue the LORD" and so he confessed as such. The root of sin that all the human beings have, including David, is "not pursuing the LORD," that is, "being separated from Him."

God Sends a Prophet After the Case Happened

David beat his brains out without leaning on God. He first tried to call Uriah and have him sleep with Bath-sheba, but he failed, and he subsequently decided to kill him. He thought he could hide his commitment of adultery through the death of Uriah, but things got out of control.

In this instance, He sends Nathan the prophet to David with a parable (2Sa 12). Nathan confronted him by telling the story of a traveler that came to a rich man, but he, instead of taking of his own flock and herd to dress for the traveler, took a poor man's only little ewe lamb that he had raised as a daughter. David repented deeply.

We can find here that God sent Nathan to David after he had had Uriah murdered on the battlefield. How wonderful it would have been if He had sent Nathan to David before things had got so completely out of control. We are sorry that He always shows Himself just after the things have happened.

However, this is the way He works. For example, he did not appear before Adam and Eve ate of the tree of the knowledge of good and evil, but afterwards. He said to them "Hast thou eaten of the tree, whereof I commanded thee that thou shouldest not eat?" (Gen 3:11)

Further, in the case of the king Saul, when Saul offered the burnt offering on behalf of Samuel after a long wait for him, Samuel arrived and told Saul "Thou hast done foolishly" (1Sa 13:9-13).

Also in this case, He sent the prophet to David after he had committed adultery and had killed Uriah. In fact, He delayed because His plan could be perfectly fulfilled only when it had reached that time. If he had only committed adultery, he would not have repented, saying to himself "I am mistaken, but most of the kings also do that."

However, he could not help repenting when he realized the wickedness of his killing Uriah. Accordingly, it suited God's timing and purpose that Nathan appeared at that time.

Great Occasion to the Enemies

Consider 2 Samuel.

> [10] Now therefore the sword shall never depart from thine house; because thou hast despised me, and hast taken the wife of Uriah the Hittite to be thy wife. [11] Thus saith the LORD, Behold, I will raise up evil against thee out of thine own house, and I will take thy wives before thine eyes, and give them unto thy neighbour, and he shall lie with thy wives in the sight of this sun. [12] For thou didst it secretly: but I will do this thing before all Israel, and before the sun. [13] And David said unto Nathan, I have sinned against the LORD. And Nathan said unto David, The LORD also hath put away thy sin; thou shalt not die. [14] Howbeit, because by this deed thou hast given great occasion to the enemies of the LORD to blaspheme, the child also that is born unto thee shall surely die. [2 Samuel 12:10-14]

In fact, according to the law David who had committed adultery and murdered should have been condemned to die. However, God forgave him his sin and kept him alive. God used his repentance for his sins to give him good things. Therefore, the series of tragic affairs for the royal family of David was not law-based chastening, even though it may appear so.

The kings of the world punish people when they have violated the law such as "Do not commit adultery," or "Do not kill" so that they may not do it again. That is the purpose of punishment. The world only wants the world without adultery and murder. However, God wants the world to repent and return to Him.

Those who are ground down by conventional ideas will also try to understand God within this restriction. So when David committed adultery and instigated murder, we have a mind to beseech Him by saying, "Please hurry to punish him for his exceeding sinfulness." If God does not punish him substantially, we will say blasphemously:

"God damn! How could He leave David alone who committed adultery and killed his man? Can He be a God?"

Please do not imagine that the enemies of God will be devil-faced and very different from us. The enemies of God represent those who are not yet born again, and so cannot understand the heart of God. They judge and reproach Him because they have no idea of what He does.

In order to shut their mouths, He allows the son of David and Bath-sheba to die, the sword never to depart from his royal family, and anxieties to occur continuously. Upon seeing what He did to him, they implicitly want all the other people to have a lesson as follows: "If you commit adultery and kill, you will be punished severely by God. So never do that." They will further praise Him by saying, "Our God is righteous in His works."

However, God who is revealed in the Scripture is not such a man-made God. Taking the transgression of David as an opportunity, He raises tragic affairs in his family, which is a way of healing his soul to give him the Holy Spirit of Immanuel, not to punish him. Of course, it is your own choice to take all these things that happened to David as punishment. As mentioned, it may look like punishment for those who are not born again. Accordingly, God's good hand is hidden in this affair that has been concealed from the eyes of His adversaries up until today.

His good hand toward David is manifested in the prayer of repentance of David.

David's Repentance and Desire – Psalm 51

Read Psalms.

⁴ Against thee, thee only, have I sinned, and done this evil in thy sight: that thou mightest be justified when thou speakest, and be clear when thou judgest. ⁵ Behold, I was shapen in iniquity; and in sin did my mother conceive me. ⁶ Behold, thou desirest truth in the inward parts: and in the hidden part thou shalt make me to know wisdom. ⁷ Purge me with hyssop, and I shall be clean: wash me, and I shall be whiter than snow. ⁸ Make me to hear joy and gladness; that the bones which thou hast broken may rejoice. ⁹ Hide thy face from my sins, and blot out all mine iniquities. ¹⁰ Create in me a clean heart, O God; and renew a right spirit within me. ¹¹ Cast me not away from thy presence; and take not thy holy spirit from me. [Psalm 51:4-11]

Psalm 51 was written by David when Nathan confronted him after he had had Uriah killed because of his commitment of adultery with Bath-sheba. David who had always walked with God, found that he had missed God's hand in these events. It was not a matter of being careful. The essential reason why he missed His hand was that he was born a sinner.

David confesses this by saying, "I was shapen in iniquity, and in sin did my mother conceive me" (Psa 51:5). This means that since his parents were human and therefore sinful he too was born a sinner. He confesses that his sin is something that is related to his born nature, which cannot be corrected by certain works.

So he stretched his hand to God to save him from this sinful nature. God also wanted to save him from such sin.

📂 David Asking the Holy Spirit of Immanuel

Then what was David's desire in this situation? Naturally, it was to be one with God always, not from time to time. He wanted to be one with Him and never be separated from Him again.

David made his supplication like this: "Cast me not away from thy presence; and take not thy holy spirit from me" (Psa 51:11).

His supplication "take not thy holy spirit from me" does not refer to the Holy Spirit he already has. The Holy Spirit of Immanuel has not yet come on David at that time. So, what he meant is that he desperately wanted to receive the Holy Spirit who will never be taken from him once given, that is the Holy Spirit of Immanuel that is given by Jesus.

Once the Holy Spirit comes on him, He never leaves him ever. He committed sin and did wicked things contrary to his intentions and instincts at the time, because the Holy Spirit had not yet come on him. The one and only solution to this trouble is to receive the Holy Spirit of Immanuel. David realized it and sought this.

The series of tragic events that occurred to the royal family of David took place in the course of the healing of his soul by God. After this process, God abided in him as the Holy Spirit forever. This was the final consequence of David's sleeping with Bathsheba under God' providence.

David and Uriah

If God had planned all this in order to give David the Holy Spirit of Immanuel, what about the case of Uriah? Uriah was a soldier of great loyalty. Being sent from the battlefield at the command of David, he refused the king's suggestion twice when the king told him to go and sleep with his wife.

Uriah said to him in 2 Samuel 11:11: "The ark and the soldiers abide in tents. My lord Joab and his men are encamped in the open fields. Shall I then go into my house to eat, drink, and lie with my wife?"

He is a real soldier and an honorable man. However, when Uriah had his wife snatched away and then lost his life, we get angry at David by saying, "How can a king do such a shocking thing to his faithful servant?"

Fortunately, we were slightly comforted since God punished him very severely. But, this book you are reading now says that all these things done by God were not done only to punish David.

How should we understand the case of Uriah then?

📂 Uriah in the Sight of God

First, God's punishment of David has consoled us for the death of Uriah. However, is this thinking supported by God? Uriah had his wife taken from him and was killed by wicked scheming. Will it be meaningful to Uriah who is already dead if God punishes David? It means nothing at all. If God had truly cared for Uriah, He should have taken steps before David killed him. With men it is impossible, but with God all things are possible. Uriah's death signifies that God did not value his life that much.

Therefore, if you think that God avenged the unfair treatment that Uriah suffered by punishing David, which is our traditional way of thinking, it is a total mistake. God had no mind to protect the life of Uriah from the outset. Considering that Uriah was loyal and honorable in our sight, why did he die in such misery? What sort of wrong did he do?

We greatly respect the life of flesh that is given to us when we are born. However, in the sight of God, our life on earth is not as precious as we would like to think. This is because such life is depraved and already 'dead.' If we hold onto the 'dead life' to live in this world and then die as we are, that life profits us nothing. The one and only thing we should do is to be born again by using our 'dead life' as a stepping-stone. This is what we are born into this world for. It is God's desire to give us new life in this world.

As for the life of the flesh, many people as well as Uriah are dying nowadays because of earthquakes, terrors, wars, diseases, and traffic accidents. Do all these people die in a haphazard fashion? No, they do not. All those things happen with the permission of God.

God sees all of our future. If a man will be a person who will live with 'dead life' to the end, there is no difference in the sight of God whether he dies now or later. God permits the death of such men if needed. God determines the time of death to be best when the death will influence neighbors to think about God.

Am *I* a David or a Uriah?

If a person sincerely hopes to receive Holy Spirit of Immanuel and have a born again life while living in this world, God will protect his life of the flesh so that he can receive the Holy Spirit. It is because God also wants him to receive the Holy Spirit.

Read Luke 11:13: "If ye then, being evil, know how to give good gifts unto your children: how much more shall your heavenly Father give the Holy Spirit to them that ask him?"

As can be understood from this story, in spite of the sins committed by David, his desire to live a born again life, caused God to help him in the end. On the contrary, Uriah was an insignificant tool needed for David to receive a born again life. And then he passed away, a loyal soldier.

Can you tell the difference between the two men? The difference lies in whether a person desires to have a born again life by receiving the Holy Spirit of Immanuel while living in the world or whether he simply tries to live a better and more noble life.

David does not mean the David the king, a figure of history. If you hope for the Holy Spirit of Immanuel and pursue it in your life, you are a David. Likewise, Uriah is not simply the Uriah you meet in this tragic story. If you do nothing but hope for the values of this world and search after it through believing in Jesus, you are Uriah.

Whose life do you want to live?
Be David!

▷ Difference Between Samson and David in Adultery

This may be a digression. What is the difference between Samson and David in terms of adultery? Samson is a Nazarite and he is the prototype of the born again man. The born again man commits no sin. It is not sin for Samson to lie with Delilah.

However, the adultery of David shows another meaning. Before being born again, he committed adultery with Bath-sheba and instigated murder. These are sins. Due to those sins, David had repented and sought to have the life of Nazarite, whereby he sins no more.

To summarize, Samson and David committed adultery that, superficially, looked similar, but which can be regarded as sin or not depending on who committed the sin. Samson is born again and is under grace, and it is no sin. David at that moment is not yet born again and is under the law, and it is therefore sin.

The Hidden Manna 127

Epilogue

This story about David reveals Jesus Christ to us. We believe in Jesus and with our utmost efforts try to have communication with Him from time to time. When we have this people will respect and commend us and we also think that we are 'at the top of the faith.' However, this is not so, as we can see from David's case. We should meet the real Jesus and our soul should be healed by destroying our 'old man' on the cross. Then we will receive the Holy Spirit of Immanuel. This is the fulfillment of the whole Bible.

We are born into this world to achieve this. Please remember! This is the purpose of our life.

Traffic Violation in San Francisco*

My family and I arrived at San Francisco International Airport on a July afternoon. We took a taxi to accommodation in Emilyville. We unpacked our bags and suitcases, and then went out and rented a car. I had to take out car insurance, and the rental company provided four or five insurance options such as physical damage of my vehicle, damage to other vehicles, and bodily injury, *et cetera*.

Each one cost $9 to $11 per day. That is, if I take out one option, I have to pay $9 per day, and if I take two, I have to $18 more for each day. The insurance cost was much more expensive than I had expected. I had no idea about how many options I had to select. So I prayed to God on this matter. He replied to me by saying, "Do as you like."

I felt really disappointed by His response. I would have been very happy if He had told me "Take out two," or "You need no insurance." But, He told me to do as I wanted, which was an unwelcome favor. I thought, "Will such an answer give me any insight for my walk with the Lord? I've already done as I wished for several decades before having met Him." Anyway, in anguish, I purchased insurance for physical damage to my vehicle.

The next morning, I drove around looking at the sights of the city. After finishing the morning itinerary, we wanted to go to the Twin Peaks.

I found the place, which was at the western end of Market Street. Since I was driving in San Francisco for the first time, it was not easy to find Market Street. Unfamiliar with the traffic signaling system, I approached Market Street but the traffic was moving in an easterly direction opposite the Twin Peaks.

I looked in vain for a suitable place to make a U-turn. I wandered here and there for a long time, and then I was about to enter Market Street from the western end. Now, if we could just proceed a little further we would arrive at the Twin Peaks. It was about 5 pm.

However, when I was turning right toward the western side of Market Street, the car behind me honked a couple of times, and having no idea of what was going on, I turned right. Immediately, a traffic policeman appeared, and he stopped me. He said that no right-turn was allowed in that area.

In Korea, drivers can turn right on nearly all roads, but this city had a different traffic rule. The officer came near to me and asked to see my driver's license. Showing him my international driving permit, I told him politely that I was a foreigner.

"I'm a stranger in San Francisco, and I'm unfamiliar with the roads."

"No right-turn sign is international."

He was filling in the traffic violation ticket. He asked for my passport number, and I told him I could not remember it because I had left it in my room in the hotel. I showed him my Korean driver's license for the purpose of reminding him that I was a traveler from another country. He returned it to me, telling that it made no sense to him. Even though he clearly knew I was a traveler, he made no allowance for me.

At any rate, he made out a ticketing sheet based on the international driving permit, and gave me a copy of it. He told me that I must present myself to the police station before the due date and provide the additional details. I did not think that this man was reasonable taking into consideration that he had ticketed me based on the international driving permit, even without my passport number.

I felt perplexed. I had got lost and wandered from place to place in a totally foreign city, and to make things worse, I had got a ticket. So I was fed up with travel and wanted to return home. In a bad frame of mind and not knowing how I would deal with the ticket, I drove on to the Twin Peaks.

While driving the car after that, I found a Safeway supermarket with a wide parking lot. I parked there and tried to focus. I got out of the car to show the ticket to the supermarket guard and asked.

"I'm a traveler here. What should I do with this ticket?"

"Well, did you tell him you were traveler here?" he asked me, thinking that it was quite unusual for the traffic police to ticket foreign travelers.

"Yes, I told him so, but I nevertheless got a ticket."

"I am not quite sure, but a fine of about $100 is quite heavy."

He also scared me by saying,

"If you don't report yourself at the police station and pay the fine, you might be arrested the next-time you visit the States."

In fact, on the way to the supermarket after I got ticketed, my wife repeatedly told me "I don't think so. It will be just a warning, and we can go without reporting ourselves to the police station." I was concerned by what the supermarket guard told me so I completely ignored her advice and decided to solve the problem of the fine first.

I calmed myself and read the details of the summons to find that I should appear in the Hall of Justice within the expiration of a notified date. At the time, I thought that it was an exaggeration to call the police station a Hall of Justice. I felt like I had been branded as a gangster.

We had to leave San Francisco in two days and having no idea of where the police station was, I thought how nice it would be if I could pay the fine at a bank in the same way as we pay traffic fines in Korea.

It was very depressing to have to search the map to find a police station; not an obvious tourist attraction! And this only to throw away precious money!

I reluctantly kept on searching for the police station on the tourist map; but to no avail. The tourist map publisher must have thought that tourists would have no necessity to visit a police station. However, some miserable people like me need to be able to find a police station on a tourist map.

While searching, I happened to see another map the rental company had given me and the notation "Hall of Justice" in clear red print at the intersection of Bryant and 7th Streets. I felt that the Lord had been kind to me!

I found the police station without difficulty and arrived there at

The Hidden Manna 131

about 6 pm. I walked to room 101 indicated on the ticket, but the man in charge told me to come back tomorrow because the office had closed for the day. So I had to return to the hotel. I sat in the room and told my hard-luck story to myself.

"How could I fall into this troubled condition?"

My wife was blaming herself guessing that the Lord had got angry at her because she had missed a church gathering in Korea and joined this trip.

Having no idea about what had happened to me, I thought about what He was doing in this case. I felt sad that the Lord had left me alone and in trouble despite the fact that He said He loved me and cared for me each time I asked Him. I will now write the conversation that I had with Him at that time.

"Did you know in advance that I was to be ticketed because of the traffic violation?"

I asked Him this question because I thought if He had already known, He would not have allowed all these things to happen to me since He loved me. In addition to this, I wanted Him to console me a little in such a difficult situation.

"Yes, I did."

It was a natural answer. Nothing He does not know and does not permit can happen to me.

"Did you allow me to get ticketed because it would give me an advantage?"

The Lord said to me, "Sure."

"Then, when I got a ticket today, did you save me out of more serious danger to come or did I do something wrong?"

"You did wrong."

I could not understand what sort of mistake I had made. I asked Him again.

"If I did wrong, did I do it while I was in Korea or after I came across to the United States?"

"You are at fault in the US."

"Do you mean that the traffic violation was my mistake when You said I did wrong?"

It was almost meaningless to ask Him this, but I tried to find my mistake through many questions to the Lord.

"No, it isn't."

He therefore means that I got ticketed because I had done something wrong to God.

"I'd like what I have to do tomorrow to be settled satisfactorily so that I may not pay the monetary penalty."

"I got it."

I asked Him again to make sure.

"Do I have to pay the fine?"

"Yes, you have to."

Up to then, even if I was required to pay the fine because of what I had done wrong to Him, I believed that He would rescue me from this embarrassing situation.

Early the next morning, I, together with my family appeared at the police station instead of going to an amusement park. I felt self pity. I stood in the line before the window under the title of "Moving Violations." I showed my ticket to the officer at the window, and he said, "This is an international driving permit!" He showed the ticket to his supervisor and asked him something. It seemed that he asked, "Does this guy with this international driving permit have to pay the penalty?" He seemed to have difficulty in inputting data to the computer. The supervisor looked at the ticket for a moment and told him to receive the payment.

The officer in charge, after coming back to his desk, asked the supervisor again saying, "How can I impose a fine on this international driving permit that is unlike an American driver's license?" and the supervisor told him "He has no option but to pay it" with a more stern expression.

At the very moment, I could see the Lord as a severe judge from the face of the supervisor. After all this, the officer at the window was forced to tell me to pay $104. I paid him and he made out a receipt for me. I still have that receipt!

Anyway, I had struggled not to pay the money, but was compelled to pay it after many ups and downs. When all these things had come to an end, I found that the general manager of these things was God.

He worked on purpose like this: I was just a traveler in San Francisco, but He allowed a hardhearted traffic officer to ticket me.

He scared me and cut off any retreat by saying through the supermarket guard that I would be arrested on the next visit if I bilked the fine. He kindly enabled me to find the police station on the map, fearing that I may fail to find the police station and pay the fine.

It was found to be an obviously exceptional case at the police station that a traveler with an international driving permit should be fined, but He had the man in charge collect the fine to the last penny.

Since I had no idea of His original plan prepared for me, and I made vain efforts praying to God over and over again to release me from the fine. Maybe, the President of the US might like this kind of God because He permitted no resistance and made me present $104 to the US government.

During the course of their work, the traffic police, the supermarket guard, and the supervisor of the police station were used by God to play their roles, not knowing they were being used by Him.

If you regret that you have no connections in the community to which you belong, stop regretting and focus on believing in Jesus. Then, the Lord will control all the people in the world to support you. Have no fear.

After the case was over, I became quietly angry. I felt sorry that God had inserted an undesired visit to the police station and the payment of a fine into the tour itinerary. If a travel agency put such program into a travel itinerary, nobody would purchase such a holiday. I would never have gone to the States if I had known about this in advance.

I asked God what on earth was wrong,

"Now that You have afflicted me as You wanted, please let me know what blunder I made." The Lord said,

"I see."

Some days passed, and then He allowed my fault to occur to me. It was the matter of insurance. When He told me "Do as you like" while I was renting a vehicle, He wanted me to express faith towards Him. In other words, when I received such a response, I should have said to Him "My Lord, please protect us, I will not purchase any insurance," and should not have contracted any insurance. This means that I put my faith in Him, not in the insurance.

So God was displeased with my decision, and He wanted to teach me through this case. He forced me to pay the fine even though I would have not paid it under normal circumstances.

In one aspect, He treated me roughly, but my faith has increased that much. The hand of the Lord works together on all occasions for good.

I pray that you all walk with the living Lord.

Blessed is the Man

[Psalm 1:1-2]
¹ Blessed is the man that walketh not in the counsel of the ungodly, nor standeth in the way of sinners, nor sitteth in the seat of the scornful. ² But his delight is in the law of the LORD; and in his law doth he meditate day and night.

We all know Psalm 1, after reading it, we make up our minds and say:

"Yes, I will not follow the ungodly even if they tempt me, I will not follow what the sinners do, and I will not hold my head high. Also, I will try to meditate on the word of God with joy always."

However, we should go further from here. "So, have I been blessed?" It is not a simple thing for us just to say "Yes, that's right. I agree" each time we read and hear this Psalm. How long are you going to continue to do this? Now we should stay alert.

If kindergarten pupils make a fuss, to calm them down their teacher says:

"Good children keep silent, do not make a noise."

Then, they stop talking and keep silent so as to be good kids.

We tend to think immaturely like kindergarten kids when reading Psalm1. That is, we try to follow the prescribed behaviors so that we may gain acceptance as the blessed ones. It is time for us to leave such kindergarten level thinking, especially, when it comes to understanding the Scripture.

The Vine and its Grapes

The passage above does not prescribe actions that must be followed so that we may be blessed. If the passage reads to you in this way, then you are under the law. The words in the passage simply define the blessed man. It can be re-arranged as "The man that walketh not in the counsel of the ungodly is blessed," and this sentence is similar to: "The vine produces grapes." This is a statement of truth and life.

Grapes only grow on the vine and not on other trees. If a man puts grapes on a thorn tree, it will not be fruit but hypocrisy and affectation. The grapes produced on the vine will only be called grapes. Not knowing that we are 'thorns,' we are absorbed in making grapes. Therefore, we insist that we have produced a lot of grapes while actually we have simply stuck many grapes on the thorns. This is hypocrisy as I have previously said.

If God instructs us to bear grapes, we should first become a vine. This is the right approach.

If we understand the word "Blessed is the man that walketh not in the counsel of the ungodly" as "I must not walk in the counsel of the ungodly in order to be blessed" and then conduct ourselves in such way, that will be a good instance of gathering grapes and sticking them onto thorns.

At this point, some of you might ask, "Should I then, try to walk in the counsel of the ungodly?" I have no option but to say, "No, you should not."

You cannot become blessed in that way.

Then, how can we be blessed? The answer is this: You can be blessed when you do not walk in the counsel of the ungodly, nor stand in the way of sinners, nor sit in the seat of the scornful.

Now I will describe the true characteristics of the man who is blessed.

The Counsel of the Ungodly

"Blessed is the man who does not walk in the counsel of the ungodly."

In this instance, the ungodly do not mean murderers, robbers, or thieves. In simple terms, the 'ungodly' means the "old man" mentioned in Romans 6:6, who is in us and is against God. The 'old man' is the ungodly, and the person who is controlled by the ungodly in him is the ungodly man. So this passage of Psalm 1 is talking about the 'ungodly man' in *us*, the 'old man,' not other people such as murderers *et cetera*.

Some people might say, "I have no mind to follow the ungodly. The one thing I want to do is to serve Jesus Christ and God only. Also, I am not controlled by the counsel of my 'old man.' However, why am I so far from being blessed?"

Are you not blessed now? Then, it proves that you are currently walking in the counsel of the ungodly, and as a consequence, you are not blessed. Maybe you never even dreamt of walking in such a way, but fact is fact.

How is the counsel of the ungodly known to us? How fortunate it would be if the ungodly were to identify himself and say, "I am the ungodly. Walk in my counsel, and I will make you prosper in everything." No one will walk in his counsel even if he promises blessings. We will thrust the ungodly away by saying, "I will not be cheated by the honeyed words." However, the ungodly does not come this way. Never!

None of the ungodly calls themselves ungodly. They put on a mask and come to us as godly men. The ungodly *in* us naturally never shows himself in his true colors. If he reveals his real nature, it is his end because nobody will listen to him. The ungodly in us is extraordinarily smart.

He deceives us, but we have no idea of the fact that we are being deceived by him. If deceived like this unconsciously, we will eventually be his slaves. We will be used as members of the ungodly. Then, we are the ungodly in both name and reality. As 2 Peter 2:19 says, "For of whom a man is overcome, of the same is he brought in bondage."

The ungodly cheats us when we are reading the Scripture. He makes us spend all of our lives keeping the legalistic meanings of the Scripture, which is the law, ignoring the truth that the law cannot make us justified. Consider Romans 3:20: "Therefore by the deeds of the law there shall no flesh be justified in his sight: for by the law is the knowledge of sin."

Sometimes we are driven to despair after having found that we cannot keep the law of the Lord, and seek other ways, but we are immediately deceived by the counsel of the ungodly that we will be gradually sanctified until death. So we are caught under the law till death even when we are believers in Jesus.

🗁 Doctrines of Men

The ungodly transforms the word of God into the doctrines of men. For example, Jesus says to us "You shall love your neighbor as yourself." The ungodly will change and interpret this word of God into "You must love your neighbor, so try to love," which is the doctrines of mankind. At a glance, it looks the same to us. However, such interpretation is not the word of God. It is the teachings of men, which are taught since kindergarten and not only by believers but also by non-believers, and by all human beings actually. Such teaching did not make one single man love his neighbor as himself. We know it from the history of humanity.

In fact, the doctrines of men mean the law, which ask human beings, the sinners, to do righteous things. It is like asking thorn trees to produce grapes; which is utterly impossible. Unfortunately, this is what we are endeavoring when walking in the counsel of the ungodly.

If we spend our lives this way, we will live ungodly lives throughout, only trying to love our neighbor, but never truly loving our neighbor. We have not been able to love, not because we were less eager or made less effort, but because we walked in the wrong way.

In order to love your neighbor, we have to be born again first as a 'love being,' *then* we can love. So the right way to love our neighbor is to meet Jesus and receive the Holy Spirit, the love that Jesus brings. This is being born again as a 'love being.'

Therefore, the word "You shall love your neighbor as yourself" does not mean to "Try to love your neighbor," which is the law, but it means, "Meet Jesus and He will give you the Holy Spirit and then you will be able to love," which is *grace*.

However, the ungodly still stirs us up to try to love our neighbors by ourselves without meeting the real Jesus. If the Holy Spirit has not yet come on us, all of us are inevitably walking in the counsel of the ungodly. When the Holy Spirit comes on us, we will no longer walk in the counsel of the ungodly. Blessed are those.

The Way of Sinners

"Blessed is the man who does not stand in the way of sinners."

This word does not mean that we should avoid what sinners do so that we may be accepted as blessed. This word characterizes the blessed man who does not stand in the way of sinners, and it is not a commandment that you should not do the things that sinners do in order to be blessed.

The sinner sins. He is eventually a sinner even if he suppresses sin once or twice, or he sits still. The only method for him not to stand in the way of sinners is to be changed into a righteous man. Then, he will become blessed and will no longer stand in the way of sinners.

To try not to commit sin, whether it is possible or not, is human, but to be re-born from sin into righteousness is a gift from God. You cannot recreate yourself as righteous; only God can do this through Jesus.

If we meditate on the word "Blessed is the man that standeth not in the way of sinners," we will find that it means: "I who am God will make you righteous through Jesus and you will be blessed."

However, believers, having been deceived by the counsel of 'old man,' will answer "No, God! Stand aside! I will try to do it alone. I will not kill, I will not judge, I will not steal, and I will love my neighbors as myself." He never fulfills all these promises. Even after he has finally failed, he will still insist saying, "It is impossible to do such things while I am living in the flesh. However, I will not be sinning any longer when I am dead after having passed through the sanctification process in this life."

This is a very dreadful word, which will destroy our soul eventually. Because once we are cheated by this word of the ungodly, we are justifying it as natural to live our whole life as sinners. Do not be taken in. If it is really so, Jesus died in vain.

We have no other option but to become righteous if we would not "stand in the way of sinners." The way to become righteous is, as I have said before, to meet Jesus and receive the Holy Spirit. God does this work for us. What we can do is only to hear, realize the true meanings of the Scripture, and walk with the Lord. When we have finished this course, we will be born again as righteous, and we will not stand in the way of sinners any longer.

The Seat of the Scornful

"Blessed is the man that sitteth not in the seat of the scornful."
The scornful in this case do not refer to those who are arrogant or overbearing, as we generally tend to think. The scornful signify those who are scornful before God.

Human beings, who were scornful, thought they could do better than God and so they ate of the tree of the knowledge of good and evil, and then they were born in this world. The idea of desiring to become righteous by sincerely keeping the laws God gave has also come out of this sort of scornfulness.

In the parable of the prodigal son, when the younger son had tried to live alone in the far country, that long period of time was his expression of scornfulness towards his father. When he was almost starved to death without any husks that the swine ate, his scornfulness was broken.

I am describing this in detail since some of you reading this book may feel unfairly criticized and say, "Have I been scornful of God? Have I ever thought that I was superior to Him?"

Does the mind of judging brothers come out of you? You are the scornful. Does the idea that "I have no big problem because I have seriously believed in Jesus for several decades" come across your mind? Yes, you are the scornful. Do you happen to think, "I have worked for God with spiritual gifts such as prophecies or interpretation of tongues?" You are the scornful also. Do you estimate that "I am freed from the law since I have understood the deeper meanings of the Scripture that few other know?" You are likewise the scornful.

If you do not want to sit in the seat of the scornful, you should experience the life of the prodigal son and receive the Holy Spirit at the father's house. After that, your position will be changed from the seat of the scornful to the seat of the meek and lowly in heart.

In His Law Meditates Day and Night

"In His law does he meditate day and night."

We can easily conclude that this generally refers to the person who reads and meditates on the word of God continuously and steadily.

However, the law referred to above does not represent the command of God written in words but signifies the Christ who is the Word coming into the heart of the born again man. He will always walk with the Lord and live his life according to His will. He is the man who has met Jesus, undergone the healing process of the soul, and then received the Holy Spirit. Thus, the Word has been written on his heart (Hbr 8:10) and so he can meditate on His law day and night.

Blessed is such a man. Whatever he does shall prosper.

From Marketplace to Vineyard

[Matthew 20:1-16]

[1] For the kingdom of heaven is like unto a man that is an householder, which went out early in the morning to hire labourers into his vineyard. [2] And when he had agreed with the labourers for a penny a day, he sent them into his vineyard. [3] And he went out about the third hour, and saw others standing idle in the marketplace, [4] And said unto them; Go ye also into the vineyard, and whatsoever is right I will give you. And they went their way. [5] Again he went out about the sixth and ninth hour, and did likewise. [6] And about the eleventh hour he went out, and found others standing idle, and saith unto them, Why stand ye here all the day idle? [7] They say unto him, Because no man hath hired us. He saith unto them, Go ye also into the vineyard; and whatsoever is right, that shall ye receive. [8] So when even was come, the lord of the vineyard saith unto his steward, Call the labourers, and give them their hire, beginning from the last unto the first. [9] And when they came that were hired about the eleventh hour, they received every man a penny. [10] But when the first came, they supposed that they should have received more; and they likewise received every man a penny. [11] And when they had received it, they murmured against the goodman of the house, [12] Saying, These last have wrought but one hour, and thou hast made them equal unto us, which have borne the burden and heat of the day. [13] But he answered one of them, and said, Friend, I do thee no wrong: didst not thou agree with me for a penny? [14] Take that thine is, and go thy way: I will give unto this last, even as unto thee. [15] Is it not lawful for me to do what I will with mine own? Is thine eye evil, because I am good? [16] So the last shall be first, and the first last: for many be called, but few chosen.

As we can see from the first sentence of the passage, Jesus is giving this parable to explain the kingdom of heaven. So the parable should be construed to portray the kingdom of heaven, which is unseen to our eyes, not the proper wage distribution scheme of the world.

This householder is very unique. We generally think in terms of hiring laborers for a day's work, first thing in the morning, but he continued to go out and hire them throughout the day. Even until 5 pm. (Eleventh hour)! Why did he do this?

Further, he paid the same one penny (*denarion* in Greek) to each of them who worked only one hour, who worked three hours, who worked six hours, and who worked eight hours. We think it is natural for the householder to give wages in proportion to working hours. The laborers who came early in the morning also thought this would be fair. Did he handle them reasonably?

Let us see what revelation about the kingdom we can get from this parable.

Parable and Its Symbols

We will first need to know what the words in this parable symbolize. I will explain them first.

🗁 Marketplace

The place where the laborers were waiting at first is the marketplace. In the marketplace, goods and services are exchanged, usually for money. If a person has given something to another, he gave it to receive something in exchange, be it money or goods. Here, although something may be given free; it is not free at all. Because the man who gave free, did so with the intention of getting back something.

This marketplace symbolizes the world. The Scripture likens

the world to the marketplace because all the actions of human beings in the world are based on the give-and-take transaction system. The motive of giving something to another already includes a calculation of what the one will receive from the other as a trade-off.

As for love, be careful if someone says to you that he loves you. He will definitely ask for something back for loving you. Therefore, when someone says that he loves you, it means, "You must love me in return for my love for you." Love between a man and a woman in the marketplace is give-and-take. As such, marriage is typically a transaction and a binding contract for life. Even if love fades, he or she has to love the partner until death. This is somehow mandated by the law of the world.

The Scripture therefore refers to men as the marketers by pointing out such characteristics of human society. In the world, they are engaged with each other, their mutual interests and the processes of buying and selling.

The Scripture likens this world to the marketplace.

📁 Vineyard

The vineyard is in contrast to the marketplace. The vineyard produces grapes and there is an increase and fruit-bearing according to the phenomenon of life.

Jesus says "I am the true vine, and my Father is the husbandman" (Jhn15:1) and "I am the vine, ye are the branches: He that abideth in me, and I in him, the same bringeth forth much fruit: for without me ye can do nothing" (Jhn 15:5).

God is the householder, Jesus is the vine, and believers are the branches of the vine that bear grapes. Believers in unity with Jesus will produce grapes that please God.

The vineyard symbolizes the kingdom of heaven, which is His church on earth. In church, the members receive the word of Jesus and produce fruit; the formation of Christ in them. Love here is unconditional, like the love of parents towards children, which is a shadow of the love that God has towards us.

In this parable, the marketplace indicates the world of transaction, while the vineyard represents the world of life ('life' in contrast with the 'law'), the kingdom of heaven.

From Marketplace to Vineyard (Mat 20:1-7)

The householder goes out to the marketplace to recruit laborers. When the laborers who were in the marketplace (that is the world of give-and-take) enter the vineyard that is the world of life, the systems of these two different worlds collide. The laborers who were hired in the morning complained about the householder, because he paid the same wages to the workers hired in the evening. This is the collision between the people from the market and the vineyard. However, those who came in the evening and worked one hour did not murmur at all but were grateful to him.

The parable depicts the process by which we, who once lived according to the worldly system, enter the church. Many people get discontented because of the collision of the two worlds, while others in the church enjoy life giving thanks to God. The former corresponds to those who came in the morning and the latter corresponds to those who came in the evening.

I will now tell you how the parable of the laborers and their behavior relates to the church and church members today.

▱ Those Hired First

The householder goes to the marketplace early in the morning and hires laborers. The chosen ones agree on a wage of one *denarion* with him for a day of work in the vineyard. They are passionate and overconfident. The called men will provide their working power to the householder and will receive a wage in return. It is the typical give-and-take transaction of the marketplace.

Those that are hired first represent those who are in the church with the following mindset and level of faith:

They are strong, and think they are men of ability who can execute many plans for the church. They are living in the 'morning time' of their life. They believe in Jesus and think that they can be of help to the church in many ways, such as praise, collection, preaching, management of church activities, or serving table. In addition to these things, and with regard to the keeping of commandments given by the Lord, they are ready to obey the words "Love one another," "Do not judge," "Do almsgiving," and "Fast" and so on.

The only reason they do these things is to receive the kingdom of heaven from Him. Accept it or not, there is no reason for them to do such things if they do not receive compensation. They believe that they provide their efforts to God and He gives them in return the kingdom of heaven as their wages.

This shows that they are perfectly armed with worldly give-and-take thinking even though they attend the church of life; of Jesus Christ. They represent believers under the law.

They are those who were hired first in the parable.

📂 Those Hired in the Middle of the Day

Some laborers were also hired and sent to the vineyard at 9 am, 12 noon, and 3 pm. They came to the vineyard not early in the morning but much later when they have half the day, or less, to labor and earn their wage. They met the householder when nobody else had hired them and so they had given up saying, "I will be hungry today and tomorrow."

At this time, they were unexpectedly called. They could not afford to make a deal with the householder in their serious situation. Therefore, when he said to them "Whatsoever is right I will give you," they did not ask, "Will it be a *denarion* or a half *denarion* a day?"

I want to be clear, they only wished in their heart, "Please give to me as much as you like." This is how they were sent to the vineyard. They were thankful that they were called to have a chance to labor. They were happy and were willing to labor because they had a job in their desperate condition. Their mindset is only half give-and-take.

These laborers represent those that are in the church with the following mindset and level of faith:

They thought at first that they could give a helping hand to God and the church and in return, they could claim the kingdom of heaven or something else based on their effort and help given. But now, they gradually realize that they themselves are the ones who benefit most by working in the church; not God and not the church. But as their faith grows in the church, they get to experience the healing of their soul by Jesus to enter the kingdom of heaven, that is, to have eternal life.

By this time, they are grateful to Him since they realize that He called them not because they were distinguished, but because He wanted to give them the kingdom of heaven freely. They begin to realize step by step that it is joyful to work in the church, and they are not so much interested in a future reward. They will only say, "Please let me have it as You see fit." However, they are not yet done, but are in the middle of the faith growing process. They must grow in faith to the level of those who are hired last.

They represent those whose give-and-take mindset is changed to partially understand the law of life and grace in the church. They are those who were hired in the middle of the parable.

🗁 Those Hired Last

Now, it is 5 pm. The work in the vineyard will be over at 6 pm. There were still some people wandering in the marketplace at that time. They stood there until 5 pm not because they hoped that anyone would hire them, but because they found no other place to go. They gave themselves up to despair and then the lord of the vineyard comes to them, saying: "Go ye also into the vineyard."

This is the gospel. They did not think that they would work that day and earn a wage. They were deeply grateful to him for calling them in their state of despair. So the vineyard owner simply told them to go into the vineyard and said nothing about the pay.

In contrast he had agreed with those he hired first on 'a *denarion*' a day, and with those hired in the middle of the day for 'whatsoever is right.' Anyway, those hired at 5 pm happily went into the vineyard and worked there, giving no thought to the wage.

Those who came in the evening represent those who have lived their own life, be it in the church or otherwise, but reached their limits and fell down. They correspond to the younger son in the parable of the prodigal son who left his father, lived life in his own way in a far country until he was entirely desolate, and then came back to the house of the father.

Whilst those who were hired first are doing their best with legalistic eagerness, they too, finally face their limits like the prodigal son. Up until then, they would not even realize that they believed under the law. Anyway, then they will realize that they cannot enter the kingdom of heaven through their efforts under the law. From that time on, they will hear the voice of Jesus and will follow Him, forsaking everything.

They will not think of whatever they do in the church as works which will be rewarded later, but will only be thankful for Him who has called them to give an opportunity to work in the church. For them, the life in the church is the life of the kingdom of heaven. Their mind is now changed to that of the lord of the vineyard. They are born again men, who are under grace.

Such men correspond to those who were hired last in this parable.

Those First And Those Last (Mat 20:8-15)

📂 **To Do What I Will With My Own**

Those hired first came into conflict with the householder because they had no idea that the vineyard operated in a totally different manner to the marketplace. When they tried to apply the principle of the marketplace to the vineyard they were frustrated and annoyed.

So, should the householder change the principle of the vineyard so as to calm them down? Absolutely, not! This is what "Is it not lawful for me to do what I will with mine own?" signifies.

The church, which is the body of the Christ, operates differently to the organizations in the world. It will be operated by the law of life in God, not by the doctrines of men from the marketplace. But those hired first will try to apply a marketplace viewpoint in the church, but God will never ever allow that kind of nonsense. It is lawful for God to do what He wills with His own.

In fact, a *denarion* signifies the 'salvation.' Salvation cannot be apportioned in accord with the amount of works done by the individual. However, those hired first thought so unknowingly and asked for such nonsense. We need to realize that, in this respect we are not so much different from those hired first.

📂 Go Your Way

Those hired first think that what the householder did to them was evil, but on the contrary, the householder says that their eye is evil. Essentially, these two parties cannot go together. So there is only one way left. Either of the parties who cannot agree should leave. The vineyard belongs to him, and so the laborers who were hired first must leave. This is what "Take that thine is, and go thy way" means.

In order for you to live in the kingdom of heaven, you must be one with God through Jesus to have same mind as Him. Otherwise, you are destined to face conflict with God, and you will have to leave the kingdom of heaven ultimately. Not because God kicks you out, but because you do not wish to be together with Him due to frustration that He will not work as *you* wish.

When Jesus starts to preach this parable in verse 1, He says, "For the kingdom of heaven is like unto a man that is an householder." According to His saying, the kingdom of heaven is not a certain 'place,' but the 'mind' of a householder.

So if you have the same mind as God, wherever you go that place is the kingdom of heaven. But if you do not, wherever you go, wherever you are, that place is hell. Are you one with God having the same mind? If not, Jesus will do it for you provided that you believe in the *real* Jesus.

For those who have a different mindset, the householder in the parable says, "Go your way."

📂 Those First to Become Those Last

The lord of the vineyard gave a *denarion* to all laborers from last to first equally. This made those hired first upset. However, the lord did no wrong to them. He agreed with them for a *denarion* a day, and he gave it to them.

The problem is that they could not receive their *denarion* with thanks. Those hired in the middle of the day, for example, did not murmur against him because they had only worked half a day and received a full *denarion*. Needless to say those who were hired last and who worked only one hour, received a *denarion*, the full-day's wage. They were only thankful for the act of grace on the part of the householder. They are the ones who can stay together with the lord, differing from those hired first.

In this instance, if you think that it will be a solution for those hired first to have patience, you miss the point. If you take the positions of the various groups of laborers, how would you have responded to what he did to you? If you were in the shoes of those hired first, you would naturally grumble at the householder. If you were those hired in the middle of the day, you could manage to work without complaint. If you were like them who were hired last, you would only thank him for what he did for you so graciously.

God treats all believers equally, but even in this equal treatment, many will complain and some will be grateful depending on their respective spiritual positions, i.e., the maturity of their faith. Therefore, this conflict will not be resolved if we tell them who were hired first to be patient rather than grumble against him. It is human nature to feel aggrieved in such a situation. Furthermore, the lord of the vineyard does not seem to accept their complaint.

Then, how could this problem be solved? The solution is that those hired first should be changed to be like those hired last. It is the only way. In this situation, they will not get angry at what the lord did, but they will feel grateful to him.

Those first will gradually change into those last, if they meet the real Jesus in their lives. All these problems will therefore be solved.

A *Denarion* Means Salvation

After the work is over, the lord of the vineyard gave each of them a *denarion* for their wage.

What does this *denarion* mean? It means salvation, the kingdom of heaven. God promised to give salvation to those who believed in Jesus. In the same way He gives salvation to all the people who come to church to believe in Jesus, whether they come in the morning or in the evening. When people come to church and confess Jesus as their Savior, they received salvation, a *denarion*.

However, as we can observe in this parable, the meaning of salvation is different from person to person. For example, for those hired first, a *denarion* is not as important as the work they have done. They misunderstand and think that salvation is something to be received based on their deeds. But, for those hired last a *denarion* means their salvation and this is a free gift of God. They understand that salvation is a born again life given by grace, which is biblical.

Therefore, it is meaningless for the lord of the vineyard to give those hired first more *denarion*. Salvation does not work in this way. They have to be changed into those hired last who can accept their salvation for what it really is, a new life freely given by the grace of God.

In the parable of the prodigal son in Luke, the elder son stayed with the father. He worked hard because he wanted his father to recognize his hard work and reward him accordingly. Living in his father's house, he had no idea of the principle of life and lived according to the principles of the marketplace. The elder son, already living in salvation, being one with his father/God, but hoped for yet more. He corresponds to those hired first in the current parable.

Compared to him, the younger son having gone through all sorts of terrible troubles returns home and does work which is not labor but pure joy for him. Through this process, the younger son is able to receive salvation. He matches those hired last.

To conclude, those hired first cannot recognize salvation as salvation, but those hired last from a position of desperation in the world of the flesh, recognize salvation for what it is, being one with God. Therefore, those hired last are those who are saved at last.

The Last Shall Be First (Mat 20:16)

"So the last shall be first, and the first last" (Mat 20:16a).

It is very difficult to understand this word because the *first* and the *last* have a double meaning.

We begin to believe in Jesus with the faith of those hired first, which is legalistic. This legalistic faith is identified as 'the first' in this verse. When we meet the real Jesus in our life, we will have the faith of those hired last, which is grace. This faith of grace is identified as 'the last.'

Regarding the legalistic faith (law) and the faith of Jesus (grace), the latter is much more glorious than the former. So, 'the last shall be first' means 'the glory of grace is much more glorious' and 'the first (shall be) last' means, 'the law is less glorious.' Consider 2Co 3:9: "For if the ministration of condemnation be glory, much more doth the ministration of righteousness exceed in glory."

"For many be called, but few chosen" (Mat 20:16b).

Those hired first are many in number, but those hired last are few. This means many people come to church to believe in Jesus, but only a few of them will be born again and saved by the real Jesus. In this sense, many are called, but few chosen.

Epilogue

Our faith starts from the position of those hired first, and will be complete as we come to the place of those that were hired last, that is, if we meet Jesus. Although the kingdom of heaven is already given at the stage of 'hired first,' we cannot realize it because of our market-mindset formed from birth in this world. When this mindset is destroyed at the cross by Jesus, we will then realize that we are in the kingdom already and will live there forever. We now have the faith of those 'hired last.'

In other words, Jesus says, "Your faith begins first with the law and is to be complete with grace. Grace is what I really want to give to you, and it is more glorious than the law." "Truly, many come to believe Jesus under the law, but only a few get to believe under grace." So watch!

Dream of Reaping Grapes*

One day in December of the year after I met Jesus, I had a dream. I saw the garden of the house that was next to mine in my old hometown, and grapes grew in clusters there. The grapevines had many bunches of grapes high up in the air and had a rectangular shape. Many people tried to reach them but they were located so high that nobody could touch them. So people threw stones to knock them down. However, they were also out of throwing distance. One of them threw a stone that just managed to graze one of the grapes in a bunch. Not anyone standing there could pick the grapes. I, however, was able to reach out and pick all the grapes with a white cloth.

God gave me this dream to give me hope and vision. He showed me what I should be doing during my life in this world. Huge numbers of churches worship Him, practice discipleship training, gather together to pray for revival, sing praises, and try everything to enlarge the churches and their members. They do all of these works in order to harvest souls. However, how many people will be harvested through these activities? Not many I guess.

This is because most of the sermons preached in churches focus on the law. Very little true understanding of God and His grace is found in them. All the efforts that are expended focusing on law based preaching will be like throwing stones at the grapes that are out of range.

God revealed through this dream what I would be doing in the future, and I am now doing it.

Martha and Mary

[Luke 10:38-42]
³⁸ Now it came to pass, as they went, that he entered into a certain village: and a certain woman named Martha received him into her house. ³⁹ And she had a sister called Mary, which also sat at Jesus' feet, and heard his word. ⁴⁰ But Martha was cumbered about much serving, and came to him, and said, Lord, dost thou not care that my sister hath left me to serve alone? bid her therefore that she help me. ⁴¹ And Jesus answered and said unto her, Martha, Martha, thou art careful and troubled about many things: ⁴² But one thing is needful: and Mary hath chosen that good part, which shall not be taken away from her.

This story begins as Martha living in Bethany invited Jesus into her house. Martha, Mary and Lazarus are the brother and sisters in this house. And Jesus loved them.

When Martha received Jesus into her house, she was quite busy cleaning up the rooms and preparing food for Him. It is very natural for her to receive Him who is so precious with all her heart. On the contrary, Mary does not have the slightest thought of working with her sister but only listens to Him, and Martha naturally complains about her. However, in contrast to Martha's thinking, Jesus speaks in favor of Mary by saying, "Mary hath chosen that good part."

Having read the passage, it is a lot easier for us to understand the standpoint of Martha than that of Mary. Why? Because we are Martha in this case. What does this mean then?

Now I will reveal who Martha and Mary are in the spiritual sense, and I hope that by this revelation we can see for ourselves where we are individually in the development of our faith.

Martha and Mary Represent Believers

First, we should know who Martha and Mary are. We will try to understand them through their behaviors. They tried to welcome and be friendly towards Jesus. Who then are they who hope to welcome and get along with Jesus these days? They are all of us who believe in Him. So, Martha and Mary symbolize believers in the church nowadays.

Now I will proceed to explain the different approaches of the two sisters.

Quite a number of people feel that life in the church is laborious and boring. Some men joke that they come to church because their wives will nag them if they do not come. Some others come to church because they are relatives of the pastor. And some come because friends have begged them to come. These people will not come to church on the following Sunday if they have some small trouble on their mind. They tend to cease for a while, and then come again when they feel better.

However, Martha and Mary are quite different from the above-mentioned people. They realize that He is precious, and so invite Him into their house deliberately, and they do their best to serve Him. They know Jesus through experiencing His mercy, healing and grace and so are very devoted to Him. These sisters are role models for the believers in today's churches.

Jesus gives the key point of faith to us through their faith. Now, let us go further.

Faith of Martha

Martha was very familiar with the works and miracles of Jesus. He did many miraculous things with great power, and so she had witnessed the evidence through which she could trust in Him as the Son of God. Since such a precious man was coming to her house, she had to prepare many things and so she was naturally busy.

If I describe Martha in a contemporary manner, she does not belong to the group of believers with weak faith. She has trustworthy evidence in herself since she has met the living God, and speaks in an unknown tongue. She admits that Jesus is the Son of God to whom all power is given in heaven and on earth, and so she follows Him. She believes that she will go to the kingdom of heaven if she believes in Him earnestly, and all of her troubles will disappear if she prays to Him. She wishes to please Jesus further. Therefore, she keeps the Lord's Day holy, serves table, sings praises, fasts, and gives her tithe. She leads a busy Christian life in doing all these things.

We accept those who have such faith as Martha as perfect believers. Pastors speak well of them and other people commend them highly, and endeavor to produce as many Marthas as possible in the church. However, such faith as Martha has is not complete from Jesus' point of view. Her faith needs to grow in a totally new direction. Why and how?

📂 The Limit of Martha's Faith

When we work hard for the church with the faith of Martha, our mind will be full with the thinking below:

"I'm doing something my Lord wants and applauds. I'm doing something very difficult while others do not even try!"

This shows that our deeds are stored in our heart as self-righteousness. And such self-righteousness functions as the basis of judging others. That is, we will judge others who are not as diligent as we are, and pressurize them by saying, "You ought to do as I do." Even though we may not actually verbalize this, it is inevitable for us to judge others in our heart in this way.

Martha served Jesus by preparing something for Him, whilst her sister Mary did not. Martha's deeds worked as self-righteousness and it automatically made her accuse her sister in front of the Lord, saying, "Lord, Mary is not working as much as I am. Please tell her to help me" (Luk 10:40).

If I change what Martha said into a prayer to the Lord, it will be like this:

"Lord, I serve table, give alms, and give donations on every Sunday. I do all of these things for You. Am I not the man who truly loves You? You said in James, 'Even so faith, if it hath not works, is dead, being alone.' Please tell those men who do nothing but fool around to work hard!" We judge others and accuse them like this. This is the nature of the faith of Martha, which provokes judgment of others automatically.

Think about her current location in this scene. Maybe she was in the kitchen whilst Jesus and Mary were sitting in the living room. She is separated from Him even though she was with Him in the house. Ironically enough, her zeal to serve Jesus caused her to be away from Him. If she works for Jesus under these circumstances, i.e., being separated from Him, she will have to accuse others based on the works she did. She cannot avoid it.

Likewise, if we do something being separated from Him, we will have to judge others based on our deeds. Martha's faith is, therefore, not complete and should grow to become one with Jesus.

📂 Troubled About Many Things

Jesus responded to Martha's complaint saying, "Martha, Martha, thou art careful and troubled about many things; but one thing is needful."

She was very busy in doing many works in order to receive Him, and she naturally felt anxiety and concern when things did not go as well as she expected. She cannot but act in that way because of the nature of her faith.

Our faith is like Martha's. To be blessed and to go to heaven, we must work hard in the church, help the poor, fasting, participate in missionary works, and give collection. These show the features of the lifestyle of believers under the law. We have to keep all the commandments of the Lord. Read James.

> For he that said, Do not commit adultery, said also, Do not kill. Now if thou commit no adultery, yet if thou kill, thou art become a transgressor of the law. [James 2:11]

Because He who said, "Do not commit adultery," said also "Do not kill," we must not commit adultery *and* must not kill. Further, since He who said, "Do not commit adultery," said also "Join the activities in the church and pray," we must do them too. We are very busy doing all these things. We are sometimes troubled about the things we have not yet finished, apologizing to Him. This exactly matches what Martha does. The Lord gives a prescription to these believes.

One Thing Is Needful

He says, "One thing is needful." He advises us to do one thing instead of being distracted with much serving — what will that be? As we can guess from Mary, it is to "hear the word" from the living Jesus. We will enter the kingdom of God not by doing a lot of things but by hearing the word of Jesus.

However, this is not a matter of choice. In other words, we cannot choose either to do many works like Martha or hear the word like Mary. Not everyone can hear the word like Mary does. Only he who has ears to hear can hear. If not, he cannot help behaving as Martha did.

Mary could hear because she had ears to hear. Jesus stood up for her. It means from the viewpoint of Jesus that he who has ears to hear is much more blessed.

Martha and Mary indicate the steps of faith. We will be able to have the faith of Mary when the faith of Martha is finished within us. While having the faith of Martha, we do not even know whether there is a faith of Mary ahead. At that stage, we all think the faith of Martha is 'the real thing.' However, we will realize through Jesus that there exists faith at Mary's level, and then we will pray for it. Martha and Mary represent the stages of faith, that is, the 'law' and then 'grace.'

Faith of Mary

What is Jesus to you? What will you ask of Him if He comes into your house? Will you ask for the kingdom of heaven after death, healings, fortune, peace in this world, or even the glory of the world? Then, you have to work hard like Martha to please Him.

However, if you realize that Jesus is the one who heals your soul and gives you spiritual re-birth with a new life, you will only hear Him like Mary. During the course of the faith of Mary, you will be healed by Jesus on the cross and your sin will be forgiven forever. This way, Jesus has come to save you.

Depending on what you want from Jesus, your behavior will differ in front of Him, either Martha or Mary's.

At the end of your 'faith of Martha' stage, your 'old man' will be desolate and collapsing and only then, can we hear the word of Jesus. You will start to have the faith of Mary at this point. Through hearing the word of Jesus, you will be entering the kingdom at the end of the day.

▷ Well Done. I Feel Bored Now!

Once a believer at the stage of Martha's faith, hears about Mary's faith and understands it, he will pay less attention to serving in the church kitchen, because he was also quietly thinking that serving is hard work. He comes to think that hearing the word of Jesus appears to be more sophisticated than dishwashing! People who are under the law will act like this when they first start to really understand the gospel.

To tell the truth, Mary will serve in the kitchen more diligently than most others because she knows that Jesus is her life. Accordingly, her works in the church such as ministering, helping with collection, and helping the poor will be true and sincere since she is doing them with the living Jesus in mind. She does not judge others based on what she does, because she does it naturally and unconditionally and therefore requires no compensation.

Martha also hears the word of God, but she hears it as a commandment, "Work hard and do various things to go to heaven." So she does. On the contrary, Mary hears the word of God and her soul is being healed by that word.

Martha is a person who works in the kitchen even while she is hearing the word, but Mary is a person who hears the word even while she works in the kitchen. Therefore, the difference between them is not caused by their deeds, but by who she is. Martha is *me* under the law, and Mary is *me* under grace. In *my* faith development, Martha comes first, then Mary.

Martha, Mary, and Lazarus

Martha, Mary, and Lazarus were a brother and two sisters living in Bethany. Consider the following passage from John:

> [1] Then Jesus six days before the passover came to Bethany, where Lazarus was, which had been dead, whom he raised from the dead. [2] There they made him a supper; and Martha served: but Lazarus was one of them that sat at the table with him. [3] Then took Mary a pound of ointment of spikenard, very costly, and anointed the feet of Jesus, and wiped his feet with her hair: and the house was filled with the odour of the ointment. [John 12:1-3]

As we have seen through verses from Luke 10:38-42, Martha was very busy with things she must do for Jesus. Mary was hearing the word of Jesus.

Here in another scene in John, Martha was again the one who was serving. Mary broke the alabaster box of very precious ointment of spikenard and poured it on Him. This act signifies that her old self is being destroyed on the cross, as a result of hearing the word of the living Jesus. So Mary was hearing the word here as she was also in Luke. Lazarus rose again from the dead through Jesus.

Once again these three characters indicate the respective stages for growing in faith. Martha's stage shows the time when we believe in Him under the law. Mary's stage represents when we meet the real Jesus and follow Him, forsaking all. Lazarus' stage represents when we are born again in the stage of Mary. Simply speaking, in faith we will be Martha-Mary-Lazarus progressively.

I have already explained Martha and Mary, so now I will describe to you some characteristics of Lazarus.

Consider John.

The Hidden Manna 161

⁹ Much people of the Jews therefore knew that he was there: and they came not for Jesus' sake only, but that they might see Lazarus also, whom he had raised from the dead. ¹⁰ But the chief priests consulted that they might put Lazarus also to death; ¹¹ Because that by reason of him many of the Jews went away, and believed on Jesus. [John 12:9-11]

Although Lazarus had been dead for four days, Jesus brought him back to life. Lazarus has some distinguishing features that are different from Martha and Mary.

First he died, but was raised from the dead by Jesus (Jhn 11:44). Lazarus symbolizes a man who was dead in trespasses and sins but receives a new life by the word of Jesus. He is the example of the born again. According to the steps of growing in faith, those who are in the Martha stage or Mary stage have not yet been born again from the dead. They will be born again when they have reached the Lazarus stage.

Second, many Jews believed in Jesus as a result of Lazarus' resurrection. (Jhn 12:11). Those who are born again can really preach Jesus because they were once dead and were raised again. By their presence alone, the power and life of Jesus is revealed. They will naturally preach Jesus to others.

Third, Lazarus is the only man out of the three (Jhn 11:2). In the spiritual context, we are brides of Jesus. We are women. Martha is the symbol of believers who have not yet received the word of God, Mary is the symbol of believers who become pregnant by hearing the word of God. When Mary has given birth to a child, the child is a man who is Jesus, Lazarus himself in this case.

In this way, a woman (Martha - Mary) is born again to be a man (Lazarus). Woman refers to a believer who is not yet born again, and man refers to a believer who is born again. The man now has the word of God and so he can sow seed (that's why he is a man), that is, preach the true gospel.

Furthermore, the man can conduct spiritual warfare and fight against evil spirits.

Epilogue

I want each of you to check where you are in the faith development process and hope for the next stage, and then God will lead you to increase your faith to that stage. Amen.

Faith Without Works Is Dead

[James 2:14-26]

¹⁴ What doth it profit, my brethren, though a man say he hath faith, and have not works? can faith save him? ¹⁵ If a brother or sister be naked, and destitute of daily food, ¹⁶ And one of you say unto them, Depart in peace, be ye warmed and filled; notwithstanding ye give them not those things which are needful to the body; what doth it profit? ¹⁷ Even so faith, if it hath not works, is dead, being alone. ¹⁸ Yea, a man may say, Thou hast faith, and I have works: shew me thy faith without thy works, and I will shew thee my faith by my works. ¹⁹ Thou believest that there is one God; thou doest well: the devils also believe, and tremble. ²⁰ But wilt thou know, O vain man, that faith without works is dead? ²¹ Was not Abraham our father justified by works, when he had offered Isaac his son upon the altar? ²² Seest thou how faith wrought with his works, and by works was faith made perfect? ²³ And the scripture was fulfilled which saith, Abraham believed God, and it was imputed unto him for righteousness: and he was called the Friend of God. ²⁴ Ye see then how that by works a man is justified, and not by faith only. ²⁵ Likewise also was not Rahab the harlot justified by works, when she had received the messengers, and had sent them out another way? ²⁶ For as the body without the spirit is dead, so faith without works is dead also.

"Therefore we conclude that a man is justified by faith without the deeds of the law" (Rom 3:28).

We all know that we are justified by faith, not by works. However, here in James, the writer emphasizes the necessity of works for salvation. He says explicitly that faith without works (deeds, *ergon* in Greek) is dead, and such faith cannot save man. We are confused whether we are justified by faith or by works. It is well known that Martin Luther also said that the book of James was an epistle of straw due to this seeming contradiction. Of course, there is no contradiction in the Scripture, but our eyes reading the Scripture can deceive us.

We are justified (saved) by faith, not by works. Basically, James does not say that we are saved by the works of the law. This is obvious if we read James 2:10: "For whosoever shall keep the whole law, and yet offend in one point, he is guilty of all." By this verse, James also says that we cannot be saved by the works of the law. In fact, James and Paul speak in the same way. How is this?

Faith and Works Are One

James says, "Faith without works is dead."

First, 'faith' is the life of Jesus, which comes to us who have the sinful life, through the life begetting process. In this process, we are to meet Jesus and follow Him to the cross to destroy our 'old man.' And when this is done, Jesus will be resurrected in us as Christ, and at this moment, we will have the life of Jesus, a new life. This is how we are justified and saved by faith.

Please keep this definition of faith in mind. It is the initiative of the life of Jesus, as grace, to give us His life. It is not through our believing initiative, i.e., legalistic efforts.

The 'works' refers to our actual obedience to the initiative of the living Jesus, the life.

Faith and works are one, and they cannot be separated. If we have sound faith, we will do sound works. If we have dead faith, our works will be 'dead.' Nobody stops going to heaven knowing that he is going to heaven, and nobody goes to hell knowing that he is going to hell.

Think about the Pharisees, the holders of dead faith, who sent Jesus to the cross. Jesus spoke about them as follows in Luke:

Then said Jesus, Father, forgive them; for they know not

what they do. And they parted his raiment, and cast lots. [Luke 23:34]

They had legalistic faith, so they did dead works unwittingly. If they had known, they would not have done so.

Likewise, so far we have known faith as our believing efforts, which is not from true faith. Consequently, we have been doing dead works unwittingly.

Faith and works are one. In this respect, the term 'faith without works' is a paradox, if we read faith here as the true faith of Jesus. It is 'dead faith,' which produces 'without works.' Needless to say, '(dead) faith without works' cannot save us.

Consider the simple illustration below.

(a) faith = works = justification
(b) (dead) faith = (dead) works (=deeds of the law) = non-justification

Paul says we are justified by faith (a), without the 'deeds of the law (b). James also says in line with Paul that 'faith without works,' which is the 'deeds of the law' (b) above, cannot justify us. Do not be confused by the terms 'faith' and 'works,' but you should be wise to know what they truly mean in context.

Let us read James together with this basic understanding.

Faith Without Works

[James 2:14] ¹⁴ What doth it profit, my brethren, though a man say he hath faith, and have not works? can faith save him?

What is the 'faith without works,' which cannot save us? When you read this word, you think that God through James urges you to do works, so you try to do works. What works are you going to do? You have done enough works so far. Under this situation, whatever you do you are not doing works.

Works come from faith. Dead faith produces dead works. So if you are not doing works, you first check whether your faith is sound. Surely, it is dead, that is why you are without works.

To be justified, we should follow the real Jesus to the cross. As long as we are doing so, our every step is the work of faith, and after all, we will be justified by such works. If we digress from this process of faith, that is, do not follow through to the cross, all our works will be in vain. In this case, the works we do have nothing to do with justification. The works we do will not be counted as works. This is the 'faith without works' that James speaks of.

We all think that we have faith, as we attend church and read the Bible and try to love neighbors, hoping for a new life. However, the faith we know is not that which is testified to by the Scripture. As mentioned above, faith is to follow Jesus to the cross to destroy our old man, and to have Jesus resurrected in us. If we have an incorrect concept of this faith, automatically the works we perform will be dead works. Can this faith save us? Definitely, not!

Depart in Peace, Be Warmed and Filled

> [James 2:15-17] [15] If a brother or sister be naked, and destitute of daily food, [16] And one of you say unto them, Depart in peace, be ye warmed and filled; notwithstanding ye give them not those things which are needful to the body; what doth it profit? [17] Even so faith, if it hath not works, is dead, being alone.

When you read this message, you may think you are not one of them who do good works only by mouth, because you practice doing good things like donation, sharing and stretching out a helping hand to the needy in Jesus' name. So you are sure that you are someone who has works and faith together, and think that these verses should be heard by the lip-service believers out there.

Actually, however, it is you who is helping the needy only with mouth. You do so, not because you want to do so, but because you do not understand what the Scripture refers to as faith and works. If you are in the process of true faith, you should already have known the meanings of 'giving clothes to the naked,' 'giving daily food' and 'giving them peace.' The meanings of these works are spiritual, not of the flesh. Read the following passages.

> For as many of you as have been baptized into Christ have put on Christ [Galatians 3:27]

> I counsel thee to buy of me gold tried in the fire, that thou mayest be rich; and white raiment, that thou mayest be clothed, and that the shame of thy nakedness do not appear; and anoint thine eyes with eyesalve, that thou mayest see. [Revelations 3:18]

Jesus gave clothes of righteousness for the naked (sinners). We have to do these works after laying down our 'old man' on the cross first.

Also Jesus gave daily food for the poor. Consider John.

> [56] He that eateth my flesh, and drinketh my blood, dwelleth in me, and I in him. [57] As the living Father hath sent me, and I live by the Father: so he that eateth me, even he shall live by me. [58] This is that bread which came down from heaven: not as your fathers did eat manna, and are dead: he that eateth of this bread shall live for ever. [John 6:56-58]

His flesh means the Word, and when we eat the Word, we can have eternal life. And this food, we should be able to give to our neighbors, when the Word is written on our hearts, after going through our cross.

Also Jesus gave us peace.

> Peace I leave with you, my peace I give unto you: not as the world giveth, give I unto you. Let not your heart be troubled, neither let it be afraid. [John 14:27]

The peace that Jesus refers to is not the peace that we generally know, but the peace between the sinful man and God, which is only possible by His crucifixion and resurrection in us. We, as believers, should be able to give this peace to others.

So you may be doing the works of good according to moral codes, but you are not doing the works spiritually. Of course, you may also say that you are giving spiritual clothes, food and peace as written in the Scripture, but in reality, you do not know what they are all about. So you cannot help them spiritually. James is enlightening this darkness within you. This is the case that "faith, if it hath not works, is dead, being alone," that is, the legalistic faith.

Devils Also Believe

> [James 2:18-20] [18] Yea, a man may say, Thou hast faith, and I have works: shew me thy faith without thy works, and I will shew thee my faith by my works. [19] Thou believest that there is one God; thou doest well: the devils also believe, and tremble. [20] But wilt thou know, O vain man, that faith without works is dead?

Faith is inside our beings and is unseen. Works are the fruit of faith, which are seen. The one who has dead faith cannot show sound works, but only dead works.

For example, the Pharisees, who do not want to know what sound faith is, have dead faith of their own. Under the circumstances, whatever they do, it has to be dead works. So they can never show their faith. Jesus rebukes such scribes and Pharisees as follows in Matthew.

> Woe unto you, scribes and Pharisees, hypocrites! for ye make clean the outside of the cup and of the platter, but within they are full of extortion and excess. [Matthew 23:25]

The Pharisees, after reading the Scripture, were only concerned with the works they do (make clean the outside). Figuratively speaking, they put grapes on thistles, and say, "Look, I have fruit." This is their faith and works, which are surely dead. They are hypocrites, the holders of legalistic faith.

They believe in God superficially, but in reality, they cannot do any works of God. That is, their faith exists in their thinking and talking, and they produce no works. This is the faith of demons (*daimonion* in Greek). A demon is a being that is considered to have a spirit only without a body. So is the faith of the Pharisees.

You can understand 'faith without works' as one term, and it is another expression of legalistic faith.

Justification Of Abraham

> [James 2:21-24] [21] Was not Abraham our father justified by works, when he had offered Isaac his son upon the altar? [22] Seest thou how faith wrought with his works, and by works was faith made perfect? [23] And the scripture was fulfilled which saith, Abraham believed God, and it was imputed unto him for righteousness: and he was called the Friend of God. [24] Ye see then how that by works a man is justified, and not by faith only.

Abraham is the prototype of man who has sound faith. He offered Isaac his son upon the altar and became a man justified by faith. We easily think of this as a historical event and praise him for his faith to offer his beloved son whom he begot at the age of one hundred. If we construe this event as such, surely Abraham is the elder of faith. So then, what is that to *me*? *I* am not Abraham.

Many believers try to have the faith of Abraham by doing works that imitate his. So they are offering everything that they have, be it mental or physical, to God.

However, we cannot have the faith of Abraham in this way. This is apparent if we think about ourselves who spent several decades trying, and do not yet have such faith. We are misguided. In order to possess the faith of Abraham, we also should offer Isaac upon the altar as he did.

Then, who is the Isaac whom we should offer to God and how? Isaac is the figure of Jesus, and we should offer Jesus to the altar according to faith. So we should meet and follow Him and during this process, our 'old man,' the body of sin, will be crucified. When this is completed, we are justified.

Read Romans.

> [6] Knowing this, that our old man is crucified with him, that the body of sin might be destroyed, that henceforth we should not serve sin. [7] For he that is dead is freed from sin. [Romans 6:6-7]

In this way, we offer Isaac (Jesus) upon the altar like Abraham, and so we will have the same faith as Abraham. James refers to Abraham as being justified by works. The works refer to the offering of Isaac on the altar.

Here, we should know that faith requires works in two stages, first, to offer Isaac on the altar for the justification and salvation of ourselves, and second, to love our neighbors as ourselves (to save others as Jesus did). And this is what Jesus says in Matthew.

> [37] Jesus said unto him, Thou shalt love the Lord thy God with all thy heart, and with all thy soul, and with all thy mind. [38] This is the first and great commandment. [39] And the second is like unto it, Thou shalt love thy neighbour as thyself. [40] On these two commandments hang all the law and the prophets. [Matthew 22:37-40]

Above verses 37 through 38 speak of offering Isaac, the beloved son of each one of us and at the same time our old man, on the altar for justification. This is explained by the cases of Abraham and Rahab in this passage.

And verse 39 speaks of the *agape* love we get from God after offering our Isaac on the cross. This is explained under the heading of "Depart in Peace, Be Warmed and Filled."

As Jesus says "And the second is like unto it," the first and the second are connected as one. That is, when we receive *agape* love through the cross, with that love we can love our neighbors.

As Abraham offered Isaac, it was said that he believed God, and so he became righteous, and was called the friend of God. We also should be so by offering Isaac.

Faith of Rahab

> [James 2:25-26] ²⁵ Likewise also was not Rahab the harlot justified by works, when she had received the messengers, and had sent them out another way? ²⁶ For as the body without the spirit is dead, so faith without works is dead also.

Rahab was justified by works. This is not to mean that Rahab was justified by one single deed. She was justified by following the process of faith to the cross.

This is signified as follows:

Rahab received the messengers of Joshua. The spiritual meaning of this is that Rahab met Jesus (the messengers of Joshua), which is the first coming of Jesus to her.

She had sent them out another way, to let them live at the risk of her life. This means spiritually that she followed Jesus to destroy her 'old man' on the cross in spite of her life ('old man') in peril in order to allow the new life to grow in her. This is her offering of Isaac upon the altar.

Then, Joshua came into Jericho where she was, and she was received by him (Jos 6:17). This means spiritually that she received Jesus in her as Christ (the Holy Spirit), which is the second coming of Jesus, and thus was justified.

Rahab was doing works according to faith, so the works saved her.

"For as the body without the spirit is dead, so faith without works is dead also" (Jam 2:26). Only works by faith can save us. 'Works by dead faith' or 'faith without works' are dead, they cannot save us.

Epilogue

James speaks of works, which should be in accord with faith. He wishes to reveal that we, the believers, are doing works not according to faith, but according to our own man-made moral codes.

So from the standpoint of the truth, we are doing no works. Such faith or works will not justify and save us. The faith without works, that is, legalistic faith, exists only in our imagination like demons. And it is dead.

Therefore, this is what James says in this passage:

"Follow the living Jesus to the cross, and this is works of faith that you should do. When you complete this, you will be justified, and you will do works of faith thereafter forever."

The Unjust Steward

[Luke 16:1-9]

¹ And he said also unto his disciples, There was a certain rich man, which had a steward; and the same was accused unto him that he had wasted his goods. ² And he called him, and said unto him, How is it that I hear this of thee? give an account of thy stewardship; for thou mayest be no longer steward. ³ Then the steward said within himself, What shall I do? for my lord taketh away from me the stewardship: I cannot dig; to beg I am ashamed. ⁴ I am resolved what to do, that, when I am put out of the stewardship, they may receive me into their houses. ⁵ So he called every one of his lord's debtors unto him, and said unto the first, How much owest thou unto my lord? ⁶ And he said, An hundred measures of oil. And he said unto him, Take thy bill, and sit down quickly, and write fifty. ⁷ Then said he to another, And how much owest thou? And he said, An hundred measures of wheat. And he said unto him, Take thy bill, and write fourscore. ⁸ And the lord commended the unjust steward, because he had done wisely: for the children of this world are in their generation wiser than the children of light. ⁹ And I say unto you, Make to yourselves friends of the mammon of unrighteousness; that, when ye fail, they may receive you into everlasting habitations.

We all know this story, but its true meaning has been hidden, so we raise questions about it over and over again. Our questions are—the lord commended the steward who privately reduced the debts without permission, and Jesus commended him saying, "Make to yourselves friends of the mammon of unrighteousness."

Then, do we have to act like the unjust steward? Or, what is the mammon of unrighteousness of which we should make to ourselves friends?

Above all, this parable is not meant to portray such worldly things as "one should not waste his master's goods" or "one should help debtors," *et cetera*. This is a revelation of the unseen spiritual world.

Through the word of God, God wants to communicate with our hearts, and to make our hearts His. So it is not His intention for us to keep his Word simply as a set of commandments. For instance, "Love your neighbor as yourself" is not a commandment for us to keep, but it is the expression of the heart of God, that is, "I will make you a person who can love your neighbor." This is what the gospel is seeking to communicate.

If we construe this word as a commandment, we will try to love our neighbor in vain, being separated from God. However, if we understand the word as gospel, then we will always keep an eye on God in our heart and follow Him to become such a person. The difference between these two understandings is life and death.

It is the tendency of the sinner to receive the word of God as a set of commandments that he then tries to keep and live up to. Superficially, it looks like nothing is wrong. However, no matter how many commandments he keeps, he still is a sinner. Keeping the commandments can never change him from being a sinner. Not even a little bit.

The parable of the unjust steward uncovers such truth for us. The word of God is meant to heal the soul of the unjust steward, but he does not want this healing. So he converts it in him as a commandment to keep, and he thinks that he has kept the word of God. He believes in God in his own way. He represents the Pharisees of Jesus' time, including all believers today.

Now, I will explain in detail.

Give an Account of Thy Stewardship

> [Luke 16:1-2] ¹ And he said also unto his disciples, There was a certain rich man, which had a steward; and the same was

accused unto him that he had wasted his goods. ² And he called him, and said unto him, How is it that I hear this of thee? give an account of thy stewardship; for thou mayest be no longer steward.

In the parable, a rich man has hired a steward and entrusted him with his goods. He hears that the steward has wasted his goods, and called him and told him to give an account of his stewardship for he may no longer be his steward. Accordingly, the steward devises a counter plan thinking to himself, "I cannot dig; to beg I am ashamed."

🗁 Who is the Steward?

Here, the rich man symbolizes God who is the richest one ruling over life and death, good and evil and the whole of creation.

The steward (*oikonomos* in Greek) is the man who works under Him, and he represents the bishops, priests, pastors or preachers doing God's work. However, we, the believers, are also stewards of God. This is because we will naturally preach the word of God that we learned at church to neighbors. So all of us are His stewards.

The steward is supposed to give out the word of God, spiritual food, to believers. Read Luke 12.

> And the Lord said, Who then is that faithful and wise steward, whom his lord shall make ruler over his household, to give them their portion of meat in due season? [Luke 12:42]

The Apostles Paul and Peter called themselves stewards. Read the following passages.

> ¹ Let a man so account of us, as of the ministers of Christ, and stewards of the mysteries of God. ² Moreover it is required in stewards, that a man be found faithful. [1 Corinthians 4:1-2]

> As every man hath received the gift, even so minister the same one to another, as good stewards of the manifold grace

of God. [1 Peter 4:10]

However, not all stewards are the same. Some are 'faithful and wise,' 'good,' or the 'stewards of the mysteries of God' as mentioned in the above passages. However, many are 'unjust' as shown in this parable (Luke 16). Then, who is the good steward, and who is the unjust? In short, the good steward is the one who is under grace and the unjust steward is the one who is under the law.

Consider the verses from 2 Corinthians.

> [6] Who also hath made us able ministers of the new testament; not of the letter, but of the spirit: for the letter killeth, but the spirit giveth life. [7] But if the ministration of death, written and engraven in stones, was glorious, so that the children of Israel could not stedfastly behold the face of Moses for the glory of his countenance; which glory was to be done away: [8] How shall not the ministration of the spirit be rather glorious? [2 Corinthians 3:6-8]

Paul speaks of two types of stewards. One is a steward of the Old Testament; of the letter of the law, which kills. He has the ministry of death. The other is a steward of the New Testament; of the spirit, which gives life. He has the ministry of the spirit. He is described as the good steward in Scripture.

The unjust steward in the parable, apparently has preached the word of God, as best he understood it, saying things such as "Do not judge," "Love one another," "Do not steal," "Do not commit adultery," and "Confess the Lord Jesus," *et cetera.*

However, the lord was not happy with what he saw as a waste of his goods, and told him to give an account of his stewardship. In what way had the steward wasted the lord's goods in carrying out his role?

In What Way Had the Steward Wasted His Lord's Goods?

The behavior of the unjust steward represents people who are under the law. He has to preach what he is under, the law in this case. And he is supposed to have wasted his lord's goods. How is that?

The word of God is the expression of the heart of God, which is the 'spirit.' But we, the believers under the law, simply understand it as a set of commandments and act to keep them. In this case, even while following God's commandments on our own initiative, we will be separated from God in our hearts. Knowing that God's wish is to be one with us in our hearts, if we act like this when hearing the word of God, we are misguided.

Nevertheless, if we choose to construe the word as the law, it is okay. In this case, however, we have to keep it strictly. By nature, the law requires outright obedience without exception. For instance, "Love you neighbor as yourself," as the law, mandates us to do this.

However, we simply cannot love others 'as ourselves.' If we fail to love our neighbor right now, we have transgressed and so we have to repent to God for forgiveness every single moment. This way, we will accumulate sin and will eventually realize that we are sinners.

Consider Romans below:

Moreover the law entered, that the offence might abound. But where sin abounded, grace did much more abound: [Romans 5:20]

As above, God gave us the law so that the offence may abound in sinners. If offence abounds, the sinner will truly repent. Then he will seek the mercy of God, and will receive mercy.

So taking all this together, the law is not meant for us to keep, but to reveal to us eventually that we are sinners who cannot live up to the law. As a result, we seek God's mercy for salvation. This is the ministration of the law (2Co 3:6).

However, we digress. We misunderstand that the law is given to us to keep to make ourselves clean. With this underlying thinking, we try to consider the law. So when we hear "Love your neighbor as yourself," not knowing that we cannot keep this commandment, we modify it to the level that we can accommodate. That is, "You shall 'try to' love your neighbor as yourself" or "You will be sanctified to love your neighbor gradually throughout your life," or "You are saved by faith, and loving your neighbor is related to the rewards in heaven," *et cetera*.

As mentioned, the law is meant to incur our debt (transgressions) to God. If we loosen the requirements of the law to a lower level, then we are wasting the Lord's goods. For instance, if a police officer catches a driver violating a traffic law, the officer should issue a fine of say, $104 for that violation. If for any reason he issues a discounted fine of say, $50, he is wasting the money of his lord, the government.

We who are represented by the unjust steward in the parable waste the goods of the Lord in this manner. This nature of the sinner is revealed repeatedly in the parable when the unjust steward says, "I cannot dig; to beg I am ashamed," and when he is reducing the debts of his master's debtors. Of course, he does not know what he is doing, as we do not know what we are doing in our efforts to follow Jesus.

📂 Give an Account of Your Stewardship

"Give an account of your stewardship!" It must have been like a thunderbolt from a clear sky to him. He had worked for his lord with zeal, but the lord wishes to dismiss him from his stewardship job. The lord may have misunderstood him, and he thinks this cannot be true. However, it happened anyway. He has no other option but to accept it.

This is when the unjust steward heard and understood for the first time the true meaning of the word of God. At the time, he was shocked; as he was hearing a completely new interpretation of the Bible. For instance, so far he understood "You shall not eat the flesh of swine" as "You shall not eat pork," but now he gets to know that it means, "You shall not receive the teachings of people under the law."

In this case, quite naturally, the steward cannot carry on with his existing stewardship, because he realizes that his current understanding is incorrect. So he ceases his existing works, and seeks to do new works according to his new understanding of the gospel, receiving it as yet another commandment. However, his old works are works and his new works are works also. No difference. No works will bring him under the grace of God. In this way, he stays under the law even though he has, for the first time, realized the true meaning of the gospel.

Anyway, this is the situation when the steward hears from the lord to give an account of what he is doing. Of course, the lord (God) does not tell him to cease the existing works. But, he himself thinks that God told him so, because he did it in obedience to the word of God. Jesus depicts this situation as follows: "Give an account of thy stewardship." What a stunning statement that only Jesus can make!

I Cannot Dig; to Beg I Am Ashamed

> [Luke 16:3] Then the steward said within himself, What shall I do? for my lord taketh away from me the stewardship: I cannot dig; to beg I am ashamed.

The steward deprived of his position had to consider his future. He thought he was not strong enough to do physical labor such as digging and he was ashamed to beg for his bread.

The steward neither wants to keep the law strictly, nor surrender to God and beg His mercy. He is neither under the law, nor under grace. In this seemingly contradictory situation, the man is in fact under the law. The law forces him to act. So if he believes under the law, he has to labor and is therefore heavy laden. It is very difficult to lead such a life. He wishes to get away from it. He therefore modifies the law to a level that he can somehow comply with. This is explained in one of the sub sections above "In what way had the steward wasted his lord's goods?"

This way he labors or 'digs' under a modified or less onerous law. Of course, this 'digging' effort has nothing to do with God, but is simply his own self-righteousness. If he keeps such a 'loosened' law, it already proves that he is saying, "I cannot dig."

This is the hidden meaning of the word of the steward, "I cannot dig."

If he really wants to get out from under the law, he should truly repent and beg God for mercy. He can truly repent only when he has reached the nadir of his life under the law, like the prodigal son in Luke, who begged his father and God to help him when he had almost perished. In this situation only, can he shed all his pride before God and wait for His mercy to create him as a new person who loves his neighbor, does not eat the flesh of swine, and so forth. At this moment, he is ready to receive the gospel as gospel, not as the law.

If he feels ashamed to beg God for mercy, he has no experience of having reached the nadir of life as in the case of the prodigal son. So he still has pride before God and so tries to keep the gospel as a set of commandments, whereas the gospel is actually an expression of his mercy.

This is the hidden meaning of what the unjust steward said to himself, "To beg I am ashamed."

🗁 Unjust Stewards of Today

Let us look at ourselves, who are in reality under the law. If I tell you to keep the law strictly, you will step back and say, "No. Sorry! I'm saved by faith. I am not under the law anymore." We do not wish to keep the law strictly, as it is difficult to do this. We are saying, "I cannot dig" as the unjust steward in this parable says. Yet, we do not have the experience of the prodigal son. So we are really saying, "To beg I am ashamed."

In this situation, we as believers, are saying, "We are saved, so now let's do good deeds." This is a weird mixture of grace and law, light and darkness. Currently, we belong to neither the law nor grace. We are neither cold nor hot (Rev 3:16).

And consider Matthew:

> [16] But whereunto shall I liken this generation? It is like unto children sitting in the markets, and calling unto their fellows, [17] And saying, We have piped unto you, and ye have not danced; we have mourned unto you, and ye have not lamented. [Matthew 11:16-17]

Jesus is saying to this generation, "If we pipe unto you, you are to dance. But you do not." It means, if He gives the law to you, you are to keep it, but you do not, saying you are saved by faith. This is what the unjust steward says, "I cannot dig."

"If we mourn unto you, you are to lament. But you do not." This means that if He tells you to beg God for mercy, you are to beat your chest and plead with God. But you do not, because you are still arrogant in front of God thinking you can do something good by yourself. This is what the unjust steward says, "To beg I am ashamed."

God wants believers to have 'grace,' 'light,' and 'love,' not a mixture of 'grace and law,' 'light and darkness,' and 'love and trying to love.' In essence, all this confusion arises from our spiritual blindness; which in turn is derived from our law based 'faith.'

Friends the Steward Made

The unjust steward called every one of his lord's debtors and asked how much they owed his lord. It is interesting that he only called his lord's debtors and tried to befriend them.

What does this mean? If someone shows interest in the gospel that we preach, he must be indebted to God, that is, a sinner. This is because he who thinks that he is not a sinner will not respond to the gospel to achieve his salvation. Therefore, the steward necessarily calls those who are the lord's debtors only.

The unjust steward tries to make friends with his lord's debtors. This symbolizes that the unjust stewards of today's churches try to make friends, promising forgiveness of sin and the kingdom of heaven to people. However, the friends that they make are friends of the world, not friends of the kingdom of heaven.

This is because they do not have the true gospel that will enable them to develop friends of the kingdom of heaven. Jesus wishes to reveal to us that we need to be healed first to have friends of the kingdom and then we will be able to make others to be friends of the kingdom.

We will now see how the unjust steward makes friends, and also that he does this in accordance with the law and not through the gospel.

Reduction of Debts by the Steward

> [Luke 16:4-7] [4] I am resolved what to do, that, when I am put out of the stewardship, they may receive me into their houses. [5] So he called every one of his lord's debtors unto him, and said unto the first, How much owest thou unto my lord? [6] And he said, An hundred measures of oil. And he said unto him, Take thy bill, and sit down quickly, and write fifty. [7] Then said he to another, And how much owest thou? And he said, An hundred measures of wheat. And he said unto him, Take thy bill, and write fourscore.

Now, upon receiving notice from the lord, the steward calls the debtors and reduces some of their debts. He stops what he has been doing and begins doing new things. By doing this, he reveals that the lord had been fair in his accusation that the steward had wasted his goods.

Probably, he newly understood the gospel that says, "Forgive your neighbors!" and he agrees with that. So he acts according to the new law, thinking he is doing so according to the gospel. And he can only implement what he understands the gospel to be teaching him regarding forgiveness. Even if he changes his deed, it does not mean that he himself has been changed. So basically he has to do the same thing in essence, which is to waste his lord's goods.

Who are the Lord's debtors? We have received many commandments from the Lord. Nevertheless, against these commandments, we hate our brothers and sisters, judge them, and slander them day and night; above all, we cannot love our neighbors as ourselves. We are the Lord's debtors because we do not carry out His commandments. Disobedience and sin constitute our debt to God.

So, in this parable, the lord's debtors represent us who have sinned against the Lord.

📁 Features of Debts Reduced by the Steward

The steward calls the lord's debtors and reduces their debts. In this instance, his reduction of debts symbolizes forgiveness of sins. The gospel tells us that forgiveness of sin comes through Jesus. When the unjust steward hears of this forgiveness, he tries to apply the same principle and grants forgiveness of debt. However, his actions are no more than a poor imitation. This is symbolized by the debt reduction offered by the unjust steward. However, such forgiveness cannot be equated to the forgiveness spoken of in the gospel.

There are two main reasons for this:

First, such forgiveness demands compensation, and this give-and-take trading paradigm belongs to the world. The true gospel demands no compensation for giving forgiveness. Life has no concept of recompense. Everything is given free. Parents give birth to kids and raise them. They do it unconditionally; just out of love.

However, the unjust steward reduced the debts hoping for a benefit in return. This clearly shows that what he did was not based on the principle of life, that is, the gospel. This is the limitation of those who are living under the law.

We, the believers, consider the forgiveness of sin to be conditional or a give-and-take transaction. For example, we think this way; "Because we are forgiven we should work hard for the Lord, should behave, and in return we should love our neighbor." This kind of sin-forgiveness, salvation and love for our neighbor are all legalistic transactions.

Secondly, such forgiveness cannot be equated to the forgiveness spoken of in the gospel since it is not perfect forgiveness. The unjust steward reduced a hundred measures of oil to fifty and a hundred measures of wheat to fourscore, but he did not remove them completely. This means that even if he preaches the gospel, he cannot give once-and-for-all forgiveness, which the gospel promises. So the parable points out that he reduced the debts only partially.

Traditional doctrines of Christianity do not give perfect forgiveness of sin. So we should sin-and-repent repetitively. We will do this until we die. What does this mean? It means that our sins cannot be forgiven during this lifetime. In other words, it tells us that we have to confess our sins and repent for the rest of our lives. This is the forgiveness of sin that the unjust stewards of today offer.

However, the true gospel gives us perfect forgiveness of sin once and forever. The unjust steward represents a man under the law who hovers between the law and the gospel mimicking the gospel. He represents Christians today.

How do the unjust stewards of today reduce the debts of the people? By preaching that our sins are forgiven historically by Jesus and if we believe, we are saved by faith. This way they make almost every law powerless, and waste the Lord's goods. Yet, they cannot give the once-and-for-all forgiveness of the gospel to the people.

📂 The Current State of Christianity

We classify the Jews who believe according to the Old Testament as non-Christians because they do not receive Jesus Christ as their Savior. Then is our Christian life, based as it is on the Gospel, really that much different to Judaism? No, it is not!

The commandments such as "Love one another," "Do not judge," and "You pray after this manner," are given by Jesus for us to keep. Having heard that the Jews believe in God in a legalistic manner, Christians quickly follow the law given by Jesus, thinking "Then, we had better act differently from the Jews. Let's believe in Jesus who is the gospel." The word of Jesus has appeared to Christians as a new law to keep. As the Jews keep the word of God as the law, the Christians keep the word of Jesus as the law. Whether a man is under the law of God through Moses or under the law of Jesus, he is under the law. There is no difference.

Today's Christianity, although having taken the form of the gospel, is an updated version of Judaism, which is a legalistic religion. The unjust steward in the parable represents believers in today's Christianity.

Why Is the Steward Unjust and What Did He Do Wisely?

[Luke 16:8] And the lord commended the unjust steward, because he had done wisely: for the children of this world are in their generation wiser than the children of light.

The steward acted unjustly by reducing the debts the lord should receive. However, the lord commended the unjust steward saying that he had done wisely! We cannot understand the lord at this point.

Why Was the Steward Unjust?

The steward reduced the debts that were owed to the lord without permission. This was where he went wrong. This means that he weakened the power of the law to a standard acceptable to the sinners. He ruined the purpose of the law of God. He is unjust in this sense.

Likewise, we do not keep the commandments strictly, because we have discounted 'tickets' issued by the unjust stewards of today, that is, "Because you are forgiven by faith already, out of thanks to the Lord, you 'try' to love your neighbors. That will be all right." This way, we have little sense of offence and transgression under the law, justifying to ourselves that we are keeping it to a certain extent, and so we will not repent to God.

Really, these stewards are unjust!

Then Why did He Commend the Steward?

If so, why did the lord commend the steward? The lord commended him not for the action itself, but for the symbolic meaning of the action, that is, exchanging 'mammon' for 'friends.'

The unjust steward exchanged 'mammon' for 'friends.' This mirrors that we can enter the kingdom of God by handing over 'mammon' and in return gaining 'friends.' So the Lord is saying, "Like the unjust steward exchanged mammon for friends, you ought to exchange mammon for friends."

Of course, the 'mammon' and 'friends' that Jesus is talking about are totally different from those whom the unjust steward dealt with. These 'mammon' and 'friends' will be explained as we go on.

Anyway, the Lord commended him seeing the significance of the action of the unjust steward, which reveals the way to enter the kingdom of God as a sign.

📂 Wiser Than Children of Light

The children of this world represent them who are under the law. They are very smart and quick-witted. The steward under the law, having realized that he will be discharged from his job, reduced the debts by using an unjust device and made friends to seek a way of making a living. All this represents wise conduct for those who are under the law. Stewards of today are also performing such wise works in churches.

However, such behavior cannot lead him to the kingdom of God and enable him to become one of the children of light. He will become one of the children of light only when he meets Jesus, and goes into the kingdom, under His leadership. The children of light become so, not by their own wise acts but by the grace and guidance of Jesus.

Illustrating this point, Jesus said that the children of this world are wiser than the children of light. This word does not mean to commend the wisdom of the children of this world, but it means that becoming one of the children of light is by grace, and it is not acquired by our own wise conduct. Read Ephesians.

> For by grace are ye saved through faith; and that not of yourselves: it is the gift of God: [Ephesians 2:8]

Make to Yourselves Friends of the Mammon

> [Luke 16:9] And I say unto you, Make to yourselves friends of the mammon of unrighteousness; that, when ye fail, they may receive you into everlasting habitations.

Let us see what the mammon of unrighteousness is. It is very difficult to understand this passage from the perspective of the law.

It has double meanings; both natural and spiritual. We generally think that 'the mammon of unrighteousness' is something like possessions that are earned by gambling or stolen valuables, as in this parable. However, Jesus always talks about the world of the spirit, not the world of the flesh.

Then what will be the spiritual meaning of the 'mammon of unrighteousness,' that Jesus is alluding to? The mammon of unrighteousness represents the self-righteousness that we acquire by keeping the law. These are the possessions of Job in Job 31, and those that Jesus mentioned to the rich young man in Matthew, "Go, and sell that thou hast (i.e., possessions), and give to the poor" (Mat 19:21). Also they are the possessions of the elder son in the parable of the prodigal son in Luke, and this is revealed by his saying, "Lo, these many years do I serve thee, neither transgressed I at any time thy commandment" (Luk 15:29). And they are the possessions of those hired first in the parable of the vineyard householder and the laborers, in Matthew 20:12: "Saying, These last have wrought but one hour, and thou hast made them equal unto us, which have borne the burden and heat of the day"; and they are the possessions of the Pharisee in Luke below.

> [11] The Pharisee stood and prayed thus with himself, God, I thank thee, that I am not as other men are, extortioners, unjust, adulterers, or even as this publican. [12] I fast twice in the week, I give tithes of all that I possess. [Luke 18:11-12]

The above possessions are called self-righteousness or the mammon of unrighteousness. Self-righteousness, which is referred to as 'mammon,' is the foundation for our judging God and our neighbors. Because of this nature, it is referred to here as the mammon of 'unrighteousness.' We have to have this mammon when we do good things under the law without being one with God, like the unjust steward.

🗁 Make Friends

"Make to yourselves friends of the mammon of unrighteousness." This signifies that we will enter the kingdom and meet friends when our self-righteousness is destroyed. In this way we have exchanged self-righteousness (mammon) for friends. The 'old man' is the origin of self-righteousness. So when the 'old man' is destroyed by being united with Jesus on the cross, self-righteousness will be gone. In this way the unjust steward becomes the good steward. Not by changing his works, but by the grace of Jesus.

To know more about the elimination of self-righteousness and the friends that Jesus is talking about, read John below:

> [13] Greater love hath no man than this, that a man lay down his life for his friends. [14] Ye are my friends, if ye do whatsoever I command you. [15] Henceforth I call you not servants; for the servant knoweth not what his lord doeth: but I have called you friends; for all things that I have heard of my Father I have made known unto you. [John 15:13-15]

Jesus said this when He was teaching the disciples shortly before He was crucified. In the disciples' case, their self-righteousness and old man was destroyed on the cross, and then they entered the kingdom of God where Jesus Christ is. At this point, they became friends of Jesus. So friend is another expression for the one who is born again, belongs to Jesus and is in the kingdom of God.

Jesus said to his disciples in verse 13 that "Greater love hath no man than this, that a man lay down his life for his friends." This does not refer simply to the heroes of this world. When a man lays down his life of the 'old man' on the cross, he will be received as a friend in the kingdom. This is how he lays down his life for his friends. In this way, he will become the one who possesses the 'great love' of God in him, as he has become one with God, who is love.

This is the greatest love that one can possibly have across the universe.

🗁 When You Fail

Jesus says, "When ye fail, they may receive you into everlasting habitations" (Luke 16:9). This does not mean that when you are in need or distressed in your life, that these friends will help you in some way. Here, 'when you fail' means when your 'old man' is destroyed in unity with Jesus on the cross. At that time, your 'mammon of unrighteousness' will fail, and you will be entering the kingdom of God, the everlasting habitation. If you enter the kingdom in which the friends of Jesus stay, it means that the friends of Jesus abiding there receive you into the everlasting habitation. This is how you make friends by discarding self-righteousness.

The word "Make to yourselves friends of the mammon of unrighteousness" corresponds to the word "Go, and sell that thou hast, and give to the poor" in Chapter 19 in Matthew.

In addition, if you understand this message as a two-step process such as: 1) "Make friends by 'using' the mammon of unrighteousness, 2) and they will receive you into the everlasting habitations when you fail," then you will have misunderstood Jesus' message.

It means that by 'discarding' the mammon of unrighteousness, you make friends and meet friends in the 'everlasting habitations' at the same time. This sentence structure is something like this; if you tear off a black tape from a white paper, the white background will appear at the same time the tape has been taken off. Likewise, if you give up the mammon of unrighteousness on the cross, you will find that you are already abiding in the kingdom where the friends are.

Basically, the unjust steward represents the believer who does not want to take up his own cross, being deceived by his 'old man,' and yet he wishes to believe. In this circumstance, he can only do various types of works of the law. The unjust steward's nature is displayed throughout Luke Chapter 16, including "The Rich Man and Lazarus."

Epilogue

Jesus says through this parable that you should make friends by using the 'mammon of unrighteousness.' As explained, the mammon of unrighteousness represents self-righteousness, and 'friends' indicate the born again who are in the kingdom of God.

Make friends in the kingdom. And this is not achieved by changing your deeds from one to another, but Jesus does this for you. Leave all your wise efforts behind, and turn your eyes upon the living Jesus. Then, you can give up the 'mammon of unrighteousness' at the cross and then make friends.

Make to yourselves friends of the mammon of unrighteousness!

Cannot Serve God and Mammon

[Luke 16:10-13]

[10] He that is faithful in that which is least is faithful also in much: and he that is unjust in the least is unjust also in much. [11] If therefore ye have not been faithful in the unrighteous mammon, who will commit to your trust the true riches? [12] And if ye have not been faithful in that which is another man's, who shall give you that which is your own? [13] No servant can serve two masters: for either he will hate the one, and love the other; or else he will hold to the one, and despise the other. Ye cannot serve God and mammon.

Confusing Law with Gospel

Jesus finishes the parable of the unjust steward with the conclusion "Ye cannot serve God and mammon." This means that the unjust steward tried to serve both God and mammon.

Why did Jesus think that the unjust steward was serving both God and mammon?

This is because if a man who is under the law meets the gospel, he will understand the gospel as another commandment and behave accordingly. So he has both the law (self-righteousness or mammon of unrighteousness) and the gospel (God or Jesus) at the same time. These two simply cannot coexist. The gospel the unjust steward understands is not the true message of the gospel. He has mistaken the law for the gospel.

He belongs to none of the two groups, and he will be rebuked by Jesus saying, "So then because thou art lukewarm, and neither cold nor hot, I will spue thee out of my mouth (Rev 3:16)."

Meeting the gospel for the first time, all believers will respond to it like the unjust steward did. Jesus gives many examples in the Bible of this sort of reaction. Read Mark.

> [21] No man also seweth a piece of new cloth on an old garment: else the new piece that filled it up taketh away from the old, and the rent is made worse. [22] And no man putteth new wine into old bottles: else the new wine doth burst the bottles, and the wine is spilled, and the bottles will be marred: but new wine must be put into new bottles. [Mark 2:21-22]

The piece of new cloth symbolizes the gospel; the old garment symbolizes people who have developed self-righteousness through following the law. The new wine signifies the gospel, and the old bottles indicate the ones who are under the law.

In the two parables, the new cloth and the new wine which are symbols of the gospel, cause damage to the old garment and the old bottles. This warns us that if one who is under the law receives the gospel, he will interpret the gospel to meet his need and lose the devotion and eagerness that he has acquired thus far. His law-based sincerity toward God will disappear whilst he does not fully understand the true meaning or interpretation of the gospel, which would lead him into a grace-based life.

In detail, He warns that if a man whose time to receive the gospel has not come, even his existing legalistic faith and zeal for God will be taken away from him (Mat 13:12). Then, he will become a man of no faith; neither of the law nor of grace.

This is the status of the faith of the unjust steward and the believers of today. This will become more explicit when we read what Jesus is saying.

This and That, the Two Different Worlds

> [Luke 16:10-12] [10] He that is faithful in that which is least is faithful also in much: and he that is unjust in the least is un-

just also in much. ¹¹ If therefore ye have not been faithful in the unrighteous mammon, who will commit to your trust the true riches? ¹² And if ye have not been faithful in that which is another man's, who shall give you that which is your own?

After having instructed us to 'make to yourselves friends of the mammon of unrighteousness,' He continues to say that we will receive that which is 'much,' the 'true riches,' and that which is 'our own,' when we have been faithful in that which is 'least,' the 'unrighteous mammon,' and that which is 'another man's.'

The comparison is summarized in the table below:

Law	Grace/Gospel
That which is Least Unrighteous Mammon Another Man's	That which is Much True Riches Your Own
Sinner	Righteous Man
Darkness	Light

These things, contrary to each other, are like darkness versus light, and the latter will come when the former has passed away completely. Light and darkness cannot co-exist. However, the unjust steward in the parable is a man of contradiction who has both the law and the gospel at the same time.

We sin because we are sinners and so we constantly and continuously commit sinful acts.

We belong to this world of darkness as we are born. Salvation represents escape from this world and entry into the world of light, and we cannot escape from this world of darkness simply by changing our law-based deeds.

Nevertheless, the unjust steward, upon hearing from the lord to give an account of his stewardship, reduces the debts of the lord's debtors, but his deed of debt reduction is powerless to change his position. Furthermore, his deed of reduction is not new; it is what he has been doing always, wasting his lord's goods. He cannot change his nature by *doing* anything.

We have not only the world in which we serve sin, but also the world of light in which we serve God. The world of light will only be given to those who have completely passed beyond the legalistic faith stage. Passing beyond the law stage means that our 'old man' is destroyed on the cross. If not, no one can come into the world of light.

📁 Least and Much

"He that is faithful in that which is least is faithful also in much: and he that is unjust in the least is unjust also in much."

The above passage does not mean that if you act honestly and live morally, the kingdom of heaven will be given to you in return. It does not signify either that the kingdom of heaven will be denied to those who have behaved unfairly and have become corrupted in this world. If you read and interpret the word in this way, it only shows that you have the give-and-take paradigm of the marketplace.

Here, that which is 'least' represents the world that is under the law, and 'much' indicates the world of grace. He that is faithful in that which is 'least' means the man who has fallen and truly repented in the world of law. He is like the prodigal son who has fallen in a far country. He is now ready to enter the world of 'much.' It will be natural for him to be faithful in the world of 'much,' as the prodigal son returned home and was faithful.

On the contrary, he that is unjust in the 'least' includes all of them whose time to leave the world of law has not come; for example, the unjust steward. They have not yet repented truly to meet Jesus who will bring the kingdom of light to them. Naturally, they cannot receive the world of 'much.' So they show an unjust attitude to the world of 'much.'

Think about the case of the elder son in the parable of the prodigal son. He refused to go into the house of his father and join the party. Read Luke 15:28a: "And he was angry, and would not go in." He was unjust in the world of 'much.'

So if someone has completed his period under the law by truly repenting he is 'faithful' and he will be 'faithfully' accepted into the kingdom of 'much.' The unjust steward was not faithful, because he did not complete his period under the law and yet he wanted to jump over to the gospel stage prematurely. So he cannot be accepted into the kingdom of 'much.'

To us who are ready to do anything we are told to do, this will sound discouraging. However, Jesus is clear in saying that sin will only be eliminated from our lives when we have moved from our current world to kingdom of God, through the death of old man on the cross.

📁 Unrighteous Mammon and True Riches

"If therefore ye have not been faithful in the unrighteous mammon who will commit to your trust the true riches?"

To be faithful in 'the unrighteous mammon' is to discard it. That is you give up self-righteousness and God gives you His righteousness.

A spirit of unrighteous mammon characterizes those who are of this world. Those who have no mammon of unrighteousness already belong to the kingdom of God and possess the true riches of God.

📁 Another Man's and Your Own

"And if ye have not been faithful in that which is another man's, who shall give you that which is your own?"

Nothing is ours, but God's, when we believe under the law. However, when we come under grace, all that is God's becomes ours. I will explain what this means. The elder son in the parable of the prodigal son is a good example of those who are under the law. Read the verses from Luke below.

> [29] And he answering said to his father, Lo, these many years do I serve thee, neither transgressed I at any time thy commandment: and yet thou never gavest me a kid, that I might make merry with my friends: [30] But as soon as this thy son was come, which hath devoured thy living with harlots, thou hast killed for him the fatted calf. [31] And he said unto him, Son, thou art ever with me, and all that I have is thine. [32] It was meet that we should make merry, and be glad: for this

thy brother was dead, and is alive again; and was lost, and is found. [Luke 15:29-32]

The elder son expected that his father would give him a kid, if he served him. He thought that he would gather favor and possessions in this way. However, the father said, "All that I have is yours," including a 'kid' of course. His and his father's understanding were quite different.

The point is that even though the father offered all that he had to the elder son, he could not (or would not) take it but thought that he must work hard to get it. This is the viewpoint of those who are under the law, toward God. Those who are under the law have no option but to think as the elder son did. However, to them who are under grace that which is God's is theirs.

Hebrews accurately defines the difference between the servant and the son.

> [5] And Moses verily was faithful in all his house, as a servant, for a testimony of those things which were to be spoken after; [6] But Christ as a son over his own house; whose house are we, if we hold fast the confidence and the rejoicing of the hope firm unto the end. [Hebrews 3:5-6]

Moses is representative of them who believe under the law. He was faithful in His house as a servant. No servant can possess things of his master. These things belong to someone else, i.e., God.

However, Christ is faithful as a son over His house. The son shares things, which are his father's. That which belongs to his father is his too. Jesus will bring us from the world of the servant (another man's) to the world of son (our own).

Two Masters

> [Luke 16:13] No servant can serve two masters: for either he will hate the one, and love the other; or else he will hold to the one, and despise the other. Ye cannot serve God and mammon.

Here, in believing in Jesus, 'serving God' means being under grace, and 'serving mammon,' which is stockpiling self-righteousness as a sinner, means being under the law. We are controlled by the master we are serving. If we are serving 'this,' we cannot serve 'that' at the same time. We cannot concurrently belong to the time of the New Testament while belonging to the time of the Old Testament. We can only belong to one of the two.

For another example, in the year 2010, all that we do is the work of 2010. However, in 2011, we can no longer do the works of 2010. Anything we do is the work of 2011. Further, we cannot concurrently belong to the year 2010 and the year 2011.

Spiritually speaking, the unjust steward while actually belonging to the year 2010 followed the acts of those belonging to the year 2011, and so he mistook himself for one of those who belonged to the year 2011. If we liken the year 2010 to the law and the year 2011 to the gospel of grace, the unjust steward tried to serve both of them through his misunderstanding of the Scripture.

We generally think we can do good deeds even if we are sinners. Likewise, we are mistaken that we can be righteous when we have done many good works. This is not true. This is the way that the unjust steward in the parable thought. We must go through mammon's era first completely, and then God's era will dawn within us in the course of the faith growing process.

Epilogue

'Mammon' does not signify possessions but it is the self-righteousness of men, such as "I have done good things!" Such 'mammon' is generated by our 'old man.' The 'old man' and God cannot live together within me. If God abides in me, the old man has been crucified, and if He does not live in me, the old man is alive within me.

The unjust steward mistakenly thinks that God is in him, but, in reality, he represents 'old man.' Due to this incorrect understanding, he thinks that his faith is sound and he will not accept the healing hand of Jesus; just like the Pharisees. This kind of faith is particularly dangerous when the person does not realize that his spiritual understanding of the Word is incorrect.

The unjust steward divulges the status quo of today's Christians.

Law and Kingdom of God

[Luke 16:14-18]

¹⁴ And the Pharisees also, who were covetous, heard all these things: and they derided him. ¹⁵ And he said unto them, Ye are they which justify yourselves before men; but God knoweth your hearts: for that which is highly esteemed among men is abomination in the sight of God. ¹⁶ The law and the prophets were until John: since that time the kingdom of God is preached, and every man presseth into it. ¹⁷ And it is easier for heaven and earth to pass, than one tittle of the law to fail. ¹⁸ Whosoever putteth away his wife, and marrieth another, committeth adultery: and whosoever marrieth her that is put away from her husband committeth adultery.

Jesus finishes off the parable of the unjust steward saying, "You cannot serve God and mammon," the Pharisees hearing this deride him. Seeing them, He says that they are those who justify themselves, and then says that the law and the prophets were until John and continues talking about adultery. It is very difficult for us to grasp what Jesus was seeking to get across.

Basically, Jesus here reveals the unrighteousness of self-righteousness, and says that in order to enter the kingdom of God, the world of grace, we should complete our individual law era completely, not like the unjust steward. He is committing adultery.

Now I will explain how these words of Jesus inter-relate.

Were the Pharisees Covetous?

[Luke 16:14-15] ¹⁴ And the Pharisees also, who were covetous, heard all these things: and they derided him. ¹⁵ And he said unto them, Ye are they which justify yourselves before men; but God knoweth your hearts: for that which is highly esteemed among men is abomination in the sight of God.

The Pharisees were those who pursued religious piety and honorable poverty. That was one of the main reasons that they were respected as religious leaders by the people. The Pharisees would not have been respected for their piety if it was true that they coveted wealth. On the contrary, they were not attached to the money, or at least superficially, they were not.

So the words 'who were covetous' is to be considered and construed more deeply. Then what will be the deeper meaning of covetous? Read Romans.

> ¹⁷ Behold, thou art called a Jew, and restest in the law, and makest thy boast of God, ¹⁸ And knowest his will, and approvest the things that are more excellent, being instructed out of the law; [Romans 2:17-18]

They 'approved the things that are more excellent,' being instructed by the law. This means that they loved and cherished valuable mental 'possessions' rather than things like money. The mental possessions in this instance represented such deeds as donation, devotion, self-denial, prayer, fasting, and loving others, *et cetera*.

They pursued such good deeds in this world, thinking them to be the will of God. However, they misunderstood the Scripture. Even though the Scripture appears to set out the law as a code of moral conduct and good deeds, this is not its original purpose. In fact, such teachings can be found in many secular books, other than the Scripture. The purpose of the Scripture is to heal the souls of readers and to create in them a new life.

They easily understood the literal meanings of the Scripture, which are the doctrines of men, and observed them. This is how the word of God is transformed into the doctrine of man. Being ignorant of this, they accumulated 'treasure' by performing good deeds.

It was a precious treasure to them because it gave them pride before men and provided the justification for them to judge others who were not doing so. This is the unrighteous mammon or self-righteousness mentioned previously. Those believers who are trying to accumulate treasures this way are called covetous.

Please do not misunderstand. I am not saying you should not do good works. No. You should do good works while you are living in this world. However, such works are not exclusive to those of us who believe in and depend on Jesus, because non-believers also pursue and approve the things that are more excellent even without knowing Jesus.

The Pharisees did not consider themselves unjust because there was no reason to call the works that they did in obedience to the law, unjust. On the contrary, others who did not obey the law were unjust as far as they were concerned. The Pharisees proudly had self-righteousness as a treasure before God and men.

The Pharisees did not understand why Jesus was saying, "No servant can serve two masters: for either he will hate the one, and love the other; or else he will hold to the one, and despise the other. Ye cannot serve God and mammon" (Luk 16:13). To their knowledge, the 'mammon' (self-righteousness) that they have comes from God, because they have done it according to the word of God. To them, their 'mammon' is the representation of God, and God and mammon are one. So they deride Him who is saying, "Ye cannot serve God and mammon."

We also entertain doubt thinking, "Is it wrong to pursue such good things?" In fact, we have all been pursuing the same things in our lives as believers. However, in contrast to our and the Pharisees thinking, Jesus pointed out the unrighteousness of such deeds (Mat 6:1-8, Mat Chapter 23) many times.

Read the verses from Matthew below:

> [1] Take heed that ye do not your alms before men, to be seen of them: otherwise ye have no reward of your Father which is in heaven. [2] Therefore when thou doest thine alms, do not sound a trumpet before thee, as the hypocrites do in the synagogues and in the streets, that they may have glory of

men. Verily I say unto you, They have their reward. [Matthew 6:1-2]

Remember, not all alms giving is good.

📂 They who Justify Themselves Before Men

From what Jesus continues to say, we can understand that 'being covetous' does not refer to coveting material possessions, but self-righteousness, which indicates mental 'possessions.' When the Pharisees mocked Jesus, He said "You are they who justify themselves before men."

If they loved material possessions, they would not have been in a position to justify themselves, but they might have felt a fear of being branded as those who want nothing but money. Therefore, "they were covetous" means that they treasured their self-righteousness. They were covetous to gather self-righteousness by doing almsgiving, showing modesty and gentleness, advocating love and peace, *et cetera*—all these are the grounds on which people are commended.

Jesus says self-righteousness is only useful for boasting before men and God sees it as an abomination.

📂 Why Is Self-Righteousness an Abomination in God' Sight?

The Scripture testifies to the living Jesus, and He will heal our souls, which is usually painful. So when we read the Scripture, we do not want to be healed, so we avoid the real intention of God embedded in it and only grasp the superficial meaning, using it to achieve the respect of men. We concentrate on the world and mankind, seeking to justify ourselves through charitable acts, giving alms, and promoting world peace. All these things are of course, highly esteemed among men.

Quoting from Isaiah 6:10, Jesus says to us as follows in Matthew:

For this people's heart is waxed gross, and their ears are dull of hearing, and their eyes they have closed; lest at any time they should see with their eyes and hear with their ears, and should understand with their heart, and should be converted, and I should heal them. [Matthew 13:15]

Basically, we have no mind to obey the word of God at all. Yet we say, "I am doing all this for the glory of God." What an abomination! God knows such hearts. If we behave like this, we are abominable in the sight of God. We are deceived by our old man inside, so we behave and believe in this way.

The Law and the Prophets Were Until John

[Luke 16:16-17] ¹⁶ The law and the prophets were until John: since that time the kingdom of God is preached, and every man presseth into it. ¹⁷ And it is easier for heaven and earth to pass, than one tittle of the law to fail.

Jesus, pointing out the self-righteousness of the Pharisees, now tells us that the law and the prophets were until John: since that time the kingdom of God is preached, and every man presses into it.

The unjust steward in the parable pursues self-righteousness according to the commandments, thinking he is under grace. To him there is no difference between the law and grace, as he has no eyes to understand grace yet. He represents the Pharisees, and so it is natural for the Pharisees to speak up for the unjust steward. Their contradiction is; they cannot distinguish the law and grace. They are only faithful in self-righteousness, thinking that is the right way to serve God. However, in reality, they serve themselves.

Jesus rebukes them, and reveals how to distinguish grace from the law by mentioning John the Baptist. Once we get passed 'the day of John' we start to be healed in the grace of Jesus, forsaking all.

🗁 Until John

Regarding "until John," here John indicates John the Baptist who was a prophet who came to make Jesus' paths straight before He began His works (Mat 3:3). John cried out repentance in the wilderness. When we repent truly we are to follow Jesus forsaking all, Jesus' path is thus straightened in our mind. This is the time of John in us, and the Scripture calls it the baptism of John (Luk 7:29, Act 1:22, 19:3). From this time on, we are ready to follow Jesus to the cross, and our era of grace to enter the kingdom of God begins.

The time of John does not specify a time 2,000 years ago, it indicates the time of our repentance to meet the living Jesus in our individual life. At this time, we finish the 'time of the Old Testament,' and begin the 'time of New Testament.'

If you can hear what I am saying here, then you will realize that you have believed thus far with your own thinking and efforts, not knowing the will of God. In other words, you have served God as you wished, without hearing from God as to how and in which way you should serve Him.

You might be perplexed because you are so sure that you serve and believe God right. But it is not so. In faith steps, we all have to go through this stage of 'we believe' first, whether we want to or not. When we repent at that stage, that will be the day of John and we will follow Jesus to start the true faith of 'Jesus leads us to believe.'

Now if you follow the living Jesus, what you are doing is pressing into the kingdom of God.

📂 Than One Tittle of the Law to Fail

The days of the kingdom of God will come to you when you have perfectly passed through the days of the law. If you keep all the law, even one tittle of it, then you will come into the kingdom of God. However, nobody can keep the law that way.

Then, how can you pass through and finish the time of the law? You can do it when you become dead to the law. To die to the law, your 'old man' should be crucified in unity with Jesus. This is the only way. Read Romans.

> [5] For if we have been planted together in the likeness of his

death, we shall be also in the likeness of his resurrection: ⁶ Knowing this, that our old man is crucified with him, that the body of sin might be destroyed, that henceforth we should not serve sin. ⁷ For he that is dead is freed from sin. [Romans 6:5-7]

Once 'old man' is dead and you are resurrected in Jesus, you will no longer see this heaven and earth of the law. You will see the new heaven and earth in grace. Thus, the law does not have dominion over you who have undergone such a process. This is the only way to fulfill the law without missing one jot or one tittle of it. Not by keeping it, but by being dead to it. Therefore, it is easier to be dead on the cross (old heaven and earth to pass), than to have one tittle of the law to fail.

The unjust steward, upon hearing the gospel, interprets it into law, and keeps it to try to escape from the world of the law, but in vain.

I say vain, because if he wants to achieve this, he has to keep every part of the law. This is impossible. He is mistaken basically because he tries to believe in Jesus but not the Jesus who leads him to the cross.

Commitment of Adultery

> [Luke 16:18] Whosoever putteth away his wife, and marrieth another, committeth adultery: and whosoever marrieth her that is put away from her husband committeth adultery.

This passage about adultery does not relate to one of the legal codes of the Old Testament. It follows on from the above word dealing with, 'one tittle of the law.' The passage reveals that if someone does not pass through the law by the death on the cross together with Jesus and he thinks that he is under grace, then he is committing adultery.

"Whosoever putteth away his wife, and marrieth another, committeth adultery" (Luk 16:18a).

The wife of the unjust steward represents those who hear from him. That is, He likens a person who gives the seed, i.e., the word, to a husband and a person who receives it, to a wife. The steward who puts away the wife is the steward staying under the law.

What does "Whosoever putteth away his wife" mean?

If the steward of the law hears the gospel earlier than his appropriate time, the time of John the Baptist, i.e., when he has become desolate to repent, he will understand the gospel from the viewpoint of the law. So he thinks that he is preaching the gospel, but he is actually preaching the law. What he teaches is, even though it imitates the gospel, it is still the law, and so it will be called the 'transformed law,' not the gospel.

If the steward of the law teaches people with this 'transformed law,' it will result in his changing his wife. This is because his previous teachings correspond to the previous wife and are no longer relevant. The new teachings, the transformed law, will now be preached. And the hearer will be a new wife, because the teachings are new.

For example, the Jews accepting the laws of Judaism are different from Christians receiving the 'transformed law' of today's Christianity. Using the concept of a wife, there are Jewish wives and Christian wives. If a Jewish steward preaches Christian doctrines, he changes his wife from Jewish to Christian. This is what is referred to as adultery.

The good steward of the gospel does not put away his wife because he has already found the truth, which cannot be changed for whatsoever reasons and so he will not change his teaching. Using the above analogy, he does not change his wife.

"And whosoever marrieth her that is put away from her husband committeth adultery"(Luk 16:18b).

'She who is put away from her husband' also indicates the person under the law. That she is 'put away' means that she has left God, her husband. The relationship to give and receive the gospel is to marry and to become one. If the steward insists on preaching the gospel to her who is put away, it proves that his gospel is a fake. If his gospel is true, he can never marry her who left her husband, as there will be no harmony between Christ and Belial (2Co 6:15).

In fact, only those who are under the law, who are adulterers already in the sense that they are not receiving the seed, i.e., the word of God, will commit adultery. All their doings, including their efforts and deeds to leave the law era, amount to adultery.

Epilogue

The Pharisees are those who love self-righteousness. Incapable of distinguishing the law and the gospel, they follow any good word of God and have it as their own mammon, i.e., self-righteousness. They are the unjust stewards. Jesus says God abominates their mammon and tells them to distinguish between the law and the gospel.

Jesus is virtually saying as follows:

"You will be mistaken if you think that you are able to receive God's grace through the gospel of Jesus Christ, while blindly following a legalistic interpretation and understanding of the gospel.

Such conduct does not lead you to enter the world of the gospel. You should first finish your days under the law if you want to go into the world of the gospel. Unless you are perfectly dead to the law, the gospel is the last thing you will be able to understand and accept. It is nonsensical for you to receive the grace of the gospel through your deeds while you belong to the law. Such acts show that you are committing adultery."

The Lord is teaching us by comparing the world of the law with the kingdom of God, and self-righteousness with the righteousness of God; starting with the parable of the unjust steward.

Now, which do you think you belong to?

The law that appears to be the gospel, or the gospel?

Trip to Charleston*

At a stage in the past, I was much absorbed in posting articles on the forum of the cyber community, discussing many topics of the Scripture with other members, and debating with them. I spent most of my hours in preparing articles to be posted on the community board, and I frequently wrote articles working until 2 to 3 am.

My wife hated this. However, I continued because the Lord was not against it. It was a great comfort to me. I was addicted to the activity in the community. At the same time, however, I was gradually losing interest in such discussions because the same topics were repeatedly argued.

In June while still associated with the cyber forum, I went on an educational visit to Charleston in the US. Before I left, my wife told me "Your sister-in-law says that the Lord wants you to reduce the time you spend on the internet."

In general, when I am told that the Lord wants me to do something, I always double-check with Him. However, as He fully supported my cyber forum activities at that time, I did not pay much attention to what the Lord said through her. Furthermore, I knew that my sister-in-law did not approve of my involvement with the internet forum, so I made light of her comment.

I wanted to continue to correspond with the internet forum during my US visit, so I tried to formulate a plan to access the Korean internet service provider while in the US. Since access to Korea from the US through an international call was very expensive, I decided to use an internet roaming service. This way, I could access the Korea cyber forum at the cost of a local call in the USA.

I learned the method of accessing the internet server in the US through a local call and then accessed the forum in Korea via the roaming service. I had a dry run before I left. Everything was okay. Now while visiting America, I would be able to connect to the forum service of Korea at the cost of a local call.

Access to Internet Service in America

I packed my notebook computer for the trip and it occupied almost half of the space of the suitcase. In fact, the notebook was not a prerequisite for the education trip. It was not a must-have item. I only cherished it and took it to America for internet correspondence. After traveling for twenty-six hours, I arrived in Charleston.

Immediately after I checked into the hotel, I booted up the notebook computer to test that it worked. I accessed the local internet service provider's server via a local call and then accessed the communication service provider in Korea so that I could reach the desired forum with no problem. I was beside myself with joy. I was connected to Korea via a cheap local call. This was the so-called internet roaming service!

I first sent an email including a message that I had arrived at Charleston to my daughter. I felt so glad to send messages and receive replies without paying an expensive international call fee. It was well worthwhile carrying my heavy notebook computer with me on the trip. I accessed the internet five or six times a day and each access was successful. I really loved this easy access.

"Why am I always successful in accessing the internet with no difficulty?"

I got into the habit of accessing Korea through the internet for brief periods between classes, and so I was sometimes late for the next class and on one occasion I cut the class altogether! I was severely addicted to the internet.

It Went Well But...

The connection was extraordinarily successful but a problem occurred two days later. Connection to the local server that was successful in the morning failed in the afternoon. The message

"Wrong password" appeared on the window and the access to the local server was disconnected. So I tested the notebook computer, checked the programs, and performed disk defragmentation. However, I was still unable to access the local server, and what made matter worse was that the performance of the notebook became seriously degraded after performing the disk defragmentation.

Anyway, I tried to access the server in Korea through an international call. That access was okay. However, it was useless because of the cost of an international call. I tried to find another server access phone number in the area of Charleston from the Korean service provider. I had to connect to the server in Korea via the international calling. When I connected, I went to the website. However, it took about 2 to 3 minutes to display one or two lines of the page. I guessed that the disk defragmentation program had generated a problem.

I just wanted to disconnect the international call in the middle of it but I waited on and on. I finally gave up after failing to receive the telephone number I needed after 30 to 40 minutes. Feeling upset, I called the man in charge of the company in Korea via an international telephone call. He replied that the problem had occurred in the local US server and so I had to get help from the US company. He gave me the telephone number of the company.

I called the help center in America by using the telephone number the Korean guy gave me. The person who took the call was very kind and tested the communication conditions in many ways. He tried to access with my ID and password, and then he made me wait a long time, saying that he had to go to his desk to sit in front of his computer. He was kind but seemed unhurried. After a long time, he finally concluded that he had done all he could and failed. He gave me the telephone number of another server company in nearby Columbia. I found later that the help center was located not near Charleston but in San Jose in the western part of America. I had to pay for a long distance call.

Anyway, I had no option but to access the server located in Columbia which was the nearest one to Charleston. In addition, the call to Columbia was charged as a long-distance call even though it had the same area code. How could things go against me like this?

Everything went haywire.

Cold Wife

In the evening of the same day, I made an international phone call to Korea for the first time because I thought that sending emails was insufficient. My wife took the call, but she said in a very angry voice.

"I think you will not need to talk to me, so I will put you through to your daughter."

She soon called our daughter and handed the telephone receiver over to her. I expected that she would be pleased to hear from me since I was calling from a foreign country, but this was just my own wish. I was thrown into confusion and her voice was extraordinarily cold. Sometimes she used to behave like this, but this time was more than simple hurt. I knew later that it hurt me so much because her cold reply included the Lord's rebuke. When my daughter came on the line, I asked her.

"Why is your mother so angry?"

"She got angry because you did not directly send an email to her or call her, but you let her know how you were getting along through your email to me."

I had only sent an email to our daughter and asked after her through our daughter, and so I had hurt her pride and she had got angry with me.

After this happened, I began to feel something was going wrong with my relationship with the Lord. In other words, I vaguely felt that He was controlling things to go amiss because I was doing things that He was not pleased with. I began to think that the local server that had worked so smoothly to start with, and had suddenly stopped functioning and the annoyance of my wife were not coincidences at all. However, I still had no idea of what had gone wrong.

Terrible Telephone Charges

The next day, I ran into the only other Korean that was attending the seminar. He told me in passing, "I called a man in Seoul collect for 3 minutes, and the hotel made a mistake and charged me $18. So I explained it to the hotel's manager and he corrected it."

"Oh, really?" I said. I quickly did some mental arithmetic and worked out that the hotel would be charging about $3 per minute for international calls. I suddenly felt quite faint. The number of minutes of international calls that I had clocked up during my visit was huge!

I had accessed the server in Seoul for about 30 to 40 minutes, I guessed. Also, I had simply forgotten that I was connected to the server in Seoul while writing an article to be posted on the forum when I saw a message displayed, "You will be disconnected because of no input for a long time." Such messages usually appear when 20 to 30 minutes have passed. Further, I had telephoned the helper in the help center located in San Jose by long-distance, unaware of the time that had elapsed. My recollection of all this left me absolutely thunderstruck!

I quietly slipped out of the seminar and went to the front desk and asked for a print out of my bill. The lady at the desk started to print out the offending document while I waited in a cold sweat.

"Chirp, chirp, chirp..."

The printer's sound hurt like something scratching at my heart. The bill was already more than four pages.

"Wow, a lot of items I have to pay!"

I was very concerned as the printer went on for what seemed an eternity. My face was flushed as the lady at the front desk looked like saying within herself, "Hey! Are you insane? Why do you Koreans make so many calls from your room?"

At last, she handed me the bill; over 6 pages long! I quickly stuffed it into my pocket and escaped to my room. Having checked the details of the bill, I was shocked. Most of the bill listed telephone charges. One call cost $214. It may have been charged when I found the local server telephone number while I was connected to the server in Seoul. Many other items were $70 or $80; the total was over $500! I was terribly ashamed. Why did I spend $500 for internet communication? Was it so important? No sane person would do such a stupid thing! I was extremely regretful, ashamed, and miserable.

The Lord Meddled

I believe that the Lord had intervened. Before I left Korea, the Lord gave me the message that I should spend less time on the internet. When I did not listen to Him, He blocked access to the local server that was working well. When I stubbornly tried to make a new internet connection, He communicated with me through the angry voice of my wife. As a finishing blow, He made me realize my stubborn stupidity through the $500 phone bill. I asked Him about this.

"Did you control all these events to show me that I was too absorbed in the internet discussion?"

"Yes," He said. Upon hearing this, I thought that I would not be hooked on the internet any longer, but I became disgusted with it at the same time. After this dialog with Him, I did not access the internet forum again until the seminar was over. I simply had no inclination. I hated myself.

We all have similar experiences. We can easily say it was just a mistake and that I paid too much money out of ignorance. So someone having no idea of how the Lord works may say, "It is a commonplace experience that anybody can undergo and you are simply putting your faults down to the Lord."

However, truly this case happened because He had actively meddled in it.

You Got Hurt!

Sometime later, the Lord told me quite unexpectedly: "You got hurt."

I did not know what this meant.

"I was in trouble in the flight because I had a cold, but I recovered from it and I am now well again."

However, I understood what He meant many days later. He was saying that I was suffering not from the cold but because I had had to pay $500 in what were really unnecessary telephone charges. He had said this to comfort me.

On hearing Him, however, I got myself into rage rather than being consoled because He confessed that He had done it with a specific objective in mind. Of course, at first, I had comforted myself by saying, "The Lord did so to raise me up," and then concluded with, "I thank the Lord who is the greatest of all for having explained it to me like that." But my heart went altogether in another direction. Anger rose up within me when I thought that He had seemed to set up a stumbling block in advance and had waited for me to fall over it. I tried to understand this, but I felt uneasy.

"Did You have to use such a method on me?"

Comfort Through a Dream

The Lord spoke to me again in a dream one night. In my dream, I saw my cousin staying with us in my father's house. My father told him to learn a skill and he did not wish to. He got mad with my father's advice, and his anger showed in his face. Then I advised him as an older cousin.

"My father spoke to you in this way because he saw your future and wanted you to succeed in your life. Why were you so angry? Have patience and listen to him."

He said "I don't know what he was talking about" and soon fell asleep having failed to understand what my father had been trying to tell him. Then, I awoke up from my dream. The Lord had given me the message "I have seen your future and I let these events happen to you so that you may succeed in your life." That was what I had been telling my cousin in my dream!

God talking to me in this way was marvelous and so I was grateful to Him. However, although He comforted me through this dream, I still felt uneasy since I had been severely enraged.

Lord's Character and my Emotion

In the course of my training under the Lord, my feelings have been hurt many times. I cannot express in words the pain of the rebuke of my wife and the coldness of her words over the telephone. Such pain is very specific and we seldom experience it in this world. You will agree with me when you have also experienced it.

When I recall the popup window of "You will be disconnected because of no user's inputs," not realizing that I was still connected on an expensive international call, I remember that it tore my heart out. I had no idea at that time, but I knew later that the Lord's message was being transmitted into my heart, saying, "Hey, hey, hey! Look! You were writing an article while connected via an expensive international call. You are in big trouble! You'll pay a lot."

I got all steamed up about Him because He, even if He was the Lord, appeared to be mocking me. I was still angry when I was in the process of leaving the Charleston seminar.

God of Thanks

After the four day seminar, I returned to Korea. In the very nick of time, there was a big spiritual revival service opening in my church. The service was led by Pastor David Cho. Many people had gathered on the upper and lower floors. I was sitting on the second floor of the church. When the sermon was over and prayer time had begun, people prayed with loud voices seeking God fervently.

While looking at this, an idea came into my mind: "The God that all these people pursue with all their heart is the very God who allowed me to get into trouble in Charleston. I am seeing Him very closely whereas they can't meet Him even though they cry out loudly in prayer."

When this idea flashed across my mind, I was terribly grateful and moved to tears. I had finally realized after I had returned home from abroad that the hand of the Lord that I had believed to have reproached me was really precious.

In the Lord, everything whether it is hard, fine, painful, or glad is precious and blessed.

I praise the God of glory and give thanks to Him who has revealed Himself intimately to me, an ignoble person.

PART THREE
The Real Jesus

The only method for us to change our position from the law to the gospel is to meet the real Jesus in our life. To meet the real Jesus will be summarized as: to feel His hand by walking with God, and to know the way to the kingdom of God through your understanding the true interpretation and meaning of the Scripture. When we know the way and walk with the Lord, we will go into the kingdom of God, our destination.

The real Jesus saves us—I hope that you will meet this Jesus.

The Real Jesus

Difference Between Believing in God and Believing in Jesus

I explained in 'Fresh Eyes to Read the Bible - Book 1' that faith grows according to the arrangement of the Bible's books. If I further simplify the process, it can be divided into the stage of the Old Testament and the stage of the New Testament, or the stage of the law and the stage of the gospel of grace.

The period of the Old Testament and the New Testament can also be classified as three stages: the Old Testament Stage, the New Testament Stage, and the Holy Spirit Stage.

The books from Genesis to Malachi represent the period of the Old Testament during which we worship God, the books from Matthew to John indicate the period of the New Testament during which we are healed by Jesus, and the books from Acts to Revelation correspond to the period of the Holy Spirit, during which we are one with God.

It will be meaningless if we simply understand the periods in relation to historical events and facts, and it is accordingly important to understand the periods as the stages of faith that each one of us will progress through. Our faith will progress in relation to the order of the period of God, the period of Jesus, and the period of the Holy Spirit. When we have received faith corresponding to the period of the Holy Spirit, faith has been perfectly fulfilled in us.

Once we attend church and make confession to Jesus as our Savior, we will be called believers. However, at this point, whom we believe is not Jesus, but God because we are living in the period of God. That is, we put Jesus in the place of God and say we believe in Jesus, but in fact, we believe in God.

Some people may say it would be all the same whether we believe in either one, Jesus or God, and thus it would be of no importance to distinguish between Jesus and God. If they say so, they are saying that Jesus did not need to come to this world to save us. They are confused because they do not know who Jesus really is. God sent Jesus because the work of God and the work of Jesus are different. Therefore, we should distinguish between the two. Jesus comes to the person whose period of God and the law is completed, and opens the period of Jesus. He can then be said to believe in Jesus.

We will be saved when we become one with God, and this will be achieved through the steps of growing in faith through Jesus. These steps are actually the revelation of the triune God to us, which is God-Jesus-Holy Spirit progressively. Details are as follows:

📂 Period of God

When we come to church for the first time, we do not know much about Jesus and we try to believe in Jesus through our own efforts. However, we do not have a correct understanding of Jesus and cannot hear Him even. If we pray hard to Him, He gives us various spiritual gifts of the Holy Spirit and allows them to experience spiritual things. Those having undergone such things make an endeavor to witness that Jesus is alive, and we are eager to believe in Jesus.

However, He is still in heaven and has not yet become one with us who are on earth. We are called believers, but distant from Him.

At this time, we think we believe in Jesus because we come to church to believe in Jesus, but in essence, we believe in God who is in heaven. So whatever we say, we stay under the law and believe in God. We have the faith of the period of God at this stage.

📂 Period of Jesus

When we complete the period of God, then God sends Jesus to

us. The meaning of 'complete' is 'being desolate and repented' in our life in faith under the law. This is the day of John the Baptist in us.

Paul the Apostle who collapsed while traveling to Damascus, the woman of Samaria who came to the well to draw water, the one lost sheep, and the prodigal son would be good examples for such persons whose time has completed in the period of God. We will meet Jesus and then begin the faith of the period of Jesus.

We can meet Jesus by hearing and understanding the true meaning of the word of God together with walking with God, which is easy to say but which is not available to anyone. It will be applied to him whose time has come, that is, the one who is exhausted and given up all hope under legalistic faith, that is, the period of God.

He who has met Jesus will undergo a process of healing and chastening by Jesus so that his 'old man' may die on the cross. This healing is given to him because he takes his cross and follows Jesus after meeting Him. During this time, he will be healed and gain a new life. If our life as a believer does not include such a healing time with Jesus, his faith will be false. There will be no salvation without this period of Jesus.

God who is in heaven came near to us in Jesus who is around us. So the distance between God in Jesus and us is reduced to very close. However, we have not yet become one with God.

This is the period of Jesus in our process of growing in faith.

📂 Period of the Holy Spirit

When we are going through the period of Jesus and having taken up our cross and are following Him with patience and perseverance, our old man will be crucified and the Holy Spirit will come on us. From that time on, our period of the Holy Spirit in faith begins. He whose faith has fully grown to reach the period of the Holy Spirit is the one who perfectly believes in Jesus. The Spirit of Christ dwells in him and so he is of the Christ (Rom 8:9).

This man has no distance from God. They become one. Accordingly, the work of salvation by Jesus has borne fruit in him. Also, Immanuel, that is, "God is with us" has been fulfilled in him in this period of time. If we are believers, we should reach this stage during our lifetime.

The Real Jesus

Jesus is a secret. Many people seek Him and call His name, but most of them do not know who He is and what He does. Jesus whom we know traditionally is the Jesus who appears in history or the Jesus who will come as a judge in the far future. And we understand Him as the one who wants us to be moral. However, such a Jesus is not the Jesus that the Scripture speaks of. He is another Jesus (2Co 11:4).

Real Jesus comes to us individually once we have completely undergone the period of God. When He comes, He will destroy our old man on the cross, and immediately after that, He comes into us again as the Holy Spirit.

Jesus will come only to those who have become desolate and have fallen down in their faith under the law. Thus, to those who do not reach such point in their life, Jesus still remains a secret.

▷ Real Jesus Shows the Way

When their time comes, their ears will be opened to hear God and their eyes will be opened to see the true meaning of the Scripture. In this instance, the true meaning represents the hidden meanings of the word that shows the 'way to the kingdom of God.' Then, the priorities in their life will be turned in the direction of seeking the kingdom of God. We can see the disciples after having met Him, left all behind and followed Jesus.

Therefore, if you cannot easily tell whether you have met Jesus or not, you can know it by checking whether you know the way to reach the kingdom of God and seek the kingdom. If you give priority to the things of the world, it means that you have failed to understand the kingdom of God and His way correctly. So the things of the world have a more important effect on you.

If you think this case applies to you, you should hear the word of God again and again, and then the kingdom and its way will become evident to you gradually, and the kingdom will be settled in you as your everything.

📂 Real Jesus Heals

Many believers think that Jesus will bring fortune, bread, health, and the glory of the world to them. Partially yes, Jesus will bring them if He sees fit. However, that is not the purpose of the coming of Jesus in the flesh. Do not be mistaken. Jesus came to heal our souls.

We, the born sinners, have been taken by Satan since our birth, and we do not realize it, even when we attend church and believe in Jesus. When we meet the real Jesus, He will heal us who are taken by Satan.

The Bible says we that are taken by Satan are described as our 'old man.' In other words, the 'old man' is *me* before I am born again. Jesus will destroy this 'old man' on the cross, and it is a spiritual healing by Jesus. After that, we will be freed from Satan. Jesus came to achieve this healing for us, not to give worldly peace, bread and glory. If a man's 'old man' is crucified, he is now forgiven his sin and has been born again as a new man.

The real Jesus is he who heals and corrects us, here and now, and differs from the Jesus whom we know from history and whom we know will come again.

📂 Real Jesus Brings Holy Spirit

Jesus who gives us the Holy Spirit by laying down the 'old man' on the cross is the real Jesus the Scripture speaks of. The real Jesus is the only One who can bring us to the Holy Spirit. Some might say that even before Jesus comes, there were instances whereby the Holy Spirit comes on people. Yes, but they were only the shadow of the body and the spirit to come. The Holy Spirit of Immanuel will only be brought to the believer by Jesus who is to die on the cross.

Let us look at the disciples' case. They spent three and half years with Jesus as a healing period, and as a result, they received the Holy Spirit. No Jesus, No Holy Spirit! Thus, the Scripture says as follows:

> But this spake he of the Spirit, which they that believe on him should receive: for the Holy Ghost was not yet given; because that Jesus was not yet glorified. [John 7:39]

Please consider whether you have received the Holy Spirit through the healing of the real Jesus.

Baptism with Triune God

Consider Matthew.

> [18] And Jesus came and spake unto them, saying, All power is given unto me in heaven and in earth. [19] Go ye therefore, and teach all nations, baptizing them in the name of the Father, and of the Son, and of the Holy Ghost: [20] Teaching them to observe all things whatsoever I have commanded you: and, lo, I am with you alway, even unto the end of the world. Amen. [Matthew 28:18-20]

"Teach all nations, baptizing them in the name of the Father, and of the Son, and of the Holy Spirit."

Jesus gave this message to the disciples after His resurrection. Is this a commandment that we should teach all nations, saying, "I baptize you in the name of the Father, the Son, and the Holy Spirit" during the baptism with water? No. He did not mean this.

What do you think He wanted His disciples to do when He commissioned them in this way? It was for the disciples to do the things that Jesus did. What did He do for the disciples? He made them healed and born again. Therefore, what He asks His disciples to do when sending them out, is to heal all the nations and enable them to be born again. Jesus has no wish other than this.

To have them born again is expressed here as baptism in the name of the Father, the Son, and the Holy Spirit. The Father, the Son, and the Holy Spirit are not simply an arrangement of words.

As we have seen above, they are the triune God, which is revealed to us as our faith grows progressively. That is, the Father (the period of God), the Son (the period of Jesus), and the Holy Spirit (the period of Holy Spirit). He who has passed through this process will receive the Holy Spirit and will become born again. So Jesus sent out the disciples and commanded them to have all nations go through this progress and be born again.

Furthermore, baptism means baptism by complete immersion. A man can go over to the next stage when he has completely finished the current one, so it sensible to say that the baptism means a complete immersion, not sprinkling water. He has to pay the very last mite to go over to the next stage.

Now God desires to fulfill in us the thing He has done to the disciples through Jesus. I hope you will receive the same thing gladly by meeting the real Jesus now.

Faith of the Centurion

[Matthew 8:5-13]

⁵ And when Jesus was entered into Capernaum, there came unto him a centurion, beseeching him, ⁶ And saying, Lord, my servant lieth at home sick of the palsy, grievously tormented. ⁷ And Jesus saith unto him, I will come and heal him. ⁸ The centurion answered and said, Lord, I am not worthy that thou shouldest come under my roof: but speak the word only, and my servant shall be healed. ⁹ For I am a man under authority, having soldiers under me: and I say to this man, Go, and he goeth; and to another, Come, and he cometh; and to my servant, Do this, and he doeth it. ¹⁰ When Jesus heard it, he marvelled, and said to them that followed, Verily I say unto you, I have not found so great faith, no, not in Israel. ¹¹ And I say unto you, That many shall come from the east and west, and shall sit down with Abraham, and Isaac, and Jacob, in the kingdom of heaven. ¹² But the children of the kingdom shall be cast out into outer darkness: there shall be weeping and gnashing of teeth. ¹³ And Jesus said unto the centurion, Go thy way; and as thou hast believed, so be it done unto thee. And his servant was healed in the selfsame hour.

    We have possibly heard this story, relating to the faith of a centurion, many times. A centurion was an officer in the army of ancient Rome, who was responsible for one hundred soldiers. The centurion appearing in this story is the envy of all believers since he was highly commended by Jesus because of his faith. We all wish to have good faith that might be commended by the Lord.

    However, when we start to think about what the reality of the centurion's faith is, we get lost. All we can say about him vaguely is "Look at the centurion. Jesus commended his faith. He is Roman but he is good and is on our side." We do not know why, and for what Jesus commended the centurion. If we fail to know the reality of his faith, any reference to him as a role model of faith becomes meaningless.

We often conclude that the centurion's faith was commended by Jesus because he trusted the power of Jesus totally. Specifically, he believed that his servant would be healed at His word only, while others might have believed that he would be healed only when He directly comes to him and lays His hand on him.

However, this is not the correct understanding of the centurion's faith. Also, such faith is not uncommon in the Scripture. For example, in Chapter 14 of Matthew, after having done the miracle of the five loaves and two fishes, Jesus instructed His disciples to get into a ship and go before Him to the other side. At night, He went to them walking on the sea. When the disciples were in trouble thinking it was a spirit, Peter said, "If it be You, bid me come unto You on the water." Then, Jesus said, "Come," and he came down out of the ship and walked on the water to go to Him (Mat 14:28-29).

Even though Peter sank, his faith resembled that of the centurion. That is, he had faith by which he could walk on the water when He spoke the word only to bid him walk on the water without holding him by the hand. Since Peter believed what He had said and actually walked on the water, his faith was no less than that of the centurion.

Considering the case of Peter, we can find that He commended the centurion not because he had the faith that was built by seeing many miracles of Jesus.

Furthermore, in the current passage of Matthew, He continued to say in a slightly excited tone, "Many should come from the east and west, and should sit down with Abraham, and Isaac, and Jacob in the kingdom of heaven whereas the children of the kingdom should be cast out into outer darkness." From this, we can imagine that the issue of the centurion's faith is something that influences our entering the kingdom of heaven.

What faith did the centurion have? What faith is it that will push the children of the kingdom out and enter the kingdom instead, as stated verse 12 above?

Now we will see the true nature of centurion's faith, which received the warm commendation of Jesus.

Two Things to Know in Advance

We should know the next two facts so as to understand the faith of the centurion.

First, these events took place in Capernaum, that is, this scene in which Jesus meets the centurion and has a talk with him does not simply refer to a historical story or event. It is symbolic of the spiritual world. Because of this spiritual symbolism, the historical records found in the Scripture become the word of God that remains the same forever and ever. Jesus has prepared the current scene as a means of explaining spiritual things to us. This scene reveals a hidden spiritual truth.

Secondly, the Scripture tells us that faith will come to us through the process of the revelation of the triune God to an individual believer. We should meet Jesus in our life, go through the healing process for a certain period of time, and receive the Holy Spirit who comes into us to be one with us. Jesus will come around us first, and when Jesus completes the building of His mansion within us, then He will come into us as the Holy Spirit. He on whom the Holy Spirit has come is already in the kingdom of God, and the kingdom is in him.

God-Jesus-Holy Spirit, this is the progressive process that we should go through one by one to have the sound faith of the centurion. We will now approach the current topic with these basic understandings.

I Am Not Worthy

[Matthew 8:5-8] ⁵ And when Jesus was entered into Capernaum, there came unto him a centurion, beseeching him, ⁶ And saying, Lord, my servant lieth at home sick of the palsy, grievously tormented. ⁷ And Jesus saith unto him, I will come and heal him. ⁸ The centurion answered and said, Lord, I am not worthy that thou shouldest come under my roof: but speak the word only, and my servant shall be healed.

As I said, the event and dialog happening in this situation symbolize spiritual aspects. Therefore, if you think from the centurion's saying, "I am not worthy that you should come under my roof, but speak the word only" that he was a very humble man who took His direct visit as an honor he was not worthy of, you have missed the point. This passage of the Scripture does not intend to teach us the humility of the world.

🗁 Knowledge We should Have

The roof or house here represents the centurion himself. When He said He would come under his roof, it signifies that He would come into him, the centurion. If we had been him, we would have said, "Wow, it's great to have You home! Yes, please come." We would have been very wholehearted, and would say, "I don't care whether it is Jesus or the Holy Spirit who will come to me. I'll welcome Him. Is the word of truth so difficult to understand? Would not that be all we needed to do just to believe in Him? I will believe. Give me faith. I'm fully ready to receive them all."

We often gather together in the church, fast and pray to wait for the coming of Jesus, saying, "Amen. Come, Lord Jesus!" You must have been leading a Christian life like this for a long time, and were you successful? I am afraid not. There is no reason why you should have been.

An old Korean proverb says, "It is no use tying a thread on the middle part of the needle." None of you will ever do needlework if you tie the thread on the middle part of the needle, no matter how sincere you are in doing so; not in ten thousand years. It is meaningless to say, "I made every effort and did my best for a lengthy period of time." If you want to do needlework correctly, you should first understand that "One should do needlework after he passes a thread through the eye of the needle." Jesus wants to reveal to us this truth in believing Jesus. Jesus in the flesh should come first and after healing us, then the Holy Spirit, that is, Jesus in the form of the unseen word. Jesus cannot be received into us even if we want Him immediately. It requires a series of steps or a process.

However, we do not want to acknowledge this. As we do not wish to be healed by Jesus (Mat 13:15), we try to do the works of self-righteousness instead. That is, however, like one trying to do needlework while binding the thread on the middle part of the needle.

People Lacking in Knowledge

The Israelites, for example, ignored this process but they thought it would be okay if only they did their best and worked hard for God. They had zeal of God but not according to knowledge. Read the following verses from Romans.

> ² For I bear them record that they have a zeal of God, but not according to knowledge. ³ For they being ignorant of God's righteousness, and going about to establish their own righteousness, have not submitted themselves unto the righteousness of God. [Romans 10:2-3]

Do you have knowledge about how the faith of Jesus comes to us? Have you realized the way to reach the kingdom of God? If not, all your zeal and efforts will prove useless; no matter how hard and how long you try. Read Hosea.

> My people are destroyed for lack of knowledge: because thou hast rejected knowledge, I will also reject thee, that thou shalt be no priest to me: seeing thou hast forgotten the law of thy God, I will also forget thy children. [Hosea 4:6]

Knowledge is a serious matter that relates to whether we are destroyed, whether God will reject us, or whether God will forget us. It also relates to whether we are cast out of the heaven or not, because Jesus said that the children of the kingdom without knowledge would be cast out. Nobody can enter the kingdom of heaven if he has no knowledge of the way to the kingdom.

📂 I Am Not Worthy

The centurion accurately knew how Jesus could be received in him. He knew it better than anyone else that He could not directly come to him no matter how urgently he wanted Him. So when He said that He would directly come into him, he answered that he was not worthy that He should come immediately. As I said, the Scripture does not mean to point out the humility of the centurion. But it intends to show that he knew the way of truth. Surely, the centurion knew the true way in which Jesus comes.

Now, I will explain what was meant when he said "I am not worthy." When we meet Jesus in our life, He cannot immediately come into us to be one with us. We need a time of healing through Jesus in order for Him to be received as one in us. This time of spiritual healing represents the period in which we are not worthy that He should come under our roof. When the time of healing has been finished, we are worthy that He should be received in us, and at this time, He comes on us as the Holy Spirit.

Regarding the case of the disciples, when they first met Jesus even though they forsook all and followed Him, He could not immediately come into their bodies to be one with them. They needed a time of healing; said to be the three and a half years. During this time frame, they were not worthy that they should receive Him in them. However, after the process of healing had been finished, they became worthy of receiving Him, and so He was received in them as one. That is, He comes on them as the Holy Spirit. In the idiom of the story of the centurion, He entered the house of the disciples as the 'word.'

The centurion had fully understood the process in which Jesus comes on a man and He is then received in him as one. Jesus tells him having knowledge of the right way of faith: "As you have believed, so be it done unto you."

Do you know the process in which faith comes to you as he did? If so, it will be done to you just as you believed it would. Of course, the knowledge of the Scripture that we are talking about here is not merely 'head' knowledge, but it is the knowledge that our whole life would move according to it.

For instance, during healing by Jesus if we stand firm to the end without giving up, then it means that we have a sound knowledge of the process. If we do not stand firm through that process, then it will prove that we do not fully understand the process.

Who is the Servant of the Centurion?

> [Matthew 8:9] For I am a man under authority, having soldiers under me: and I say to this man, Go, and he goeth; and to another, Come, and he cometh; and to my servant, Do this, and he doeth it.

The centurion wanted to have his servant healed of the palsy. The servant is also a symbol of spiritual reality. Now, let us see what the servant with palsy symbolizes.

📂 Human Being Made up of Two Parts

To understand this, we should first know that the human being is composed of two parts: the body that contacts the material world, which is seen, and the soul that cannot be seen. The visible body and the invisible soul are combined to form a person. In fact, a human being consists of spirit, soul, and body (1Th 5:23), the triune attribute of man. Since the spirit and the soul that cannot be seen can be combined into one, we can divide the human being into two parts as I said. Consider Matthew and James.

> And fear not them which kill the body (*soma* in Greek), but are not able to kill the soul (*psuche* in Greek): but rather fear him which is able to destroy both soul and body in hell. [Matthew 10:28]

> For as the body (*soma* in Greek) without the spirit (*pneuma* in Greek) is dead, so faith without works is dead also. [James 2:26]

In general, in Greek the spirit is *pneuma*, the soul is *psuche*, and the body is *soma*. However, the 'spirit and the soul' are considered as one sometimes in the Scripture, and are called either the soul *(psuche)* or the spirit *(pneuma)* as the case may be. So each person is composed of the 'spirit and soul' that cannot be seen and the 'body' that can be seen.

The soul which is unseen controls the body which is seen.

🗁 The Soul is Commander of the Body

We are wearing clothes. If we wear clothes, the clothes follow us as we move. The clothes cannot move by themselves, but they are moved by the body. It is similar to the relationship between our soul and body. The body corresponds to the clothes of the soul in the above analogy and does not act nor move by itself, but moves according to the commands of the soul.

The body of a living man moves. Imagine that a man has just died. The body that the soul has left cannot move. Based on this, we know that the body is not capable of movement without the soul. The body can be active only with the soul in place, and the soul activates the body. The Greek *soma* meaning the 'body' is usable for the dead body as well as the living body. See the following cases:

> Then took they the body (*soma*) of Jesus, and wound it in linen clothes with the spices, as the manner of the Jews is to bury. [John 19:40]

> But Peter put them all forth, and kneeled down, and prayed; and turning him to the body (*soma*) said, Tabitha, arise. And she opened her eyes: and when she saw Peter, she sat up. [Acts 9:40]

As we know, the body has no vitality without the soul.

The passage of Scripture below describes the scene in which Jesus resurrects the 12-year-old daughter of the ruler of the synagogue. Consider Luke.

⁵³ And they laughed him to scorn, knowing that she was dead. ⁵⁴ And he put them all out, and took her by the hand, and called, saying, Maid, arise. ⁵⁵ And her spirit (*pneuma*) came again, and she arose straightway: and he commanded to give her meat. [Luke 8:53-55]

When her spirit left her, the body died and could not move. However, when the spirit came again, the body became alive and began to move again. We find that the thing that makes her alive again and enables her body to move is her soul/spirit.

Our beings consist of the soul and the body, and the soul controls the body. Many people think that if they die, that is the end of the story. However, this is definitely not true. The source of life is not in the seen, material world, but rather in the unseen spiritual world. Not many people understand this.

▱ Servant and His Paralysis

Shall we return to the case of the centurion with this basic understanding? The centurion says to Jesus "I am a man under authority, having soldiers under me: and I say to this man, Go, and he goes; and to another, Come, and he comes; and to my servant, Do this, and he does it."

Now, we can understand the spiritual meaning of what he said. He talks about the relation between the soul and the body through the example of the officer and the servant, and the master and the servant. In other words, the body is the follower and the servant of the soul, and so when the soul gives a command, the body follows.

Why did he say this? I mean, why did he mention that the body is the servant of the soul in connection with receiving Jesus into his house? In fact, what he said reveals a deep truth.

The Scripture compares the sinner to the sick and mentions various diseases such as palsy, leprosy, physical handicaps, blindness and deafness. The servant of the centurion indicates his body, and the fact that the servant is sick of the palsy signifies that the body serves the soul that has sin and thus the body commits sins. The centurion knows that he himself sins because he is born a sinner. And he knows that his body will be naturally healed, that is, stop sinning, when his soul is healed by Jesus.

Read Romans.

> Neither yield ye your members as instruments of unrighteousness unto sin: but yield yourselves unto God, as those that are alive from the dead, and your members as instruments of righteousness unto God. [Romans 6:13]

The above passage has the same logical connection as the story of the centurion and his servant. If a man has a sinful soul, his members (i.e., body) become instruments of unrighteousness, and when his soul is healed to be one with God, his members will be changed to instruments of righteousness. The same members will be either the instruments of unrighteousness or the instruments of righteousness depending on the state of the soul. The members are servants of the soul. Therefore, the soul should be healed so as to heal the members.

This knowledge may sound obvious at first, but it requires a long period of hard experience under the law in order to realize this. Dependence on the law represents human attempts to control bodily members by suppressing or encouraging certain deeds. After having realized that the dependence on the law produces no fruit, we can then speak as he did.

As You Has Believed, So Be it Done unto You

> [Matthew 8:10] When Jesus heard it, he marvelled, and said to them that followed, Verily I say unto you, I have not found so great faith, no, not in Israel.

We can imagine from what the centurion said that he realized that he was a sinner and he knew how to be free from sin. His statement of "I am not worthy that you should come under my roof" signifies that he had an accurate idea of how He will come to him. Further, he clearly understood that his sin would be perfectly forgiven when Jesus corrected his soul.

Upon hearing it, Jesus said "I have not found so great faith, no, not in Israel." When Jesus comes on us as the Holy Spirit, it means that we receive faith. The Holy Spirit whom we receive through Jesus is faith itself. Faith comes to us not by man's hope or effort but by the grace of Jesus. Faith does not come to us even if we try to believe, and the Holy Spirit does not come to us if we seriously seek baptism in the Holy Spirit.

Jesus will bring faith to those who followed Him through the process. To the centurion knowing all these things and hoping for the same, Jesus says, "Go thy way; and as thou hast believed, so be it done unto thee" (Mat 8:13). If we also have clearly understood through what process Jesus comes into us and forgives our sin, we already have the same knowledge of faith as the centurion. It will be done to us as we have believed, i.e., we will receive the faith of Jesus.

Works of Jesus, Hidden Completely

In fact, up to the current dialog between Jesus and the centurion, the reason why He came to the world was completely hidden. The centurion says to Jesus "I am not worthy that you should come under my roof: but speak the word only," and he continues that he has soldiers and when he issues a command, they follow him.

Because of usage of the word 'soldiers,' his saying 'speak the word only' may be apt to be interpreted as that if Jesus gives an order by 'word,' the palsy will obey Him. It would seem that there is no other interpretation of this statement. However, as described, what it means is that, when Jesus heals the centurion and He is then received by him as the 'word (i.e., Holy Spirit),' his soul will be healed and his sinful body will stop sinning and be forgiven.

Let us think carefully. Did Jesus come to heal our bodies or save our soul? It is natural that He came to the world to save our souls. So it would be a misunderstanding if we simply think of Jesus as the man of power who heals the palsy only by speaking. God does have such power. So there is no reason for Jesus to come into the world to carry out such miracles in place of God.

You have rightly understood this passage only when you can

find the very Jesus who has come to save souls and forgive you of your sins.

Children of the Kingdom into Outer Darkness

> [Matthew 8:11-13] [11] And I say unto you, That many shall come from the east and west, and shall sit down with Abraham, and Isaac, and Jacob, in the kingdom of heaven. [12] But the children of the kingdom shall be cast out into outer darkness: there shall be weeping and gnashing of teeth. [13] And Jesus said unto the centurion, Go thy way; and as thou hast believed, so be it done unto thee. And his servant was healed in the selfsame hour.

There are many people who are eager to believe in Jesus but do not know how. Few people among them have the knowledge of faith as the centurion has.

When you, the believer, get to know the faith of the centurion, it is not right that you simply commend his faith and think no further. Because Jesus is now saying that you cannot go into the kingdom if you do not have the faith and knowledge of the centurion.

The children of the kingdom represent the Israelites who first received the word of God. Concurrently, the believers in Jesus are included in this definition of the children of the kingdom. We, the believers, received the word of God first but, in contrast to the centurion, do not interpret and understand the word correctly. We worked hard at *achieving* the kingdom and God's blessing. However, this is based on our own understanding and knowledge, which, in turn, is based on misinterpretation of the Scripture. This is quite evident when we think about the centurion and his sound knowledge of the faith.

If we believe in Jesus in our own way, we will not be able to enter the kingdom. Since we cannot go into it, we are not saved, and since we are not saved, we are living in outer darkness. God does not cast us out, but we are still living in a place of outer darkness in our current situation. We will weep and gnash our teeth in frustration and disappointment at our fruitless efforts.

📂 Qualification for the Kingdom

The natural descendants of Abraham, Isaac, and Jacob are the Jews, but the three characters appearing in the Scripture are the symbols of those who have faith. In fact, spiritually, the sequence of 'Abraham-Isaac-Jacob,' which can also be expressed as 'God-Jesus-Holy Spirit,' reflect the steps for growing in faith.

This sequence corresponds to 'Called-Justified-Glorified' as is said in Romans 8:30: "Moreover whom he did predestine, them he also called: and whom he called, them he also justified: and whom he justified, them he also glorified." So when we complete this process, we will be glorified, as in the case of the centurion.

Therefore, if the Jews do not have the faith of Abraham, Isaac, and Jacob although they are regarded as their natural descendants, they have no spiritual connection with them. From a spiritual perspective, the centurion shows the faith of, Abraham, Isaac, and Jacob but their natural descendents, the Jews, do not. The man who acts in faith as Abraham did will be actually called a descendant of Abraham.

Read John.

[37] I know that ye are Abraham's seed; but ye seek to kill me, because my word hath no place in you. [38] I speak that which I have seen with my Father: and ye do that which ye have seen with your father. [39] They answered and said unto him, Abraham is our father. Jesus saith unto them, If ye were Abraham's children, ye would do the works of Abraham. [40] But now ye seek to kill me, a man that hath told you the truth, which I have heard of God: this did not Abraham. [John 8:37-40]

Jesus admits that the Jews are the natural descendants of Abraham, but the Scripture says that the spiritual descendants of Abraham are his 'true' descendants. The spiritual descendant who will go into the kingdom and abide with Abraham is symbolized or represented by the centurion in the current passage. We, therefore, should be the centurion to enter the kingdom.

How did the centurion who was a heathen become accepted as a descendant of Abraham and go into the kingdom? It has already been described. He understood correctly the way to the kingdom, but the Jews had no idea. The centurion naturally enters the kingdom and if the Jews continue to follow misguided doctrine, then they will finally fail to get there. Here, the Jews represent the believers, and we might be one of them.

Jesus said to the centurion, "Go thy way; and as thou hast believed, so be it done unto thee." And his servant was healed in the selfsame hour. The centurion symbolizes the man whose sins are forgiven by Jesus and who has gone into the kingdom.

Disciples vs. Centurion

Some might query that if the centurion's faith was so great, then how about the faith of the disciples who were actually following Jesus. Should not their faith be better than that of the centurion?

Jesus revealed the way to faith by means of the story of centurion. So when He highly commended the faith of the centurion, He wanted to demonstrate to us the correct way to come to faith. As for the disciples, they were those who were actually on the right track. In the end, the disciples would become men who received Jesus as the Word at Pentecost. And this was foreshadowed in the story of the centurion. In short, the centurion's case is taken as the sign of the correct faith, and the disciples' case is the reality of progress to the correct faith.

Epilogue

To conclude, faith comes to us in the order of 'Jesus' and then, the 'Holy Spirit.' We need to understand this properly. Then, it will be done to us as we have believed, and we will be forgiven our sins perfectly.

I pray we all meet the real Jesus and be healed to receive Him in us as the 'word.' Thus, we activate all the glory and promises that God has given to us. Amen.

Unjust Judge and Widow

[Luke 18:1-8]

¹ And he spake a parable unto them to this end, that men ought always to pray, and not to faint; ² Saying, There was in a city a judge, which feared not God, neither regarded man: ³ And there was a widow in that city; and she came unto him, saying, Avenge me of mine adversary. ⁴ And he would not for a while: but afterward he said within himself, Though I fear not God, nor regard man; ⁵ Yet because this widow troubleth me, I will avenge her, lest by her continual coming she weary me. ⁶ And the Lord said, Hear what the unjust judge saith. ⁷ And shall not God avenge his own elect, which cry day and night unto him, though he bear long with them? ⁸ I tell you that he will avenge them speedily. Nevertheless when the Son of man cometh, shall he find faith on the earth?

What matters to us in believing in Jesus is to pray and bear our suffering and not to lose heart. This endurance looks trivial but it is the motive force to fulfill our faith. Without it, we can neither receive faith nor enter the kingdom of God.

This parable gives us the message that during the course of our 'old man' being destroyed, we should have patience and endure without being weary or faint no matter how hard the journey is.

Some people misunderstand what this parable teaches and conclude that it is telling us that we should pray to God with persistence. So they say that we must pray with tenacity as the widow did, and that we ought to keep on praying to Him even if He does not appear to hear our prayers. Of course, He does sometimes grant prayers offered with persistence. However, it is not because of the persistent demands that the prayers are granted but because He had other reasons to answer their prayers.

This parable does not teach us to continue to pray to God with persistence. It tells us what we should do while the 'old man' is being destroyed on the cross in the process of growing in faith.

Now, let us get started.

Who is the Judge?

> [Luke 18:1-3] ¹ And he spake a parable unto them to this end, that men ought always to pray, and not to faint; ² Saying, There was in a city a judge, which feared not God, neither regarded man: ³ And there was a widow in that city; and she came unto him, saying, Avenge me of mine adversary.

The city represents the world we are living in. The judge is Jesus Christ. It is appropriate to define the judge as Him because God gave Him power to judge the living and the dead. However, we do not like to interpret the parable in this way, because the judge is described as the one who is lacking in common sense, and does not fear God or hold man in high regard. In addition, Jesus calls him an unjust judge and so we reject the interpretation that the judge is Jesus Christ. Nevertheless, this is the expression of the truth, which is very exquisite, wise and valuable and is contrary to common sense.

📂 A Judge who Feared Not God

The judge is portrayed as he who does not fear God, but it does not mean that he pays no attention to God and looks down on Him. 'Fear' is *phobeo* (verb) and *phobos* (noun) in Greek, which is interpreted into two ways.

One is 'to reverence.'

We should fear God in this sense. Consider Romans 3:18: "There is no fear of God before their eyes," and 2 Peter 2:17: "Honour all [men]. Love the brotherhood. Fear God. Honour the king."

The other meaning is 'to be afraid of.'

The judge does not fear God because God is His father who loves Him. Paul says in Romans 8:15: "For ye have not received the spirit of bondage again to fear; but ye have received the Spirit of adoption, whereby we cry, Abba, Father."

If you fear God, it proves that, even if you believe, you are still under the law, having a spirit of bondage. On the contrary, if you are able to call God father because of being born again of Him, you no longer know Him as the One to Fear. He is the father of love who understands you and cares for you. You are sons of God.

Jesus instructed His disciple not to fear Him. Read Matthew 14:27: "But straightway Jesus spake unto them, saying, Be of good cheer; it is I; be not afraid."

If we fear God, we are not made perfect in love. Read 1 John 4:18: "There is no fear in love; but perfect love casteth out fear: because fear hath torment. He that feareth is not made perfect in love."

The wicked servant in Luke 19 feared Jesus. Read Luke 19:21: "For I feared thee, because thou art an austere man: thou takest up that thou layedst not down, and reapest that thou didst not sow."

So we should not fear Jesus and God, as Jesus does not fear God.

The Judge Who Did Not Regard Man

The judge is also depicted as he who does not respect man, but it does not signify that he despises other men. It means that he neither depends on man nor trusts in him. Read John.

> [23] Now when he was in Jerusalem at the passover, in the feast day, many believed in his name, when they saw the miracles which he did. [24] But Jesus did not commit himself unto them, because he knew all men, [25] And needed not that any should testify of man: for he knew what was in man. [John 2:23-25]

Jesus performed miracles and many people believed, but He was not convinced of the durability of their faith because He knew the fundamental nature of their mind that could vacillate at any time. We remember that Peter declared that he would not forsake Jesus with his life but in the end, he denied Jesus at His trial (Mat 26:69-75). Man's will or zeal is unreliable, unless he is born again. In this sense, Jesus does not rely on man.

Unlike Jesus, the Pharisees always regarded men. Consider Matthew.

> Take heed that ye do not your alms before men, to be seen of them: otherwise ye have no reward of your Father which is in heaven. [Matthew 6:1]

They tried to do righteousness before men, to be seen by them, and Jesus rebuked it. In this sense, we should not regard man, as Jesus did not.

Well, you will now have eliminated the concern that was caused by my assertion that the unjust judge in the parable, who neither feared God or had regard for man, was Jesus. One thing that I still need to explain is why Jesus called the judge appearing in the parable the 'unjust judge.' I will explain this later. In the mean time, I will proceed on the basis that the judge is Jesus Christ.

Who is the Widow?

The widow is defined in the dictionary as a woman whose husband had died and who had not married again. Following this interpretation of widow, we are widows to whom Jesus Christ, the true husband, has not yet come. Hence, the woman represents us who believe in Jesus.

This widow comes to the judge and troubles him to avenge her of her adversary. This symbolizes us who come to church, pray to Jesus, and trouble Him to achieve something. The judge finally decides to avenge her because of her persistent demand.

Now, we have things to think about.

Who is her adversary? The adversary does not indicate a person who did damage to her, but represents her 'old man' that is herself ruled by the devil. We all have this 'old man' in us. The spirit of this 'old man' separates her from God and controls her inclination to sin. So the 'old man' is called the adversary.

She represents, like the centurion (whose case we discussed earlier) believers who have sound spiritual knowledge about salvation, and she has begged Jesus Christ to avenge her of this adversary.

First, she knew that she was separated from God to remain as a sinner because of the 'old man' in her, who is the root cause of sin. So she wanted to have him destroyed.

Many people believe in Jesus, worship God, pray to Him, and participate in church activities unaware of the 'old man' that continues to live in them. Such belief and church activities will be meaningful only when they come to the realization that he should be destroyed first. Because, we can never be set free from sin as long as the 'old man' in us is alive, which is, in fact, sin itself.

Secondly, she knew accurately who Jesus was. She knew that nobody, except Jesus, could destroy her 'old man,' the adversary inside her. So she prayed to Jesus in this regard.

Unlike this widow, we are praying to Jesus to get possessions and health or something similar in this world. This is not so bad, as long as they are sought in conjunction with the laying down of 'old man,' the first priority in following Jesus. Unfortunately, however, most of us do not know who the 'old man' is.

The widow is symbolic of believers who had believed under the law, but now met Jesus through true repentance. She is now beseeching Jesus to have the 'old man,' her adversary, crucified so that she can be born again. She knew the real Jesus and sought the real thing from Him.

Consequently, she received what she wanted from Him. Not because she paid visits and troubled the judge day and night, but because she asked him to hold a trial which was his duty and avenge her of her adversary. In this way she could get what she was hoping for. She asked the judge for the right thing.

▷ What are We Seeking Now?

Do you know Jesus as she does? What are you seeking from the judge?

Is it food to eat? Money to pay the rent? Or, some spiritual gifts to revive the church and do missionary work? Or, do you seek judgment on your 'old man' as the widow did?

Jesus has come to judge our 'old man' and give the kingdom of God to us. So if we pray in this manner, we are seeking the right thing from the right person. Read Matthew.

> ³¹ Therefore take no thought, saying, What shall we eat? or, What shall we drink? or, Wherewithal shall we be clothed?
> ³³ But seek ye first the kingdom of God, and his righteousness; and all these things shall be added unto you. [Matthew 6:31 & 33]

Seeking to avenge herself against her adversary in the case of the widow is symbolic of her journey of faith seeking the kingdom of God and his righteousness. This is the only prayer that we need to pray as believers. When we pray as such, the kingdom of God and his righteousness shall come to us, as we prayed the right thing to the right person.

The widow is such a believer.

He Would Not, For A While

> [Luke 18:4-5] ⁴ And he would not for a while: but afterward he said within himself, Though I fear not God, nor regard man; ⁵ Yet because this widow troubleth me, I will avenge her, lest by her continual coming she weary me.

For what reason did he refuse to avenge her for a while? It is because she is unworthy of being avenged immediately. So a predetermined time was needed for her.

We generally think that if we believe in Jesus, He will immediately receive us. This is not true. We need a predetermined period of time until He can be received in us. In this sense, the centurion that we saw in the previous section said, "I am not worthy that you should come into my house" when Jesus said, "I will come" (Mat 8:7-8).

During this time period, He lays down our 'old man' on the cross, and then we are changed to be able to receive Jesus as Christ in us. Superficially, He looks like He is not listening to our prayer during this time, but this time period is required to destroy the 'old man' as a life and faith growing process.

The disciples, for example, followed Jesus, but He was not received by them immediately. In three and a half years' time, He is received in them as the Holy Spirit. If we describe this according to the parable's expression, it would be like this: He would not hear the disciples' prayer to avenge their adversaries for three and a half years. This 'three and a half years' corresponds to the period of 'for a while' in the parable.

🗁 Period Always to Pray and Not to Faint

The period of time when she was required to pray continuously and not to faint was the period of 'for a while' during which the judge would not grant her wish. Spiritually, this period covers the time span from the time when you meet Jesus in your life and follow Him to the time when your 'old man' is crucified, being united with Jesus. It corresponds to the stage of the Synoptic Gospels in steps for growing in faith. For these steps, please refer to the 'Fresh Eyes to Read the Bible - Book 1.'

Why did He say you ought to pray and not faint during this period? During this period, your 'old man' is exposed and destroyed, and you suffer painful experiences. Think about the case of Peter when he was severely rebuked by Jesus, saying, "Get behind me, Satan!" When you are rebuked by Him, you will feel a severe and intense pain in your heart. Only those who have undergone such rebukes will understand what it is. Furthermore, you do not experience a single rebuke but rather a whole series of rebukes as you are healed during this process.

You may have similar experiences as he did, which may be stronger or weaker depending on your specific case, and you *must endure and not faint*. If not, you will not be able to receive faith and you will not be saved. You must always pray and not faint in this time, and the parable is given to show this.

He will Avenge Them Speedily

> [Luke 18:6-8] ⁶ And the Lord said, Hear what the unjust judge saith. ⁷ And shall not God avenge his own elect, which cry day and night unto him, though he bear long with them? ⁸ I tell you that he will avenge them speedily. Nevertheless when the Son of man cometh, shall he find faith on the earth?

If you do not know the course of salvation, you can never follow Jesus who leads you. For example, if you do not know that you must go through the cross, being led by Jesus to salvation, when Jesus actually brings you there, you will figuratively curse and stone Him, thinking that He is trying to kill you. This is what actually happened to the case of the Jews.

However, He will speedily save you if you know the way of salvation and so endure, pray and not faint. Having a good look at us who endure and pray while our 'old man' is being destroyed, Jesus says to Himself, "I will avenge them speedily. If not, they will stare fully at me and wait for me until I avenge them of their adversary."

He will surely do this speedily. Many believers do not even know from what they should be saved. All of us, with no exception, should be saved from the adversary, which is sin, in each of us.

📁 The Unjust Judge — Was He Really Unjust?

I interpreted the judge as Jesus Christ in the current parable, and Jesus calls him the 'unjust judge.' This was difficult to understand. Now I will explain.

Apparently, the judge was unjust because he delayed her trial. It is his duty to deliver justice as soon as he receives the case in order that justice is served. But he delayed. From this perspective, He seems to be unjust. However, the delay of the trial was inevitable in order to 'lay down' or destroy the 'old man' and to give the widow new life. Therefore, the delay was actually just and good, not unjust.

Sure enough, the unjust judge appearing in the parable is Jesus

Christ.

📂 His Own Elect

Verse 7 reads:

"And shall not God avenge his own elect, which cry day and night unto him, though he bear long with them?"

Here above, 'elect' is *eklektos* in Greek. The widow is 'elect' while she is praying and is not fainting, because she will be avenged and saved at the end. If she stops praying and gives up, naturally she cannot be 'elect.' She is 'elect' on condition that she always prays and does not give up.

Read Matthew 22:14: "For many are called, but few are chosen." Here, 'chosen' is *eklektos* in Greek same as 'elect.' The widow is 'chosen' as long as she prays always and does not give up. If she gives up, then she is 'called, but not chosen.'

The believer who knows the way to salvation prays always and, just like the widow, does not faint. He will surely be God's elect. He will avenge them speedily and save them. However, those who know the way to salvation, but do not pray always and faint during the course of their trials, are described as, "called but not chosen."

We should stay awake and alert because many are called but few are chosen.

📂 When the Son of Man Comes, Shall He Find Faith?

"When the Son of man cometh, shall he find faith on the earth?"

Jesus connects the time when He will avenge them to the time when He comes again. In this instance, the earth represents us, and the time 'when the Son of man comes' indicates the point of time when He comes into us again as the Holy Spirit. This time will be the judgment day that the widow has been eagerly expecting for so long. After this day is passed, she will serve Jesus Christ as her husband and will live with Him forever.

Jesus wants to avenge us speedily and come into us. However, if He does it quickly without thinking our readiness, we cannot take

Him. So He will gradually destroy our 'old man' over the time of 'for a while.' From this, we also know that the judge delayed giving her justice not because he was lazy but because the widow was not ready.

His word "When the Son of man cometh, shall he find faith on the earth?" signifies that the Son of man strongly desires to come, but He cannot, because we, the earth, are not ready to receive Him. At first, Jesus is working around the earth, which is us, for the period of 'for a while' to build a mansion in which He can live. When this is finished, the Son of man comes.

He has other names like, Faith, the Word, the Holy Spirit, Jesus, Jesus Christ, Christ, Christ Jesus and so forth. Therefore, when the Son of man comes, Jesus can see Faith, Jesus Himself, in us. If the Son of man has not yet come, it means that Jesus cannot yet see Faith in us. Let Him see Himself in us. Read Galatians 4:19: "My little children, of whom I travail in birth again until Christ be formed in you."

Christ in us is the sign of our faith, salvation, the kingdom of God, eternal life and being born again.

Epilogue

Our 'old man' is exposed while we meet the real Jesus and follow Him. During this period, we might feel pain, but we ought always to pray and endure without losing hope. Let us have patience and perseverance in this period, and therefore receive Jesus Christ in us.

*Daybreak Prayer and A Traffic Accident**

Some time ago I was knocked down by a motorcycle and broke my left ankle. I had to spend three months in hospital.

One very cold day in December, I was crossing the road to go to daybreak prayer in the church, and I was hit by a motorcycle delivering newspapers. I can't remember exactly what happened. What I do remember was that I wore a muffler around my neck for my journey to the church, and after the accident I regained consciousness hearing a faint buzz of people in the hospital.

As I was told later, it was a misty day, and when I tried to cross the road, a motorcycle came towards me at a high speed. Seeing it, I may have hesitated before crossing the road, fearing that I may be hit. However, instead of waiting for the motorcycle to pass, I may have thought it safe to hurry across and I was hit. The motorcycle driver later said that he did not think that I would cross the road when he saw me hesitate.

Anyway, after the accident, I had many thoughts in hospital. I questioned:

"If God is alive, how can I meet with an accident while going to church for daybreak prayers?"

Before my accident, I had heard that a family, returning home after daybreak prayer, had driven off the Han River bridge and all of them had died. I was very shocked by the news at the time.

"Is God really alive? Is it true?"

I felt really confused since I had had a similar accident while my question had not been answered.

I will now describe my case in further detail so that I may share how God worked in and for me. On December 12, I finished my business trip abroad, and took a night flight back home. I arrived home at about 8 am, I did not go to the office, but slept all day. That evening, while still drowsy, I heard my wife talking with my sister over the phone.

In those days, my wife was running a gift shop, and she was the leader of a bible study group.

However, it seemed that she was having difficulties with leading the Bible study group. Over the phone, she was complaining severely to my sister about the pastor of the Bible study group.

"It's very hard to serve as a cell leader. The pastor knows I have a full-time job, but tells me to gather cell members with only one-day's notice. The pastor causes me inconvenience. Surely, I am going to stop serving as a cell leader next year" and *et cetera.*

She criticized the pastor and made a resolution to quit. I guessed she was very upset and angry, and she talked over this issue for thirty to forty minutes. Half asleep, I thought, "She must somehow have a reason to say so" and then I fell asleep again. The next morning, I had the accident.

I was transferred to a bigger hospital and had an operation. I prayed to God in tongues while I was moved to a theatre for a bone connecting operation. In the operating room, the doctor asked the other interns.

"What language is he speaking now?"

It seemed that he heard it for the first time. I heard then "Quiet please," and stopped it. Soon afterwards, I was anesthetized. When I was transferred to the ward after the operation, I found four small holes drilled in the bone of my leg with protruding metal supports to stabilize my broken bones. The bones would take about three months to knit and heal. I had to remain in hospital for this period.

I knew that my accident was connected to my wife's complaint concerning the pastor of the Bible study group. She also realized this accident happened because of her complaints of the previous evening. Through this accident, God said many things to us.

First, He connected the complaint she had made the previous day to the accident so that we would realize that He is the living God.

Second, He was pleased with the Bible study group, which may have seemed a mere trifle to men.

Third, He gave a message to my wife, "Do you think it is so annoying for you to have one or two days off because you serve as a cell leader? Look, if God does not protect you, one of your family may be injured and you may not be able to work for one or two months, instead of one or two days." Actually, she could not manage her shop for a long time because of being needed to nurse in the hospital.

Fourth, the person who judges the servant of the Lord cannot please Him. A few days later, she received the word from God, Chapter 12 in Numbers. It was the story of Miriam and Aaron who spoke against Moses and then Miriam became leprous.

I had to stay in the hospital, restricted by my broken leg, sometimes shedding tears. I could endure this because He comforted me each time I lost heart. By His help, I could receive my full salary for the three months, and my office paid the hospital expenses.

My acquaintances having heard about my accident were all disappointed with God. This was because, at that time, I used to admonish my relatives regularly and tell them to come to church. My accident would have driven them to think that it would be useless to believe in such a savior as Jesus and take Him seriously. They would have thought in their mind as follows:

"If the God Mr. Chung believes in is a real God, could He not have protected him from that accident? Now I'm sure his God can't be true."

They would not come to church again, which they were, at the time, doing reluctantly. However, this cannot be helped. One of my friends who visited me in the hospital said to me.

"Hey, you told me you met God, but didn't He tell you in advance how to escape the accident?"

I talked to myself, "Why did this guy visit me? Another one of them asked me by saying,

"Ah, you are very serious about church, aren't you? I know now that you even go to daybreak prayers!"

Their visits seemed to cut me to the quick. If I had had an accident on the way to a bar instead of going to church, it would have been a good lesson for them. So I asked God,

"Lord! Why did you allow me to meet with an accident while I was on the way to daybreak prayer of all times? Why did you not allow it while I was heading for bad things? In that case, it would be a good lessen to everybody."

He answered me by saying, "You'll know later." His reply meant that He had allowed the accident to happen to me to fulfill His purpose.

Also, what I learnt later was this:

Even though I had broken my leg while going to church, I kept on telling people around me to believe in Jesus. The profound thing about this is; believing in Jesus is something I cannot give up even if I had broken my leg. If I can abandon believing in Him since my leg is broken, my faith is nothing special. However, if a man although having had his leg broken continues to preach Him, he naturally says that God is far more important and precious than his physical injury. So I spoke to my neighbors like this:

"I had my left leg broken while I was going to church to pray to Jesus early in the morning. However, I still urge you to believe in Jesus. It is because He is something so precious to me that I cannot give up in spite of such an accident."

My power and authority was doubled when I told them of my experience. They may wonder:

"What is Jesus? Why does this guy not give up but keep on believing in Him even though he had his leg broken?"

They who listened to me had a chance to think deeply about Him. God supported my word with double power by allowing me to experience such an accident on my way to church.

Furthermore, I thought of God who always gives believers only good things such as, good health, riches, winnings, long life, glories in this world and so forth. But I realized that even if He does not, He is a God of love.

In fact, He will give us eternal life by means of all these things happening to us. God may cause the weak in faith to return to Him through an accident on their way to the bar, but He may let the strong in faith know more about God by an accident on their way to church. Thus, the unexpected accidents or disasters cannot always be construed as the punishment of God.

These are the reasons why He allowed me to meet with a traffic accident on my way to attend daybreak prayer.

On the other hand, up until that time, my wife was terribly afraid of my quitting my job to become a pastor. Because she could see that many pastors were as poor as church mice. However, after this accident she hung up a white flag in surrender to God, raising no further objections to my becoming a pastor. Thus, He prepared my way.

Praise the Lord!

A Certain Nobleman and Ten Minas

[Luke 19:11-27]

[11] And as they heard these things, he added and spake a parable, because he was nigh to Jerusalem, and because they thought that the kingdom of God should immediately appear. [12] He said therefore, A certain nobleman went into a far country to receive for himself a kingdom, and to return. [13] And he called his ten servants, and delivered them ten pounds, and said unto them, Occupy till I come. [14] But his citizens hated him, and sent a message after him, saying, We will not have this man to reign over us. [15] And it came to pass, that when he was returned, having received the kingdom, then he commanded these servants to be called unto him, to whom he had given the money, that he might know how much every man had gained by trading. [16] Then came the first, saying, Lord, thy pound hath gained ten pounds. [17] And he said unto him, Well, thou good servant: because thou hast been faithful in a very little, have thou authority over ten cities. [18] And the second came, saying, Lord, thy pound hath gained five pounds. [19] And he said likewise to him, Be thou also over five cities. [20] And another came, saying, Lord, behold, here is thy pound, which I have kept laid up in a napkin: [21] For I feared thee, because thou art an austere man: thou takest up that thou layedst not down, and reapest that thou didst not sow. [22] And he saith unto him, Out of thine own mouth will I judge thee, thou wicked servant. Thou knewest that I was an austere man, taking up that I laid not down, and reaping that I did not sow: [23] Wherefore then gavest not thou my money into the bank, that at my coming I might have required mine own with usury? [24] And he said unto them that stood by, Take from him the pound, and give it to him that hath ten pounds. [25] (And they said unto him, Lord, he hath ten pounds.) [26] For I say unto you, That unto every one which hath shall be given; and from him that hath not, even that he hath shall be taken away from him. [27] But those mine enemies, which would not that I should reign over them,

bring hither, and slay them before me.

Many people have tried to interpret this parable of the *minas*, but they generally fail to clarify what it really means. Their conclusion is usually this: the nobleman is Jesus who will come in the future to judge us according to our deeds.

We tend to believe that we will go into the kingdom of God sometime in the future. However, the kingdom of God that the Scripture repeatedly describes refers to the kingdom that comes to us in this world. Furthermore, the kingdom is Jesus Christ Himself who comes into us as the Holy Spirit.

This parable will reveal that those who think the kingdom of God will come in the remote future are the wicked servants who will lose the *mina* (pound) they already have.

Let us uncover the hidden meaning of the parable.

The Kingdom of God In Us

> [Luke 19:11] And as they heard these things, he added and spake a parable, because he was nigh to Jerusalem, and because they thought that the kingdom of God should immediately appear.

Verse 11 begins by "And as they heard these things." Here, 'these things' are the word He gave to Zacchaeus, the publican in the previous verses. Read these verses of Luke.

> ⁹And Jesus said unto him, This day is salvation come to this house, forsomuch as he also is a son of Abraham. ¹⁰ For the Son of man is come to seek and to save that which was lost. [Luke 19:9-10]

This story happened when Jesus went into the house of Zacchaeus. Jesus compares His entrance into his house with salvation. When He entered his house, it signified the spiritual fact that Zacchaeus had received Him into himself. Jesus is the kingdom of God, and so to receive Him means to go into the kingdom. Accordingly, he is saved and the kingdom has come on him.

However, the Jews thought that the kingdom of God should come in front of their eyes when Jesus would arrive at Jerusalem and overcome evil with mighty power. This is the meaning of the word "they thought that the kingdom of God should immediately appear."

The kingdom of God that we have in mind is no different to that which the Jews of the past understood. We believe that Jesus will come in the clouds, put down evil in this world, and bring the kingdom of God universally. We and the Jews, imagine the same sort of kingdom of God.

As we can see in the case of Zacchaeus, the kingdom of God is a spiritual one, not a physical one that we can observe. Read the passage below:

> [20] And when he was demanded of the Pharisees, when the kingdom of God should come, he answered them and said, The kingdom of God cometh not with observation: [21] Neither shall they say, Lo here! or, lo there! for, behold, the kingdom of God is within you. [Luke 17:20-21]

Each Symbol of the Parable

> [Luke 19:12-14] [12] He said therefore, A certain nobleman went into a far country to receive for himself a kingdom, and to return. [13] And he called his ten servants, and delivered them ten pounds, and said unto them, Occupy till I come. [14] But his citizens hated him, and sent a message after him, saying, We will not have this man to reign over us.

Jesus narrates a parable to correct the prevailing view of the kingdom of God that comes on earth and that the Jews and the

Christians cling to. In this parable, four types of people appear; the servant who gained ten *minas*, the servant who gained five *minas*, the servant who kept the *mina* laid up in a napkin, and the citizens who did not want the nobleman to reign over them, and were slain.

All these people represent believers nowadays as follows:

First: The ten *minas* servant represents the believer who is really born again with the life of Jesus.

Second: The five *minas* servant represents the believer who is born again, but yet to grow in faith to become adult like the ten *minas* servant.

Third: The one *mina* servant represents the believer who thinks that he is born again, but in reality is not.

Fourth: The citizens represent the believers who are not so keen to follow Jesus, and are indifferent to Jesus even though they are said to be Christians. They are quite different from the servants who are keen and eager to follow Jesus, i.e., enthusiastic believers.

The above four types of believes will be explained further one by one.

Let us examine the servant group first. The servants are believers who regularly attend church services, participate in gatherings, study the Bible, pray, make donations, and try to care for others in the name of Jesus. They are the disciples of Jesus.

📂 *Mina* Means Life

The nobleman calls his servants, gives them each ten *minas* (pounds), and instructs them to trade until he returns. Here, I personally prefer to use the original monetary unit of *mina*. That is because the *mina*, after all, indicates spiritual things, not the corresponding value of modern currencies.

The nobleman, of course, refers to Jesus. Then, what does the *mina* delivered to the servant mean? To answer; what do we receive when we follow Him as Savior and become His servant? It is '(eternal) life,' which is the purpose of our believing in Jesus. Please note that eternal life is not that which will last forever in time, but it is the 'life of Jesus.'

When we believe in Him, eternal 'life' is given equally to each of us. This is what is being referred to by the nobleman giving *minas* to his servants in the parable. However, when we first receive '(eternal) life' (*mina*), this life is not complete and full as yet. It needs to grow to become complete 'life,' which will bring forth many lives.

In fact, when we first receive 'life,' this is the pregnant stage and it should grow to the delivery stage. Only at this delivery stage will our '(eternal) life' become complete and we will be empowered to bring forth many lives thereafter.

The difference between the ten *mina*s servant and the one *mina* servant is that the former is walking with the living Jesus after pregnancy matured into full delivery of life in Christ. However the latter is concentrating on doing various works, expecting Jesus to come in the future, and so he fails to achieve life in and through Jesus Christ.

With this basic understanding, let us try to interpret the parable. In the parable, the nobleman returns and calls the servants to whom he had given the money so that he might know how much every man had gained by trading. Please do not imagine a scene with ten servants standing in a row in front of the nobleman. This parable is applicable to each of the servants spiritually and individually.

One thing I want to explain in advance is that I will use the terms 'nobleman' and 'Jesus,' *minas* and 'life,' and 'servants' and 'believers' interchangeably. This will not affect the intended meanings in the parable.

I will now describe how this parable is applicable to us.

Ten *Minas* Servant

> [Luke 19:15-17] [15] And it came to pass, that when he was returned, having received the kingdom, then he commanded these servants to be called unto him, to whom he had given the money, that he might know how much every man had gained by trading. [16] Then came the first, saying, Lord, thy pound hath gained ten pounds. [17] And he said unto him, Well, thou good servant: because thou hast been faithful in a very little, have thou authority over ten cities.

The servant who gained ten *minas* from one *mina* ('ten *minas* servant'), is the believer who has completed the process and received (eternal) life. He can be described as follows:

"He met Jesus in his life (pregnancy: receive one *mina*), and after having lain down his 'old man' by following Jesus, he received the Holy Spirit (delivery: return of nobleman). By the Holy Spirit in him he became someone who could give life to others (gained ten *minas*). And thus the kingdom of God came to him."

The ten *minas* servant who belongs to Jesus is able to give life to others as Jesus did.

The Return of Nobleman

In the case of the ten *minas* servant, the return of nobleman to him in itself makes him the servant who can gain ten *minas*. So the nobleman commends him for the ten *minas,* allowing him or granting him ten cities.

It should read in this way: "The nobleman returns to him" means "The servant becomes the ten *minas* servant;" "The servant shows ten *minas* to the nobleman;" and "The servant receives ten cities." All these things are happening at the same time through the return of nobleman.

We can find a same situation in Luke 12.

> [42] And the Lord said, Who then is that faithful and wise steward, whom his lord shall make ruler over his household, to give them their portion of meat in due season? [43] Blessed is that servant, whom his lord when he cometh shall find so doing. [Luke 12:42-43]

When the Lord comes in him, due to the presence of the Lord in him, he becomes the faithful steward. He cannot be the faithful steward without the Lord in him basically.

In the main parable, the ten *minas* servant has the return of nobleman inside of him, which is salvation, whereas the one *mina* servant has the return outside of him, which is judgment.

🗀 Ten Cities

We traditionally think that if we believe in Jesus, we will get a superb mansion in our afterlife in heaven. However, this is a misunderstanding. Why?

To believe and to follow Jesus is to get the eternal life of Jesus, and this life will be given to us within our lifetime on earth. To expect something in the afterlife means that we did not receive the life of Jesus now. And if we do not get this life during our stay on earth, we will never be able to get it in the afterlife.

Therefore, if you hold on to doctrines that tell you that eternal life will only be given to you after you die, you are being deceived. Make sure you have eternal life from here to eternity. Why do you wish to defer it?

In the parable, the servant received ten cities. The ten cities are not given as some sort of prize. The ten cities are the ten *minas* itself that he gained. Therefore, ten cities are given to ten *minas*, not five nor eleven, but just ten. When our life becomes fruitful and multiplies, that is all there is. There can be no additional prize for being fruitful. For instance, no one will bear a child simply to win a prize! The child, the new life (*mina* in the parable) itself, is the prize if you want to call it that.

🗀 The Case of Peter Fitted into the Parable

The model of the ten *minas* servant in the Scripture also relates to Jesus' disciples. I will describe the process by which they gained ten *minas* by using Peter as an example.

Refer to the illustration of the life of Peter below:

	Meet and follow Jesus	Receive Jesus in him as Holy Spirit (Return of Nobleman)	
	Receipt of One *Mina*	One *Mina* gains Ten *Minas*	
		Cross	

	ⓛ Pregnancy	② Delivery	▶▶
Fisherman's Life	Healing process by Jesus ('Occupy till I come' Period)	→ Ten *Minas* Life	
Birth			Death

The Real Jesus

First, Peter left all and walked together with Jesus when he first met Him (Luk 5:11). He received one *mina* according to the terminology in the parable (point ① above). At this time, he received life, but it was at the 'pregnancy stage.' It needed to mature to the delivery stage (point ② above) to become a full life that could also give life to others. Peter was finally delivered into a complete life when He breathed on him so that Peter could receive the Holy Spirit as described at the end of the Gospel of John.

Read the passage below.

> ²¹ Then said Jesus to them again, Peace be unto you: as my Father hath sent me, even so send I you. ²² And when he had said this, he breathed on them, and saith unto them, Receive ye the Holy Ghost: ²³ Whose soever sins ye remit, they are remitted unto them; and whose soever sins ye retain, they are retained. [John 20:21-23]

Jesus came on Peter as the king. He had returned with the kingdom. When His return had been achieved in Peter, he became a servant who could give life to others due to the in-dwelling of Jesus in him. At this time, Jesus had said that he would be able to forgive the sins of others, which meant that Peter could give new life to others.

This is the return of the nobleman and second coming of Jesus to Peter.

📂 Occupy Till I Come

"Occupy till I come!"

This is what the nobleman told his servants, when he was going into a far country. In Peter's case, this 'occupy till I come period' corresponds to the period from when he first met Jesus and became pregnant with new life (point ①) to when he received the new life in full by the delivery (point ②) at the cross. This period was three and half years.

What had he been doing during this period? He had been following Jesus, taking up his own cross (Mat 10:38) so that his 'old man' may be destroyed together with Jesus on the cross. This is what Peter did, and is the spiritual meaning thereof.

Following Jesus and taking his own cross to the crucifixion and resurrection, is the key. We should also do this during this period without postponing our relationship with Jesus until His second coming in the future. In this way, we shall be a ten *minas* servant as Peter was.

If Jesus stayed with Peter from his pregnancy, then why did the nobleman in the parable go into a far country and then return? In those days, Peter looked forward to Jesus ascending the throne as king of the world. So, from the viewpoint of Peter, even though Jesus was with him, He, as a king, was not there. He, as a king, would return in the future. So according to the metaphor of the parable, Jesus went into a far country to receive for Himself a kingdom, and then returned to Peter.

Five *Minas* Servant

> [Luke 19:18-19] [18] And the second came, saying, Lord, thy pound hath gained five pounds. [19] And he said likewise to him, Be thou also over five cities.

The five *minas* servant is symbolic of the immature Christian who is to grow up to be like the ten *minas* servant.

For the disciples their period of the 'five *minas* servant' corresponded to the time from the crucifixion to Pentecost and during this period, they were afraid of the Jews and sought to avoid them. They returned to their original job, fishing. Nevertheless, they matured to be ten *minas* servants when Pentecost came to them.

One *Mina* Servant

> [Luke 19:20-23] [20] And another came, saying, Lord, behold, here is thy pound, which I have kept laid up in a napkin: [21] For I feared thee, because thou art an austere man: thou takest up that thou layedst not down, and reapest that thou didst not sow. [22] And he saith unto him, Out of thine own

mouth will I judge thee, thou wicked servant. Thou knewest that I was an austere man, taking up that I laid not down, and reaping that I did not sow: ²³ Wherefore then gavest not thou my money into the bank, that at my coming I might have required mine own with usury?

Now, I will describe the third type of the servants, the servant who kept the one *mina* laid up in a napkin. I will call this servant the 'one *mina* servant.' He represents Pharisees and scribes, and all the believers of today who endeavor to believe in Jesus through their own efforts. They all have to produce self-righteousness, which is the same as unrighteous mammon.

In the parable, the one *mina* servant also spoke to the nobleman who returned to his kingdom. However, unlike the two previous servants, he was condemned as wicked and his original *mina* was taken away. The time when this servant received the one *mina* corresponds symbolically to the time when he confessed his sins and turned to Jesus with all his heart (pregnancy by the Word). He thinks in the following manner:

"Now I am saved and I have life in Jesus. Let me work hard and preach the word of God to others so that I may be commended as a good and faithful servant when the nobleman returns or when I die and go to heaven. He is the king of kings."

This is his mindset after receiving the one *mina* and the commandment of "Occupy till I come." He thinks that the nobleman will return at some time in the future, which will correspond with the second coming of Jesus. So he tries to be watchful and work hard because men cannot know when that day will be. He imagines the day as an awards ceremony with all the servants gathered and the winners receiving prizes, e.g. ten or five cities, according to their deeds. In this servant's world, Jesus does not abide here, but He is gone and will come back in the future, as the Lord of judgment.

However, Jesus does not actually go and return. He is always here. The incorrect thinking and understanding of this servant makes Him go away in the servant's mind. In this case, he ignores Jesus of the here and now because of his misguided belief that He will return at some unspecified time in the future. The thinking creates the reality.

Therefore, he lived the 'Occupy till I come period' without Jesus, the life-giving spirit, and naturally he could not have life of the pregnancy stage to grow to the delivery stage. Under these circumstances, he would simply be working hard by himself, which has nothing to do with life.

🗁 The Only Way to Trade

The one *mina* servant thought that he should be thankful for the fact that he had received one *mina*, (eternal life) so he wanted to be loyal to the nobleman by doing something good. He surmised that the works of loyalty and good deeds would correspond to ten *minas*, and he would gain ten cities as the prize.

In order to gain ten *minas* out of one, we should follow Jesus to lay down our 'old man' on the cross, and resurrect with Him. That is the only way. Read John.

> Verily, verily, I say unto you, Except a corn of wheat fall into the ground and die, it abideth alone: but if it die, it bringeth forth much fruit. [John 12:24]

If we are deceived by 'old man,' we will postpone this healing until death, which is too late. No cross, no new life!

🗁 I Have Kept it Laid Up in a Napkin

The *mina* laid up in a napkin implies that his life is wrapped up by the law. This one *mina* servant represents the believers who know God only according to the law. Their eyes are blind to the true meanings of the Scripture, as they are being veiled by the napkin, the law. That is why they read all the Scripture as commandments. So they are separated from God by the napkin.

Consider 2 Corinthians.

> But their minds were blinded: for until this day remaineth the

The Real Jesus

same vail untaken away in the reading of the old testament; which vail is done away in Christ. [2 Corinthians 3:14]

The 'veil' in this instance is *kaluma*, and the 'napkin' found in the parable is *soudarion* in Greek. The 'veil' and the 'napkin' have the same function of covering or hiding, so both can be interpreted as the 'veil' that separates them from God. They believe in Jesus and work hard for Him but in the process completely miss the true, living Jesus Christ who is to take them to the cross.

The Jesus whose return is postponed into the future and the Jesus based on human moral codes is the Jesus who is wrapped by the napkin. We need to meet the living Jesus, person to person now. Then the napkin will be done away with, and we can bring forth ten *minas*.

🗁 Why Did He Mention Bank Usury?

This servant thought of Jesus in this way:
"Jesus is the man of power. He fed five thousand men with two fish and five loaves of bread; He walked on the water, and healed many incurable invalids. He is now working with the same power in my life. He heals me when I am sick, and He fills me when I need money and pray to Him. He is worthy to be praised and worshipped. He is fearful and austere and will punish the disobedient without exception. He promised to come back again to live together with us in heaven, and I will be faithful to Him until that time comes. I am prepared to die for the Lord. I love you Jesus!"

I do not mean that Jesus has no such power. But if we believe in Jesus based on His mighty power and miracles, the faith is not of God, but of man. The real faith will only come to us when we go through the cross together with Jesus. What is described above relates to the affairs of the world, not to the cross.

He says to the nobleman, "Thou art an austere man: thou takest up that thou layedst not down, and reapest that thou didst not sow" (Luk 19:22b).

The one *mina* servant did not know that believing in Jesus is the process of receiving life. So he neglected the life receiving process by postponing the coming of Jesus into the future, and yet he expects to receive the life and the kingdom of God. Maybe he worked hard to achieve eternal life in return, however he was misguided, and he cannot reap what he did not sow. He is deceived by his 'old man' who wishes to escape the cross by ignoring the living Jesus here.

"Wherefore then gavest not thou my money into the bank, that I might have required mine own with usury?" said the nobleman. Outwardly, what he seems to be saying is that he expected to at least get interest on the money that he gave to the servant. And he would punish him who neglected to do so, by taking the original *mina* from him. However, this is incorrect. When he mentioned interest, he meant the following:

"Life is a process of sowing and reaping and increase will only come through giving birth. You know this.

Now think about the way you see eternal life. You are investing all your efforts and good deeds to achieve this and you expect to get ten cities in heaven as compensation. However, life will never increase in compensation for your works; not like bank interest." The nobleman mentioned bank interest to enlighten the one *mina* servant about the principle of life.

If you only know and serve Jesus as a man of power and authority in relation to the affairs of this world, you will be rebuked like this servant on the judgment day. Jesus wishes to give you life, by going through the cross together with your 'old man.'

Take and Give the *mina* to Ten *minas* Servant

> [Luke 19:24-26] [24] And he said unto them that stood by, Take from him the pound, and give it to him that hath ten pounds. [25] (And they said unto him, Lord, he hath ten pounds.) [26] For I say unto you, That unto every one which hath shall be given; and from him that hath not, even that he hath shall be taken away from him.

The Lord takes the *mina* from him who has kept it laid up in a napkin, and gives it to the ten *minas* servant, and says, "That unto every one which hath shall be given; and from him that hath not, even that he hath shall be taken away from him."

It sounds like a very severe, unreasonable judgment, such as he who has will have more, and he who has little will lose the little that he has. However, this is true love. It is natural for Jesus to take one *mina* from him and give it to the servant who had obtained ten *minas*, because in this process the one *mina* servant dies since he was not walking with Jesus when he received his original *mina*.

When the time comes, the one *mina* servant will meet the ten *minas* servant, and will follow him, as a new start to receive the real *mina* from him. This means that when we, the believers, become as desolate as the one *mina* servant, God will guide us to meet the ten *minas* servant, the apostle. At this time, our existing legalistic thinking about eternal life will be destroyed by the gospel of the ten *minas* servant. This way, our one dead *mina* is taken, to be replaced by a new *mina* that will grow hopefully to the delivery stage. This is the meaning of "Take from him the *mina*, and give it to him that hath ten *minas*."

The one *mina* is not given to the five *minas* servant because he needs to grow further in Christ. The ten *minas* servant is the only mature believer who is able to give life to others. Accordingly, the judgment is the love of Jesus that He presents to this servant, the one *mina* servant.

Also, this is what the verse 26 "For I say unto you, That unto every one which hath shall be given; and from him that hath not, even that he hath shall be taken away from him" means.

🗁 Today If You Hear His Voice...

We think that our faith is okay, that there is nothing to be corrected, nothing more to hope for. However, this is not true. Please pray to God and open your heart to the Word that comes to you. Then, you will get an opportunity to meet the ten *minas* servant. If you hear him and realize your true position, you will find that your faith is misguided and is legalistic.

Read Hebrews.

> [15] While it is said, To day if ye will hear his voice, harden not your hearts, as in the provocation. [16] For some, when they had heard, did provoke: howbeit not all that came out of Egypt by Moses. [Hebrews 3:15-16]

'All that came out of Egypt by Moses' represent 'all who come to church to follow Jesus.' You cannot rest assured even though you come to church and eagerly follow Jesus in you life. The one *mina* servant was a serious Christian too.

Now, you can hear the message of the true gospel from the ten *minas* servant. This message is the word of judgment clearly exposing that you have kept the *mina* laid up in a napkin. Do not be upset at this word. All believers should start faith from the position of the one *mina* servant. It is the natural process that we all must go through to grow in faith. He who hears this message and correctly understands it will discard his existing dead faith, and will proceed to have new faith. Blessed is he who loses that which he has.

Further, please pray that this judgment may happen to you while you are living in this world. Then, you will live eternally. If not, you will have to maintain your dead faith and be judged after you are dead, which is too late.

Enemies

> [Luke 19:27] But those mine enemies, which would not that I should reign over them, bring hither, and slay them before me.

I will now explain the fourth type of person found in the parable. Who are they that do not want the nobleman to reign over them? They are also classified as believers. Some of you feel uncomfortable with this classification; however, they are also believers, being 'his' citizens as described in this parable.

Also read John 1:11: "He came unto his own, and his own received him not." Those who did not receive Jesus are believers also, described as 'His own.'

In contrast to the servants, the citizens are not given one *mina*.

From this, we can know that they represent those who are not so keen to follow Jesus even though they are known as believers. So, the citizens may include those who do not know Jesus as the Savior or who are not serious believers. They do not really need Him to be their king, as they do not know they are destined to die due to sin.

This is what it means in the parable that "his citizen hated him and send a message, saying, we will not have this man to reign over us" (Luk 19:14).

In spite of their wish, the nobleman received the kingdom, returned, and said "But those mine enemies, which would not that I should reign over them, bring hither, and slay them before me."

In this part of the parable, we are very reluctant to accept that the nobleman represents Jesus. He seems so cruel. However, paradoxically enough, we believe that those who belong to the anti-Christ will be slain in His presence at the judgment day.

We have to think deeply here. All human beings are separated from God, who is life itself, when we are born. We are therefore dead. God sent Jesus to resurrect those who are dead. Jesus says, "I am the way, the truth, and the life" (Jhn 14:6). He is our life. Therefore, until the time that He comes and reigns over us, we remain dead, as we were before.

When the whole world is full of the dead, the dead are not recognized as dead. It is like when there is nothing but darkness, darkness is not recognized as darkness. So the dead tend to think they are the living because they have no reference point for life. However, when they come before Jesus who is the real living one, they will be recognized as the dead.

This is the true meaning of the word "Bring hither, and slay them before me." Only after his coming to the realization that he is dead, will he repent and follow Jesus for salvation.

Epilogue

The servants and citizens show the process in which our faith grows: Our faith begins and grows from 'his citizen'—'one *mina* servant'—'five *minas* servant'—'ten *minas* servant.'

His 'citizens' need to meet the gospel and should realize that they are dead spiritually. When they become enthusiastic for salvation, they will become one *mina* servant. The one *mina* servant is to follow Him forsaking all to receive Him as the Holy Spirit. Please remember, 'following Him forsaking all' does not mean working hard by himself, but to hear the voice of the living Jesus and to follow to the cross. The five *minas* servant needs to grow further. The ten *minas* servant represents those who are truly born again. He will do what Jesus did for the rest of his life.

Through this parable, you should understand the real meaning of the return of the nobleman, i.e., the second coming of Jesus in your faith. This is the kingdom of God that comes into you, and Jesus eagerly wants to give this kingdom to you.

'Coming of the kingdom' is not an event that will happen sometime in the future, but is an event that should happen within your lifetime. In this process, you should not send or postpone Jesus into the future until His second coming universally, but should walk with Him now and until His second coming as the Holy Spirit in you. Once it happens to you, you will become the servant who shows ten *minas* and gains ten cities.

Thy kingdom come!

One Sows, and Another Reaps

[John 4:31-38]

³¹ In the mean while his disciples prayed him, saying, Master, eat. ³² But he said unto them, I have meat to eat that ye know not of. ³³ Therefore said the disciples one to another, Hath any man brought him ought to eat? ³⁴ Jesus saith unto them, My meat is to do the will of him that sent me, and to finish his work. ³⁵ Say not ye, There are yet four months, and then cometh harvest? behold, I say unto you, Lift up your eyes, and look on the fields; for they are white already to harvest. ³⁶ And he that reapeth receiveth wages, and gathereth fruit unto life eternal: that both he that soweth and he that reapeth may rejoice together. ³⁷ And herein is that saying true, One soweth, and another reapeth. ³⁸ I sent you to reap that whereon ye bestowed no labour: other men laboured, and ye are entered into their labours.

To enter the kingdom of God, we need to go through two stages, first is the stage that we are currently in, and the second is the stage that we will reach later when we meet the real Jesus. Jesus of the first stage is a false Jesus, and the second one is the real Jesus that the Scripture testifies of. Both the first and second stages speak about Jesus, but the Jesus described in each stage is completely different by nature.

How different? The difference is the 'world' and the 'kingdom of God.' You would not know the difference until the real Jesus comes to you. However, I am saying this in advance so that you may not be wandering what to do when the time comes.

In your life in faith, you should experience this second stage to be saved. This passage will substantiate what I have just said.

Outline

On the way to Galilee from Judaea, Jesus went through Samaria, reached a city called Sychar, and sat at the well to meet a woman. He had her repent and believe in Jesus while in dialogue. The disciples went to get something to eat during that time, and returned to Him. When they say "Master, eat," He says to them "I have meat to eat. It is to do the will of God." Starting from this, He touches the truth of "one sows, and another reaps," in the passage above.

In this message, I will explain what the meat of Jesus is, the meaning of four months to reap, and who the sower and the reaper are respectively. And we will see the reason why the sower and the reaper are different, because normally the farmer does both jobs himself.

Does it simply mean that if we sow the gospel, someone else will reap it later; or someone sows and we reap? So should we sow even if we cannot reap? No, that is not the true meanings of what Jesus said. If we interpret it in that way, we are converting the gospel into the law unwittingly. It reveals the truth that in the course of salvation, there should be a sower and a reaper separately. Let us see.

Meat of Jesus

> [John 4:31-34] [31] In the mean while his disciples prayed him, saying, Master, eat. [32] But he said unto them, I have meat to eat that ye know not of. [33] Therefore said the disciples one to another, Hath any man brought him ought to eat? [34] Jesus saith unto them, My meat is to do the will of him that sent me, and to finish his work.

The disciples went into the city and brought food to Him while He was changing the woman through the Word. They might have bought some Big Mac from the McDonald's at a Samaritan outlet. They came to Him and said "Master, eat!" If He would have said,

"Okay, well done. Let us eat," and had eaten it and had left for Galilee, we would be more comfortable. If so, we would not have trouble with the words; which are difficult to understand.

Regardless, before eating He says, "I have meat to eat that ye know not of." Of course, this does not mean that He does not eat food like hamburgers but only eats spiritual food. Jesus takes every opportunity to reveal the truth; in fact, all of His life itself is the revelation of the truth. He intends to teach us what the spiritual food is. In this instance, we are sensible enough to know that the meat of Jesus signifies the woman of Samaria. So His meat is to meet those whose time is full like this woman, and change them.

The woman had changed husbands many times and the current one was not even hers. Consider John.

> [16] Jesus saith unto her, Go, call thy husband, and come hither. [17] The woman answered and said, I have no husband. Jesus said unto her, Thou hast well said, I have no husband: [18] For thou hast had five husbands; and he whom thou now hast is not thy husband: in that saidst thou truly. [John 4:16-17]

Some people think that this woman is adulterous having many men. Further, as Jesus says she has one now but not hers, they surely think they are right. However, the woman says that she has no husband now. Is she lying? There is no reason for her to lie. We can know from this that the husband that Jesus is talking of is different from what she conceives. She conceives the husband that we normally know, but He means the husband of the law. Under the law, she needs to change her husband every now and then.

For example, when we are under the law, we pursue 'studying the words,' 'doing movement of spiritual gifts,' 'giving alms,' 'movement of repentance,' 'healing,' *et cetera*, thinking that they are the truth. Each of them is our husband. Nevertheless, none of them can give us satisfaction as the truth. So we change them one after another. Also, the one that we have now, whatever it may be, is not our husband. We are desolate and worn out in such life. At this moment, we are facing the true husband, Jesus Christ, as she is now. She and we are the meat of Jesus.

In addition, what I would like to explain is this: What we normally understand is that the flesh of Jesus, which is known as the word, is our meat to eat. For example, we need to eat and drink His flesh and blood for eternal life (Jhn 6:54).

However, here the woman is the meat of Jesus, the other way round. How is that? When we eat and drink the body and blood of Jesus, our spirit is changed to suit the heart of Jesus. Thus, by eating His flesh we are eaten by Him eventually. Here, the woman was eating the flesh of Jesus, the word, and thus, she was being eaten by Jesus to have eternal life. To eat Him is to be eaten by Him.

📁 Who Are All Which He Hath Given Me?

Jesus says, "My meat is to do the will of Him that sent me." What is the will of Him that sent Jesus? It is that all who are given to Him, He should raise up to save at the last day.

Read John.

> [38] For I came down from heaven, not to do mine own will, but the will of him that sent me. [39] And this is the Father's will which hath sent me, that of all which he hath given me I should lose nothing, but should raise it up again at the last day. [John 6:38-39]

He will quicken not everybody but those God sent to Him. When He came to the earth, many people met Him, but not all of them were saved. Great multitudes followed Him, but they all left Him, and substantially 120 people who were baptized with the Holy Spirit finally reached salvation (Act 1:15). The Pharisees and the Sadducees, far from being saved, were judged by Him. He does not raise everybody up again. No, He cannot. He only saves those God has given Him.

Those God has given represent them who are exhausted in their life and their time has ripened like the woman of Samaria. What He does in this world is to save the ripened souls. Remember that He saves not everyone but the ripened ones who's time has come. They are ready to harvest.

Yet Four Months, and Then Comes Harvest

> [John 4:35] Say not ye, There are yet four months, and then cometh harvest? behold, I say unto you, Lift up your eyes, and look on the fields; for they are white already to harvest.

Jesus always speaks about the spiritual world. When the disciples said, "There are yet four months, and then cometh harvest?" They meant general cereals. He said "You are right," but He did not mean to confirm the law of nature that corn would be reaped in four months. He is saying here that He will harvest spiritual corn in four months. In other words, the disciples say that they can harvest general corn in four months, and Jesus says that He can reap spiritual corn in four months.

The two groups use the same terminology, but the one explains the spiritual world whilst the other mentions the natural world. The two look like they are communicating with each other, but they are referring to totally different things in fact. This kind of dialogue is very common between Jesus and His disciples.

🗁 Meat Requiring Four Months

The corn that Jesus speaks of harvesting signifies the person whose time has come like the woman of Samaria. Now, what does the word 'to harvest the corn in four months' mean?

The spiritual meaning of the four months indicates the period in which God chastens men or the period of preparation before manifestation of the glory of God. For example, the Egyptians kept the Israelites in bondage for four hundred years so that they were disciplined and trained, and then, they came out of Egypt. And they wandered forty years in the wilderness during which they were chastened by God.

After crucifixion and resurrection, Jesus led the disciples forty days to let them be baptized with the Holy Spirit on the day of Pentecost. In consideration of all these cases, the number four implies the period in which God chastens men. Therefore, the word "There are yet four months, and then cometh harvest," means it requires a period of four months to be meat edible by Jesus. I am saying this figuratively. This indicates the period in which we continuously try to keep the law over and over again but we repeatedly fail and become desolate.

For forty years, the Israelites walked the way of salvation to Canaan, passing through the wilderness. This period of forty years matches the four months Jesus speaks of in this Scripture. The Israelites could be harvested into Canaan after all of them had died in the wilderness during the forty years.

In this instance, some of the readers may ask how the people who died in the wilderness could go to Canaan. However, the Scripture is written to explain the spiritual world, and so when I say that they died in the wilderness, it means that the 'old man' who was living in this world fell desolate in the wilderness.

Consider the prodigal son when he said, "How many of my father's hired men have food to spare, and here I am starving to death"(Luk 15:17b). He is one who is ready to be harvested. Accordingly, we also can be harvested in four months to be His meat.

He can see many people whose time to be reaped has come. So he said, "They are white already to harvest." According to this meaning, the time to harvest has come now, and now is the time to harvest.

One Sows, and Another Reaps

> [John 4:36-38] ³⁶ And he that reapeth receiveth wages, and gathereth fruit unto life eternal: that both he that soweth and he that reapeth may rejoice together. ³⁷ And herein is that saying true, One soweth, and another reapeth. ³⁸ I sent you to reap that whereon ye bestowed no labour: other men laboured, and ye are entered into their labours.

In general, the sower reaps what he sows. Nevertheless, why did He say distinctively, "One soweth, and another reapeth?" Because it is so.

Jesus reaped the woman of Samaria as meat, but He met her there for the first time. So He sowed nothing to her and made no efforts to cultivate her. He just harvested the woman whose time had come, that is, the woman whose four months had passed. That is, one sowed and He reaped.

Well then, who is the one having sown to her and prepared her for the harvest? It is he who taught this woman under the law. There may be many teachers, but all of them stood before her with the law. In other words, she became ripe by the law of Moses. Judging from the dialogue between her and Jesus in John Chapter 4, she has been sincere to God, even though she could not worship God in spirit and truth. Hence, when we believe in Jesus under the law with zeal, we are to face the end of our rope, and then it is time for *us* to be harvested, i.e., to meet the real Jesus.

Thus, before a soul is reaped by Jesus, there must be a man who sowed and toiled. He is Moses, the symbol of the law. So Moses, or the men who belong to him, are they who sow, they who make the effort, and who facilitate the ripening process.

🗁 Moses and Joshua

The harvesting of the soul is the journey of salvation as demonstrated by the journey of the Israelites who came out of Egypt and went into Canaan. There were two leaders during this journey.

One of them was Moses who led them for forty years in the wilderness after the Exodus, and the other was Joshua who led them to cross the Jordan into the land of Canaan. Joshua symbolizes Jesus. During this journey, Moses worked harder and toiled longer than Joshua. Joshua however, led them across the Jordan into Canaan within a relatively short time after the people had become desolate in the wilderness.

This also describes the process of salvation that we are now undergoing. We think that we believe in Jesus up to now, but in reality, we labor and are heavy laden under the law of Jesus in the wilderness. Actually, this Jesus is Moses in essence. If we meet the real living Jesus now, we will go into Canaan and conquer it within a relatively short period of time.

Moses cannot give life. Only Jesus can. Nevertheless, Jesus cannot come without Moses before Him. Moses, the law, has an important role in coming to life in Jesus. That is the reason why Jesus came to the Israelites, a people who were already under the teachings of Moses. In this sense, Jesus reaped "that whereon He bestowed no labor." This way, both he that sowed and he that reaped rejoiced together.

Present day pastors can be classified into two groups according to what and how they preach. One group is aligned with Moses and the other with Jesus. Most churches are being led by Moses, and very few are being led by Jesus. The churches of Moses sow and the churches of Jesus reap. They will rejoice together after all.

He Receives Wages

What does "he that reapeth receiveth wages" mean? (Jhn 4:36a). The reaper represents the disciple of Jesus, the born again person. He who is born again pursues no wages when he gathers the fruit of life. Only those who belong to this world will expect compensation for what they did.

The born again have moved their world into the kingdom, having left the trade based, give-and-take world. So everything they do is for nothing, and is natural. They look forward to receiving no return, as they have left behind that sort of compensation paradigm of the previous world. This is what "He receiveth wages" means. He has spiritually overcome the level in which people work for wages.

Epilogue

In order to be saved, we must first go though the days of Moses and after that come the days of Jesus. Up until now, we the believers have been under Moses whether we intended to or not, wanted to be or not, knew or did not know. And this is the natural process of obtaining eternal life.

Now if we meet and follow the real Jesus, we will be harvested and belong to Jesus in due course.

My Time is not yet come:
but Your Time is Always Ready

[John 7:1-9]

¹ After these things Jesus walked in Galilee: for he would not walk in Jewry, because the Jews sought to kill him. ² Now the Jews' feast of tabernacles was at hand. ³ His brethren therefore said unto him, Depart hence, and go into Judaea, that thy disciples also may see the works that thou doest. ⁴ For there is no man that doeth any thing in secret, and he himself seeketh to be known openly. If thou do these things, shew thyself to the world. ⁵ For neither did his brethren believe in him. ⁶ Then Jesus said unto them, My time is not yet come: but your time is alway ready. ⁷ The world cannot hate you; but me it hateth, because I testify of it, that the works thereof are evil. ⁸ Go ye up unto this feast: I go not up yet unto this feast; for my time is not yet full come. ⁹ When he had said these words unto them, he abode still in Galilee.

Normally we think that our sin is taken by Jesus and He died on the cross due to our sin. Thus, we have imputed our sin to Him, giving Him as a ransom. Consider Matthew 20:28: "Even as the Son of man came not to be ministered unto, but to minister, and to give his life as a ransom for many."

How can our sin be imputed to Jesus? Is it reasonably possible? For example, I have stolen something. Can this sin be imputed to Jesus, and so I am free from the sin? No. that is not possible at all. Unfortunately, however, that is how we see the issue of sin-imputation to Jesus.

Then, how can our sin be imputed to Jesus? We are to die on the cross, being united (planted together) with Him. When this is done, we have paid the price of sin, which is death. However, we maintain our life by the death of Jesus, and get eternal life by His resurrection in us. Thus, our sin is imputed to Jesus. The secret is for us to die being united with Jesus on the cross.

What does 'being united with Him' mean and how do we achieve this? We should not be deceived into believing that we are united with Him, through knowledge, thinking, or our imagination. We should meet the real Jesus in our life, person to person and follow Him forsaking all. That is the being united with Him. And once we go through the cross that will give us sin-forgiveness.

Outline

Jesus has been walking in Galilee, in the north, but he would not go to Judea because the Jews had tried to kill Him. The temple was in Jerusalem, and many people used to gather there at the times of the feasts. Shortly before the feast of tabernacles, the brothers of Jesus tell Him "If you want to become distinguished, stay here in Galilee no longer but go to Judaea where a lot of people gather and do what you want to do. There will be no man who does anything in secret and seeks to be known openly."

The Scripture says His brothers said so, because they did not believe Him. He answers them: "My time is not yet come, but your time is always ready. The world cannot hate you but it hates me because I testify of it that the works of the world are evil. I will not go up to this feast yet for my time is not fully come." After saying this he stayed on in Galilee.

We have several points to think about here.

Firstly, if He would show Himself to the public, should He leave Galilee and go to Jerusalem, which is a much bigger town, as His brothers had pointed out? We may have the same opinion as his brothers, but He did not listen to them. Why did he not He listen to them?

Secondly, the Scripture says His brothers said this because they did not believe in Him. Why is that?

Thirdly, what is His time "that is not yet come," and what is their time that is "always ready?" We are not sure what the terms represent, but His words suggest to us that He was too lazy to be ready. What is the 'my (your) time' that Jesus refers to?

Let us see what the passages mean with regard to the above questions.

Show Yourself to the World

The brothers of Jesus advised Him to go to a bigger place and display miracles before many people. They persuaded Him to show Himself to the world so that the world might know that the Savior, that had so long been anticipated, had come. We would also have advised Him in the same way. However, verse 5 says His brothers said so, because they did not believe in Him. Are we those who do not believe in Him?

If they had believed in Him, they would have understood what He meant by 'showing Himself.' It does not refer to showing Himself in public, but showing Himself in the bodies of the disciples.

Read the following passage from John below.

> [21] He that hath my commandments, and keepeth them, he it is that loveth me: and he that loveth me shall be loved of my Father, and I will love him, and will manifest myself to him. [22] Judas saith unto him, not Iscariot, Lord, how is it that thou wilt manifest thyself unto us, and not unto the world? [John 14:21-22]

At first glance this word appears to indicate that Jesus would only manifest Himself to his disciples at some secret location. However, Jesus did not mean this. The place where Jesus shows Himself is in His disciples. He showed Himself to His disciples when He had come as the Holy Spirit into them after resurrection. At that time, the disciples could not think where He would show Himself when He had returned.

If a person thinks that Jesus will show Himself to the world, it means that He has not yet shown Himself to that person. He who has received Jesus, who appears in him as the Holy Spirit, is the one who actually believes in Jesus. Therefore, His brothers who did not comprehend who Jesus was at that stage had no understanding of how He would manifest Himself and fulfill the Scripture.

Likewise, if we think He will come again universally with great wonders and glory and show himself to public, we will be like the brothers of Jesus who did not believe in Him. Jesus will show Himself in believers individually.

My Time and Your Time

> [John 7:6] Then Jesus said unto them, My time is not yet come: but your time is alway ready.

What does the 'time of Jesus' imply? It is the time when He will die on the cross. At that time, He will complete the spiritual healing of the disciples. So the 'time of Jesus' referred to here signifies His time to die on the cross.

Then, what does it mean that the time of the disciples is 'always ready'? The time of the disciples also refers to the time of the cross, as they would be healed by Jesus completely on it. Read Romans.

> [5] For if we have been planted together in the likeness of his death, we shall be also in the likeness of his resurrection: [6] Knowing this, that our old man is crucified with him, that the body of sin might be destroyed, that henceforth we should not serve sin. [7] For he that is dead is freed from sin. [Romans 6:5-7]

Here above, the meaning of 'plant together' (*symphytos* in Greek), which is translated as 'united with' in NIV, is referring to the seed giving and receiving relationship of a man and a woman to conceive a baby. Of course, the man refers to Jesus while the woman refers to the disciples or ourselves; the seed is the word, and the baby, Jesus Christ. Considering this, 'plant together' is a better choice for the Greek, *symphytos*.

Anyway, when the disciples meet Jesus for the first time, that is the beginning of 'plant together' or 'united with (Him),' and when Jesus, together with the 'old man' of the disciples, suffers crucifixion on the cross, it is the fulfillment of this statement. Therefore, the time Jesus is mentioning is the time of the cross. Because they are united or planted together, His time and the disciples' time are the same.

Then, it confuses us because it gives an impression that the disciples are superior to Jesus, because the disciples are ready, but Jesus is not ready. I will give an analogy to explain this.

🗁 Analogy of Doctor and Patient

A patient who is dying of cancer is lying awaiting an operation. Once the operation is successful, the patient who was dying will have a new life. In this instance, both the doctor and the patient hope in common for the time when the patient receives this new life. At that stage, the doctor would have successfully operated on the patient.

During this process, the patient has nothing to do. What is needed is for him to leave his body in the doctor's care completely, lying on the bed from start to finish. So from the viewpoint of the patient, he is always ready to receive a new life. He is available now, one hour later, or anytime.

However, the doctor is in a different position. He is the only one who can give new life to the patient, and he has to control everything, including the condition of the patient during the operation. He must check if the patient is strong enough to undergo the operation, and he should reinforce his strength if he is weak. After having checked all these things, he can conduct the operation. Thus, the operation is not always available due to the condition of the patient.

In this analogy, the doctor indicates Jesus, the patient the disciples, the sinners, and the operation starts when they meet Jesus first and it finishes at the cross. They gain new life in both His time and their time. This time is the time of the cross.

To tell the truth, the time for Him to show Himself to them is always ready and available, even if their time has not yet arrived.

That is, the time of the crucifixion of Jesus is delayed because of their problems, not because He is not ready.

Once we entrust ourselves to Him, Jesus will do everything for us and when finished He will show Himself to us. Then, we shall receive the new life. So in this sense, He said that His time was not yet come and that our time was always ready.

This time and scene of 'planting together' or 'united with Him' on the cross is sin-forgiveness or sin-imputation to Jesus so that we may receive eternal life.

The World Cannot Hate You

> [John 7:7-9] [7] The world cannot hate you; but me it hateth, because I testify of it, that the works thereof are evil. [8] Go ye up unto this feast: I go not up yet unto this feast; for my time is not yet full come. [9] When he had said these words unto them, he abode still in Galilee.

He continues to disclose that they belong to the world by saying in verse 7, "It is substantially you whose time is not ready. You are one with the world, and so the world does not hate you, but it hates me who testifies that the works of the world are evil."

In this instance, the 'world' represents man who has left God.

When such men gather together, they are able to communicate easily with each other. They can agree easily to build three or four churches, issue a declaration of the true faith, and help the needy. Accordingly, those of the same world can communicate with and understand each other's sentiments. Therefore, they do not hate each other.

However, Jesus belonging to heaven will bring to light the filthy mind of them who are of the world and will point it out. This is the feature of the man of heaven, and this is His love. But, the worldly people hate such love and also hate Him who loves. The Jews did in the past. We are doing it now.

Epilogue

Jesus will change us who are of the world into those who are of heaven through the cross. He shows Himself in us. This is what Paul was saying in Galatians 2:20: "I am crucified with Christ: nevertheless I live; yet not I, but Christ liveth in me: and the life which I now live in the flesh I live by the faith of the Son of God, who loved me, and gave himself for me."

Jesus will do all these works for us. Simply follow Him forsaking all.

A Boy That I Met in Orlando*

Sometime ago, during our kids' vacation, I had the opportunity to visit Disney World in Florida with the whole family. We rented a car and visited attractions by ourselves without a guide. We were staying at one of the tourist class inns there. It was a large three storey building complete with a swimming pool.

One morning we drove into downtown Orlando, did some sightseeing, and then returned to the inn in the early afternoon. My kids went downstairs to the swimming pool. My wife wanted to remain in the room, but I changed into swimming trunks, and went down to the swimming pool to join the children.

The swimming pool was triangular, and the deepest place in the pool was more than 8 feet. A few high-teenagers were swimming and having fun in the center of the swimming pool. They looked really good swimmers. My kids did not dare to approach the deep end. They just watched them, holding on to the side of the pool.

I myself was not a confident swimmer. All I could do was swim a short distance using my unique swimming style that is not registered with any swimming association! However, being tempted by being in the foreign land, I dared to swim across the deepest part, and I could just manage to reach the opposite side safely, but I was almost completely worn out.

This is what caused the problem. Having watched me swim successfully across the pool, my thirteen-year-old daughter, encouraged by dad's swimming prowess followed me. I had no time to stop her and she had reached the deepest part of the pool. I prayed to God earnestly in my heart that she would get across safely since I was not a good enough swimmer to save her.

Just as I was wondering whether God had heard my earnest prayer, she suddenly screamed "Dad! Dad!" and started to sink in the middle of the pool. I was instantly very concerned that she would drown. Before considering how I could rescue her, I instinctively swam to the center of the pool, towards her. However, I could not even think of how to rescue her since I had no experience of this situation.

As I struggled desperately to rescue her, I was utterly exhausted and kept sinking as I simply could not tread water. I became very frightened that I was going to drown and then the thought flashed through my mind, "I am dying here meaninglessly." I felt all was vanity and I was dying absurdly and ridiculously in a strange place. I called in panic to youngsters who were swimming near me, "Help! help!"

However, coldheartedly, they did not seem to understand the emergency in the least. They watched me pushing my daughter out toward the poolside but they thought I was having fun with her. So they approached and were enjoying watching us while swimming around us. They thought my urgent cry for help was a joke. They were swimming around me, but never offered any help. They seemed to be saying, "You are putting on a very realistic act! Good show!" It was one of the most absurd things in my life.

In the end, I was saved by a teenage boy who assisted me to get to the side of the swimming pool. Once the emergency had passed and I was clinging in exhaustion to the poolside trying to recover.

I fell on my face at the side of the pool and told the boy to save my daughter. Fortunately, she had swum by herself to the side of the pool and got out holding her brother's hand. I lay flat on the ground until I recovered.

Meanwhile the boy was telling his friends how he had bravely saved a drowning man. I was so ashamed and wanted to find a hole in the ground and hide myself in it. I could not believe that I had so nearly drowned. It was ridiculous how this incident could occur with so many people so close at hand. I was ashamed in front of these boys. However, unless the boy had rescued me, I would have gone on my last journey. He saved my life.

When I had regained my strength, I walked over to him and

thanked him. We introduced ourselves to each other. He said that he had come to Orlando with his relatives from Puerto Rico. After a short conversation, I had nothing further to say and so I said goodbye to him and went up to the hotel room with my kids.

Back in my room, I could not easily forget the embarrassing accident that had happened so recently. It occurred to me that I should see the young man again and give him a present. I hesitated for a while thinking that I could not neglect this. I tried to find something to give as a gift, but nothing satisfied me. I concluded that I should rather express my thanks to him in words so I put on clothes and went down to the swimming pool.

He was still there amusing himself with his friends. I called him. We sat on a bench near the poolside, and I gave him my business card, saying, "If you come to Seoul, call me." He said that he might visit Seoul and asked me about LotteWorld that his friends had told him about. I briefly explained as much as I knew of it.

I was still wondering what could be the best gift I could give with all my heart to him who had rescued me, so I simply introduced Jesus who walks with me. This is the most valuable thing that I have, and it would also be the most precious thing that I could give him.

I first asked if he went to church, and he said that his family attended a Catholic church and that he also attended it sometimes. He added, "My brother died young, so I always feel that I might also die young like my brother." I answered him, "God gave us life because it is indispensable to us, so it is very much important. Please trust in Him with eagerness and never easily think about dying. God sent you into this world according to His will. He had a purpose for you when He sent you to this world, and you should seek to find it."

He listened to me sincerely and very seriously. During our talking, one of his friends came to him and asked him to go with him to his room, but he let him go and wanted to hear more from me. I continued to talk for a long time after that. When I was finished, he was sincerely grateful to me for the words of encouragement. Then we parted.

In retrospect, I felt quite empty and even absurd; not quite believing that it had happened. I knew later that God had worked this case according to His will. I prayed to the Lord.

"How could this kind of thing happen to me?"

"I did it to have you tell him about Jesus."

Feeling so ashamed and victimized, I asked Him again:

"If so, You could have moved me in my heart to speak to him. Why did You allow me to suffer like that in the pool?"

He answered,

"You could only have reached him in this way."

Still feeling victimized, I said to Him,

"Please speak to me in future. I will obey You."

He said,

"I got it."

Later when thinking about the whole sequence of events I started to question whether I could have spoken to the teenager or indeed whether I would have had this opportunity without the ordeal that I went through. Frankly speaking, I guessed I could not.

God saw he was seized with fear and obsession, such as, he would die young, so He wanted to tell him that he would not. He planned this apparent misfortune to open the way for me to address the really serious issues that the young man was wrestling with and enable me to give him God's message. The boy saved me, which was a divine providence, and consequently, he could hear about precious Jesus and God's plan. In order for God to reach out to the young man, He had used me and in order to do this effectively, he allowed me to get into difficulty in the swimming pool. I was struck with reverence as I got to think that the gospel we hear now may be brought to us through the imperilment of preachers.

The itinerary started from San Francisco, passed through Orlando, ended in Chicago, and then returned to Seoul in Korea. When I arrived in San Francisco, the first destination, I prayed to God to make this journey a valuable and most memorable one. As it turned out, that journey was the most joyful and memorable one of my life. During the trip, I could find His hand working in every place that I visited.

I wish all of you to meet this living Lord in your life.

Go, and Sin No More

[John 8:3-11]

³ And the scribes and Pharisees brought unto him a woman taken in adultery; and when they had set her in the midst, ⁴ They say unto him, Master, this woman was taken in adultery, in the very act. ⁵ Now Moses in the law commanded us, that such should be stoned: but what sayest thou? ⁶ This they said, tempting him, that they might have to accuse him. But Jesus stooped down, and with his finger wrote on the ground, as though he heard them not. ⁷ So when they continued asking him, he lifted up himself, and said unto them, He that is without sin among you, let him first cast a stone at her. ⁸ And again he stooped down, and wrote on the ground. ⁹ And they which heard it, being convicted by their own conscience, went out one by one, beginning at the eldest, even unto the last: and Jesus was left alone, and the woman standing in the midst. ¹⁰ When Jesus had lifted up himself, and saw none but the woman, he said unto her, Woman, where are those thine accusers? hath no man condemned thee? ¹¹ She said, No man, Lord. And Jesus said unto her, Neither do I condemn thee: go, and sin no more.

"A woman caught in adultery." This is one of the most well known stories of the Scripture. Many of us will understand the story as instructing us to forgive the sins of others, as Jesus forgave this woman. Yes, we should do so.

However, do we know the meaning of His forgiveness? We need to know the true meaning of His forgiveness so that we can forgive others as He did. His forgiveness is not the forgiveness that

The Real Jesus 291

we traditionally know, but is the forgiveness of once-and-for-all. What then is the nature of His forgiveness?

The storyline is very simple. In short, a woman was caught in adultery by the Pharisees and brought to Jesus. Jesus forgave her by saying, "Go, and sin no more." This simple story reveals clearly to us the way to eternal life. Using this passage, I will explain the role of the law, what the once-and-for-all forgiveness of Jesus is and what the kingdom of God that comes right after His forgiveness is.

Purpose of the Law

> [John 8:3-5] ³ And the scribes and Pharisees brought unto him a woman taken in adultery; and when they had set her in the midst, ⁴ They say unto him, Master, this woman was taken in adultery, in the very act. ⁵ Now Moses in the law commanded us, that such should be stoned: but what sayest thou?

The law consists of the commandments of God. Those who hope for and seek something good from God must keep these commandments. However, it is not easy because of our sinful nature. We cannot suppress our desire to sin completely.

Why is this? Sin is not merely a matter of certain misguided deeds, but it is something that is related to our born nature, which cannot be changed at all with our own efforts.

An old Korean poet said "Keep yourself, the snowy heron, from mingling with the crow." It teaches how the snowy heron should behave in order not to be dyed black. We, the believers, consider that we are clean snowy herons and God gave us the law so as to keep ourselves from uncleanness. This is how we understand the law. However, that is not the correct understanding of the law. The snowy heron will still be a snowy heron even if it gets dirty, and the crow will be a crow even if it is bathed clean. Read Jeremiah.

> Can the Ethiopian change his skin, or the leopard his spots? then may ye also do good, that are accustomed to do evil. [Jeremiah 13:23]

No matter what type of law we have, we simply cannot keep it, as the leopard cannot change his spots. The matter of sin relates to the intrinsic nature of man, and so the law is completely powerless regarding our sin, which is intrinsic. That is the only reason why we keep on sinning in spite of what the law says. Not knowing this, we keep on trying not to sin but have to sin until the end of time. So we are eventually locked in a vicious circle of sinning and repenting.

If you are a sensible believer, by now you should realize that you cannot keep the law. It is apparent that you repent every Sunday for not being able to keep the law in the previous week. If you cannot solve this sin problem, you have to face the wage of sin at the end of the day. So when you are desperate to be free from sin, you will need someone who will save you from sin. This person is Jesus Christ.

In fact, God did not give us the law with the intention that we make our bodies holy by keeping the law. He gave it to us so that we may realize that we are born sinners who cannot keep it no matter how hard we may try. The Scripture speaks of the law in Romans as follows:

Moreover the law entered, that the offence might abound.
But where sin abounded, grace did much more abound:
[Romans 5:20]

It says that the law is given for the purpose of inducing us to commit offence further. If a man has realized that he is a sinner under the law, he will seek grace from God wholeheartedly. Then he will be ready to follow Jesus with all his heart and his sin will be forgiven once-and-for-all.

The woman taken in adultery has this feature. She could not but commit adultery. Then she was taken by the scribes and Pharisees, and so she had to be judged. Under the law, she is doomed to death unless God comes down from heaven and instructs them not to kill her.

In the Scripture it says, "For I through the law am dead" (Gal 2:19). She is found dead under the law.

📂 The Law is Schoolmaster to Bring Us Unto Christ

This woman when she faced death was brought to Jesus by the scribes and Pharisees. They are the symbol of the law. So the law made her face death, and as a consequence, she was brought to Jesus. In a similar manner, we have to spend time under the law and when becoming completely desolate, facing death, we will repent and be brought to Jesus. In this sense, Paul says that that law is the schoolmaster who will bring us to Jesus. This is what the law does. Read Galatians.

> Wherefore the law was our schoolmaster to bring us unto Christ, that we might be justified by faith. [Galatians 3:24]

If we meet Jesus Christ and follow Him forsaking all, we will then be justified like her. Her justification will be explained later in this message.

Where to Write the Law

> [John 8:6] This they said, tempting him, that they might have to accuse him. But Jesus stooped down, and with his finger wrote on the ground, as though he heard them not.

When they took her to Him and tempted Him, He wrote something on the ground. God only knows what Jesus wrote on the ground because it is not revealed in the Scripture. However, instead of being curious about what He wrote on the ground, we should know what His gesture signifies, since He is answering them through this gesture.

The meaning is this. The law, represented by the Ten Commandments, is written on tablets of stone. The time will come when the law is to be written on the hearts of men by Jesus Christ. Therefore, His act of writing on the ground signifies the declaration that "The law is not given to you to condemn each other. The law should be written in your heart, and this is what I came here for."

As we learn in the parable of the sower, the ground signifies our heart. Consider this passage of Hebrews also.

> For this is the covenant that I will make with the house of Israel after those days, saith the Lord; I will put my laws into their mind, and write them in their hearts: and I will be to them a God, and they shall be to me a people: [Hebrews 8:10]

Writing 'the laws in the heart' does not mean memorizing the Scripture. It does not mean that we should always meditate on the word of God in our hearts either. It does mean that Jesus Christ, the Word, comes into us after healing our soul. Then we become the epistle of the Christ. Read 2 Corinthians.

> Forasmuch as ye are manifestly declared to be the epistle of Christ ministered by us, written not with ink, but with the Spirit of the living God; not in tables of stone, but in fleshy tables of the heart. [2 Corinthians 3:3]

The present scene shows the law being written in the heart of the woman, and she will become the people of God.

He That is Without Sin, Let Him First Cast a Stone at Her!

> [John 8:7-9] [7] So when they continued asking him, he lifted up himself, and said unto them, He that is without sin among you, let him first cast a stone at her. [8] And again he stooped down, and wrote on the ground. [9] And they which heard it, being convicted by their own conscience, went out one by one, beginning at the eldest, even unto the last: and Jesus was left alone, and the woman standing in the midst.

Not understanding what Jesus' gesture meant, they pressed Him, so He said, "He that is without sin among you, let him first cast a stone at her." At this word from Jesus, they were convicted by their conscience and left the place one by one, and only Jesus and the woman were left there.

📁 **Conviction by the Conscience**

We probably have negative feelings towards the scribes and Pharisees and so we think of them as heartless people without a conscience. However, this kind of thinking is completely biased. Upon hearing the word of Jesus, they were pricked by their conscience; they immediately dropped the idea of stoning her. Maybe they thought deeply, and could not deny the fact that they could also commit adultery anytime. In fact, some of them may have committed adultery but they may not have been caught.

Jesus' comment is very powerful. And this word is broadly cited amongst believers and non-believers. However, this sort of interpretation is not what He wanted. It is neither the will of Jesus nor the gospel. Jesus made the comment to prevent the woman from being stoned. However, it was not the fundamental solution for this matter. He did not come to suppress our sinful acts once or twice, but to give us a life without sin.

For whatever reason, the scribes and Pharisees hearing what He said left Him. This is meant to imply that they left the eternal life, Jesus, for the law. 'Leaving for the law' means that they would keep the law more earnestly, and would come back to Him with a more refined self-righteousness. This was not what Jesus wanted. What Jesus wanted was to heal their souls to make them into new men. Anyway, they misunderstood His meaning and acted contrary to what Jesus was teaching.

Therefore, when we are under the law, even when convicted by our conscience we can be hindered from reaching Jesus.

📁 **Meanings of 'He that is Without Sin' and 'Cast a Stone'**

Then what is the true meaning of "He that is without sin among you, let him first cast a stone at her?"

First of all, 'he that is without sin' does not refer to a mythical human being who has never sinned. It refers to the man whose sin has been forgiven once-and-for-all and for this reason, has no sin. *This* is the man without sin. This will become clearer when you have a proper understanding of the expression: 'cast a stone at her.'

The 'stone' is translated from the Greek, *lithos*, and it symbolizes Jesus Christ. Read the following verses where the stone is used to refer to Jesus Christ.

> Whosoever shall fall upon that *stone* shall be broken; but on whomsoever it shall fall, it will grind him to powder. [Luke 20:18]

> To whom coming, as unto a living *stone*, disallowed indeed of men, but chosen of God, and precious, [1Peter 2:4]

Also the 'stone that was cut out' in Daniel 2:34 and 45 in the Old Testament indicates Jesus Christ. Having known the meanings of the important words in this verse, we can re-phrase the verse as follows:

"He that is perfectly forgiven his sin by Jesus among you let him first cast Jesus Christ (stone) at this sinner." That is, "Let him, who has once-and-for-all forgiveness, give the same forgiveness of Jesus, which is the salvation, (to this woman)."

Now we realize that the words to 'cast a stone' in the Old Testament does not imply throwing real stones to kill people, but means that we should 'preach the gospel of Christ to sinners and have them forgiven of their sin and saved.'

What the scribes and Pharisees could do to the woman taken in adultery was throw stones at her, or they do not do it by the conviction. This is the maximum they could do who are under the law. They completely failed to save her in any way, even thought they had the word of God and taught the people with it.

Jesus, however, could throw stones at her in a spiritual sense, and give her once-and-for-all forgiveness, or salvation. As a disciple of Jesus, we should be able to do what He did. Jesus says in John:

> Verily, verily, I say unto you, He that believeth on me, the works that I do shall he do also; and greater works than these shall he do; because I go unto my Father. [John 14:12]

> Whose soever sins ye remit, they are remitted unto them; and whose soever sins ye retain, they are retained. [John 20:23]

If we can cast a stone at someone, (I am saying this in the spiritual sense) we should first become without sin. Are you without sin now? Or are you expecting to be without sin only in the afterlife? If this is the case, your faith is meaningless. That's because you, as a disciple of Jesus, will not be doing what Jesus did in this world.

Having made His statement, He wrote on the ground again. His second gesture of writing on the ground signifies that He was writing the word on the heart of the woman. This is the healing process of the woman, and during this time, all those who condemned and accused her will be gone from her heart.

Go, and Sin No More!

> [John 8:10-11] [10] When Jesus had lifted up himself, and saw none but the woman, he said unto her, Woman, where are those thine accusers? hath no man condemned thee? [11] She said, No man, Lord. And Jesus said unto her, Neither do I condemn thee: go, and sin no more.

Outwardly, the scribes and Pharisees committed no adultery, they were convicted by their consciences and felt ashamed of casting a stone at her, and so they left Jesus. This separation from Jesus was made by themselves. They were judged by the word of Jesus and through their own thinking excluded from the kingdom.

However, the woman remained on the spot to be with Jesus seeking His mercy. 'To be with Jesus' signifies to have sin forgiven once-and-for-all, be saved and go into the kingdom of God.

These two types of believers are clearly shown in the passage of Luke below.

> [10] Two men went up into the temple to pray; the one a Pharisee, and the other a publican. [11] The Pharisee stood and prayed thus with himself, God, I thank thee, that I am not as other men are, extortioners, unjust, adulterers, or even as this

publican. ¹² I fast twice in the week, I give tithes of all that I possess. ¹³ And the publican, standing afar off, would not lift up so much as his eyes unto heaven, but smote upon his breast, saying, God be merciful to me a sinner. ¹⁴ I tell you, this man went down to his house justified rather than the other: for every one that exalteth himself shall be abased; and he that humbleth himself shall be exalted. [Luke 18:10-14]

The scribes and Pharisees represent those who are not yet dead under the law. They are filled with their own self-righteousness, and this separates them from Jesus.

On the other hand the woman was completely dead under the law, so she could not go, but remained with Jesus, seeking the mercy of God. Those in whom sin did not become exceedingly sinful (Rom 7:13) cannot stay with Him.

When all the people were gone, Jesus said to her "Woman, where are those thine accusers? hath no man condemned thee?" And the woman said "No man, Lord." She was in Christ. Yes, this is a scene from the kingdom of God. No condemnation, no accusation even from the Lord. Read Romans 8:1: "There is therefore now no condemnation to them which are in Christ Jesus, who walk not after the flesh, but after the Spirit."

📂 Go, and Sin No More! — Declaration of the Kingdom

"Go, and sin no more!"

If we understand this word according to traditional understanding and thinking, it will be something like 'Go, and commit adultery or theft no more. Or else!' We understand it as a stern warning.

However, any man, if he is sensible, will not be comfortable with such an interpretation. Because, even though He told her not to sin, she will sin again. The commandment "You shall not commit adultery" (Exd 20:14) is given by God. Could she who had failed to keep the law, keep Jesus' commandment? No way. She will sin again for sure even if she receives a stronger commandment than this. Then, she will be brought to Jesus again, and He will forgive her again, saying, "Go, and sin no more." And she will go round in

The Real Jesus 299

such circles. If she continues her life in this way, she will walk with sin for her entire life.

This is not the Jesus, who gives us the once-and-for-all forgiveness as in the Scripture. The Jesus 'who forgives us each time we come to Him and repent after having committed sins repeatedly' is 'another Jesus' (2Co 11:4). If a person knows Him in this manner, he believes in 'another Jesus' even if he may say he is a serious Christian. Where can you find in the Scripture that Jesus forgives sin repeatedly throughout our whole life? The real Jesus forgives sin once and forever. Do not be deceived by the forgiveness that is offered by 'another Jesus.'

Then what is the real meaning of "Go, and sin no more!" It is a declaration! "You are dead to the law in the world, and now you've come into the world of grace where there is no sin."

📂 "Let Them Not Turn Again to Folly"

Like this woman, I had an experience of receiving "Let you not turn again to folly," which corresponds to "Go, and sin no more." It was when the Lord gave me the verses of the Psalms, saying my salvation is near at hand.

Read the following passage of Psalms.

> [8] I will hear what God the LORD will speak: for he will speak peace unto his people, and to his saints: but let them not turn again to folly. [9] Surely his salvation is nigh them that fear him; that glory may dwell in our land. [10] Mercy and truth are met together; righteousness and peace have kissed each other. [11] Truth shall spring out of the earth; and righteousness shall look down from heaven. [12] Yea, the LORD shall give that which is good; and our land shall yield her increase. [13] Righteousness shall go before him; and shall set us in the way of his steps. [Psalm 85:8-13]

The early part of Psalm 85 describes those who are distressed by the wrath of God under the law and from verse 8 onwards it speaks of salvation, i.e., coming out of the law and going into the kingdom of God.

I jumped for joy as soon as I heard this message since it said that the time for me to enter the world of glory, which I had been desperately hoping for, was drawing near. However, I was concerned about the word 'let them not turn again to folly' in verse 8. I could not guarantee to myself that I would not be foolish again. Anyway, this word weighed on my mind for a long time.

However, now I can tell you the true meaning of this verse. This Psalms has the same message as "Go, and sin no more." That is, it declares that the born again will never turn again to absurdity. Therefore, it is not a commandment, "Do not turn again to folly," but is a declaration that he has become the man who does not turn again to folly.

The word is a blessed declaration.

Epilogue

Three types of believers appear in this scene: the scribes and Pharisees, the woman taken in adultery, and Jesus. These three types of person show different faith by stages for growing in faith.

The first stage is characterized by the scribes and Pharisees who believe in God under the law according to their conscience. They left Jesus, so they had no part with Him. They are the believers under the law.

The second stage is characterized by the woman who believed in Jesus under the law, became desolate in such faith and was taken to Jesus. From this point on, she is a real believer in Jesus. She is the symbol of those who truly repent to meet Jesus, be healed, and whose sins are forgiven by Him.

The third stage is the faith of the ones who can forgive the sins of others. They can forgive sin because in them Christ lives. And they are saved and in the kingdom of God. If you are a true believer in Jesus, you will reach this stage.

The woman taken in adultery has a negative image. However, she is the one who is greatly blessed because she has been moved from the world of sin to the world without sin, the kingdom of God.

May you hear the following blessed declaration from the Lord.

"Go, and sin no more!"

Finishing This Book...

'Fresh Eyes to Read the Bible - Book 2' sheds light on you who are zealous about Jesus and thus laboring, and being heavy laden. Up to now, you did not understand the hidden meanings of the Scripture correctly and did not have the desire to know better. Because you have thought that everything is all right. We all have to go through that stage, which is the stage of living under the law unwittingly.

Now is the time for you to believe in Jesus according to the real meanings of the Scripture. Under the law, you tend to believe in Jesus as you wish, that is, a 'self-created' Jesus, because you are still young and energetic in your relationship with God. However, when you become old and exhausted in that faith, you will be ready to follow the real Jesus, forsaking your self-created Jesus.

Read John.

> Verily, verily, I say unto thee, When thou wast young, thou girdest thyself, and walkedst whither thou wouldest: but when thou shalt be old, thou shalt stretch forth thy hands, and another shall gird thee, and carry thee whither thou wouldest not. [John 21:18]

Whilst you yourself believe in Jesus, you are under the law. When you are really led by Jesus in believing Him, you are under grace. You should think about this seriously.

God loves you so much. So He led you to read this book. I know many authors say this, but I have to say this also, not as an author, but as a man who has the life of Jesus in me. You decide. I sincerely want all you readers to check your current faith, and hope for even greater glory in Jesus.

One more thing, what I have said through this book is the gospel, which shows the way to heaven through the hidden meaning of the Scripture. If you truly understand what it means, then you are conceived by the Word, however, that is not enough. Because that life needs to grow to the delivery stage, and to the Pentecost stage ultimately.

At this moment, you are still under your 'old man,' and he will manipulate what you read in a way to make him survive in you. Think about the Bible, the word of God, that you have been reading. Your 'old man' has been guiding you to understand the Bible legalistically. He will do so with this book, too.

Therefore, you need to meet the person who has the word of God. By the person-to-person contact with this man, the life in the gospel will be transferred to you fully and completely. Do not worry, even if you do not have one around. If you are ready to have eternal life wholeheartedly, it is God Himself who will send you the man. Think about the cases of woman by the well in Samaria (Jhn 4), the one lost sheep (Luk 15), the evil spirit possessed man in Gadarenes (Luk 8), and so on.

Whilst I have been writing this book I have developed a great desire to meet those who are reading it. Let us pray that God moves in such a way that enables this to happen.

Grace be to you and peace from God our Father and the Lord Jesus Christ. Amen.

TITLES

Haggai Books plans to publish the author's titles in English one after another. The Haggai Books' titles are:

Published Titles:-

Fresh Eyes to Read the Bible I: Biblical Steps for Growing in Faith
This title will present the steps for growing in faith by considering the arrangement of the Bible's books. You will gain a very different but true perspective, to issues like 'Inheritance of Adam's Sin,' 'Parable of the Prodigal Son,' 'End Times,' 'Law and Grace,' *et cetera*. The contents are simple and strong.

Fresh Eyes to Read the Bible II: The Real Jesus
This title will let the readers know that the true spiritual meanings of Scripture are quite different from the morals and ethics of the world, and will reveal the real Jesus, who we should meet here and now for our salvation.

Forthcoming Titles:-

Fresh Eyes to Read the Bible III: Good, Evil, and the Resurrection
This title will touch on such subjects as fellowship with God, tithes and offerings, the true nature of devil/Satan/demons, and the Word and resurrection.

A Spiritual Reading of First, Second, and Third John
This title will reveal a fresh way to have no sin during your lifetime through once-and-for-all forgiveness by Jesus Christ.

ADDITIONAL ORDER

To order additional copies of this title, please contact one of the following distributors: Ingram, Amazon.com, Barnes & Noble or visit our website at haggaibooks.com

www.ingramcontent.com/pod-product-compliance
Lightning Source LLC
Chambersburg PA
CBHW031134160426
43193CB00008B/140